The General Linux I Cram Sheet

This Cram Sheet contains the distilled key facts about the LPI 101 exam. Review this information right before entering the test room, paying special attention to those areas where you feel you need the most review. You can transfer any of the facts onto a blank piece of paper before beginning the exam.

GNU AND UNIX COMMANDS

1. The shell is the interpreter between the operating system and the user. Most versions of Linux offer more than one shell, and users can choose the one that best suits them. Among the common shells found in most implementations of Linux are:
   - *bash*—The Bourne Again shell (heavily tested in this exam)
   - *tcsh*—Tom's C shell
2. The **cat** command is the simplest way to view all of a text file (use **tac** to review the file in reverse order). If you only want to view the top, you can use the **head** command, and if you only want to see the bottom, you can use the **tail** command.
3. The **cut** command can pull fields from a file, and they can be combined using either **paste** or **join**. The latter offers more features than the former and can be used conditionally.
4. The **expand** command can change tabs into spaces, the **fmt** command can crop text to fit a line's character limitation, and the **pr** command works with pagination. Lines can be numbered in the display with the **nl** command, and **sort** can place items in alphabetic or numeric (using the **-n** parameter) order.
5. The **od** command can display portions of non-text files by performing an octal dump. The **tr** command can convert one character set to another, and **wc** can count the number of lines, words, and characters in a file.
6. Files can be copied using **cp** or moved using **mv**. Files can be deleted with **rm**, and directories (which are created with **mkdir**) can be removed with **rmdir**. In all situations, you can specify target and source items using either absolute or relative addresses, and you can use wildcards as well. To change directories, use the **cd** command (when used without parameters, this will move you to your home directory), and to see what directory you are presently working in, use the **pwd** (present working directory) command.
7. Standard input (stdin) is traditionally the keyboard, and standard output (stdout) is traditionally the monitor. Both can be redirected, as can standard error (stderr). Methods of redirection include using the symbols >, >>, <, and |. You can also utilize the **tee** command to send output to two locations.
8. Commands can be joined on the command line by the semicolon (;), and each command will run independent of one another. Command history allows you to run commands over again without needing to retype them and allows for editing prior to execution. When run, every command spans at least one process, and processes can be viewed with **ps** or **top** (which continues to update the display dynamically).
9. Jobs running in the foreground can be suspended by pressing ^Z (Ctrl+Z). They can be

- *seventh*—This is the user's shell. If it is left blank, the default shell is applied.

37. Passwords can be moved to the /etc/shadow file for greater security (with the **pwconv** utility—the opposite of which is **pwunconv**). When this is done, an "x" appears in the second field of the /etc/passwd file. Passwords are changed with the **passwd** command.
38. Users can be added by manually editing the configuration files or using the **useradd** command (and they can be removed by using **userdel**). Adding a user in this way will also create his or her home directory and copy to it the template files found beneath /usr/skel.
39. Group definitions exist in the /etc/group file. Passwords can also be there, or they can be moved to /etc/gshadow for greater security (with the **grpconv** utility—the opposite of which is **grpunconv**). The **groupadd** utility can be used to create groups (and avoid manual editing of the configuration files), and **groupdel** can be used to remove groups. Groups can be modified with **groupmod**, and users can change between groups with the **newgrp** command.
40. The /etc/profile file holds variables that you want to apply to all users. When the users log in, this file runs and sets up their environments before going to any individual .profiles that may exist beneath their home directories. To see the last time each user logged onto the system, use the **lastlog** command, which extracts its data from the lastlog file. To just see who logged on most recently—and may currently be on (which **who** shows)—you can use the **last** command.
41. The system log daemon (**syslogd**) logs most events to the log files, with the main file being /var/log/messages. The **logrotate** command can be configured to automatically archive these logs and perform maintenance as configured in the /etc/syslog.conf file. You can manually write entries to the log files using the **logger** command.
42. To schedule a job to run in unattended mode one time only, you can use the **at** command. Scheduled jobs can be viewed with the **atq** command and deleted prior to execution with **atrm**.
43. Restrictions can be placed on who can use the **at** service (**atd**) by creating an at.allow file and only placing valid usernames beneath it. Alternatively, you can create an at.deny file and place within it only the names of users who cannot use the service (meaning that everyone else can).
44. If you need to schedule an unattended job to run at any sort of regular interval, you can create a **crontab** (cron table) entry for it. The crontab files are read by the **cron** daemon, which looks every minute to see if any jobs need to run.
45. Restrictions can be placed on who can use **cron** by creating a cron.allow file and only placing valid usernames beneath it. Alternatively, you can create a cron.deny file and place within it only the names of users who cannot use the service (meaning that everyone else can).
46. There are six fields to each entry in the **cron** tables:
    - The minute the job is to run (0 to 59)
    - The hour the job is to run (0 to 23)
    - The day of the month (1 to 31)
    - The month of the year (1 to 12)
    - The day of the week (0 to 6, with 0 equal to Sunday)
    - The path to the executable that is to run
47. Backups must be done in order to protect your data in the event of a catastrophe. Backups can be done with the **tar** command (which can combine multiple files into a single archive) or **cpio** (which can copy files in and out between media).
48. In addition to archiving, you can also compress files with the **compress**, **gzip**, or **pack** command. To uncompress files, use **uncompress**, **gunzip**, or **unpack**.
49. Backups can be full or partial. If they are partial, they can be incremental (everything since the last full or incremental backup) or differential (everything since the last full backup). Differential and incremental backups cannot be mixed and matched—you must use one or the other.
50. As important as backups are, it is equally important that you verify that restores can be done on a regular basis. Only by testing the quality of the backups and the restore procedure can you verify that you will be ready when an emergency does occur.

files on your system. This database can be updated by running the **updatedb** command (which can be automatically configured via the /etc/updatedb.conf file).

BOOT, INITIALIZATION, SHUTDOWN, AND RUN LEVELS

24. The Linux Loader (LILO) is used to boot the system and can allow you to choose other operating systems to boot into. LILO can be configured through the /etc/lilo.conf files, and it can load additional modules identified in either /etc/conf.modules or /etc/modules.conf.
25. The "system" log file is /var/log/messages. This is where the majority of events are written to by the system log daemon (**syslogd**). Messages related specifically to LILO can be viewed with the **dmesg** command.
26. The **init** daemon is responsible for maintaining proper running of daemons at specified runlevels. The system attempts to go to the runlevel specified as the default in the /etc/inittab file upon each boot.
27. Runlevels can be changed with the **init** and **shutdown** (also known as **halt**) commands. The valid runlevels defined as standards are:
    - *0*—Powered off
    - *1*—Single-user mode
    - *2*—Multiple-user mode without NFS
    - *3*—Multiple-user mode with NFS
    - *5*—X environment
    - *6*—Reboot

DOCUMENTATION

28. Manual files exist for most standard utilities and can be read using the **man** command. The pages are displayed one screen at a time using **more**, **less**, or any similar utility defined by the **PAGER** variable.
29. There are a number of subdirectories beneath /usr/man that hold the manual pages. The most important are:
    - */man1*—Holds definitions for shell utilities and user commands.
    - */man2*—Holds pages for system calls.
    - */man3*—Holds descriptive pages for libc calls.
    - */man4*—Holds pages of device descriptions.
    - */man5*—Contains descriptions of configurable files, such as those found beneath /etc.
    - */man6*—Holds manual pages for games.
    - */man7*—Holds manual pages for Linux system files and conventions.
    - */man8*—Contains administrative utility definitions.
30. To see a man page other than in the first directory a match is found, you can use the **man** command followed by the subdirectory number (for example, **man 2 nice**).
31. Third-party software should write documentation in the /usr/doc directory, creating a subdirectory that consists of the name of the utility, followed by a hyphen (-) and the version number.
32. The **whatis** command shows what manual pages are available for an entry (**apropos** allows you to find noncomplete matches), whereas **whereis** shows the location of the file and all related files (including any manual pages).
33. Many standard utilities allow you to enter the executable name followed by "**—help**" to obtain help only on the syntax. The **info** command shows help files stored beneath /usr/info.
34. A great deal of additional documentation can be found on the Internet at the Linux Documentation Project and other sites (including individual vendors). You can also find help to problems by subscribing to newsgroups and mailing lists.
35. It is important to document fully all changes you make to the system and to make documentation, and other forms of support, available to all users.

ADMINISTRATIVE TASKS

36. In order for a user to access the system, he or she must have a username and password. The username is stored in the /etc/passwd file as the first field. Other fields of this file are:
    - *second*—This can hold the user's password if it has not been moved to /etc/shadow.
    - *third*—This is the user's unique ID number. The root user is always 0, and system accounts typically have low numbers. Standard users typically start at 500.
    - *fourth*—This is the group ID number. The root group is number 0, and system groups have low numbers.
    - *fifth*—This is free text describing the user that is returned by **finger** queries and similar utilities.
    - *sixth*—This is the user's home directory.

moved to the background with the **bg** command, and background jobs can be brought to the foreground with the **fg** command. Running jobs can be listed with the **jobs** command, and processes can be eradicated with the use of **kill**.

10. The priority level of a job can be altered before it starts with the **nice** command. After the job has started, only **renice** can change its priority.
11. The **sed** editor can be used to change text as it is displayed, using a defined set of parameters it is given. The **grep** utility (and its counterparts, **egrep** and **fgrep**) can be used to find matches for strings within files.

DEVICES, LINUX FILESYSTEMS, AND FILESYSTEM HIERARCHY STANDARD

12. The **fdisk** command is used to create partitions, which can then be formatted using **mkfs**. The **mkfs** utility allows you to format a number of different filesystem types, including msdos, and others.
13. The filesystem contains an inode (a unique entry) for every entity stored on it. This inode (number visible with **ls -i**) holds information about the entity, including permissions, owner, group, and associated dates for creation/access/modification (which can be changed with the **touch** command).
14. The **du** command can show how much of the disk is used, whereas the **df** command shows how much is free. The main troubleshooting tool for disks is **fsck**, which can check filesystem structure, including inodes.
15. The root filesystem must always be mounted, but remote ones can be mounted with the **mount** command or unmounted with the **umount** command. To have mounting automatically occur at start-up, add the entries to /etc/fstab.
16. Quotas can restrict the amount of disk space users or groups can utilize. Quotas are initialized with the **quota** command, and they're toggled on and off with **quotaon** and **quotaoff**. They can be changed/modified with **edquota**, and reports can be generated with **repquota**.
17. File permissions can be expressed in terms of symbolic or numeric values. When files are first created, the default permissions are equal to 666 minus any **umask** value. The default permissions on directories are equal to 777 minus any **umask** value. When you're computing numeric permissions, the ability to read is worth 4, to write is worth 2, and to execute is worth 1.
18. File and directory permissions can be changed with the **chmod** command (which accepts numeric and symbolic values). Adding 1,000 to the value turns on the "sticky bit," whereas adding 2,000 turns on the SGID permission, and 4,000 turns on the SUID permission.
19. The owner of a group can be changed with the **chown** command, whereas the **chgrp** command allows changing the group associated with the file.
20. Links are created with the **ln** command. A "hard" link is nothing more than an alias to the file, and all aliases share the common inode. A symbolic link is created with **ln -s** and is an actual file (of very small size) with its own inode. The symbolic link contains a pointer to the original file and can span across filesystems (whereas a hard link cannot).
21. A number of directories are created by default during the installation of Linux. Among them are the following:
    - */bin*—Holds binary (executable) files accessible by all users.
    - */dev*—Holds device definitions.
    - */etc*—Used for files that differ from machine to machine (configuration files).
    - */home*—Holds the users' home directories.
    - */mnt*—Used for mount points.
    - */root*—The home directory for the root user.
    - */tmp*—Used for temporary files that need not survive a reboot.
    - */usr*—Holds documentation and other entries that do not change often. Among the subdirectories are those holding additional executables.
    - */var*—Keeps data that changes. This includes log files, spools, and the like.
22. The **find** command can be used to search the system for files/directories that meet any number of criteria. When these entities are found, the **xargs** command can be used to look deeper within them for other values (such as in conjunction with **grep**).
23. The **which** command will tell where the first executable by a given name can be found by logically moving through your path statement. The **locate** command looks for matching entries in the locatedb database and can help you find

LPI General Linux I

Emmett Dulaney

LPI General Linux I Exam Cram

The Coriolis Group, LLC
14455 N. Hayden Road
Suite 220
Scottsdale, Arizona 85260

(480)483-0192
FAX (480)483-0193
www.coriolis.com

Library of Congress Cataloging-in-Publication Data
Dulaney, Emmett A.
LPI General Linux I exam cram / by Emmett Dulaney.
p. cm.
Includes index.
ISBN 1-57610-923-2
1. Electronic data processing personnel--Certification. 2. Operating systems (Computers) --Certification. 3. Linux I. Title.
QA76.3 .D8237 2001
005.4'32--dc21 00-050883
CIP

Printed in the United States of America
10 9 8 7 6 5 4 3 2 1

President and CEO
Keith Weiskamp

Publisher
Steve Sayre

Acquisitions Editor
Sharon Linsenbach

Development Editor
Deborah Doorley

Product Marketing Manager
Brett Woolley

Project Editor
Sally M. Scott

Technical Reviewer
Julian Laredo

Production Coordinator
Wendy Littley

Cover Designer
Jesse Dunn

Layout Designer
April Nielsen

The Coriolis Group, LLC • 14455 North Hayden Road, Suite 220 • Scottsdale, Arizona 85260

ExamCram.com Connects You to the Ultimate Study Center!

Our goal has always been to provide you with the best study tools on the planet to help you achieve your certification in record time. Time is so valuable these days that none of us can afford to waste a second of it, especially when it comes to exam preparation.

Over the past few years, we've created an extensive line of *Exam Cram* and *Exam Prep* study guides, practice exams, and interactive training. To help you study even better, we have now created an e-learning and certification destination called **ExamCram.com**. (You can access the site at **www.examcram.com**.) Now, with every study product you purchase from us, you'll be connected to a large community of people like yourself who are actively studying for their certifications, developing their careers, seeking advice, and sharing their insights and stories.

I believe that the future is all about collaborative learning. Our **ExamCram.com** destination is our approach to creating a highly interactive, easily accessible collaborative environment, where you can take practice exams and discuss your experiences with others, sign up for features like "Questions of the Day," plan your certifications using our interactive planners, create your own personal study pages, and keep up with all of the latest study tips and techniques.

I hope that whatever study products you purchase from us—*Exam Cram* or *Exam Prep* study guides, *Personal Trainers*, *Personal Test Centers*, or one of our interactive Web courses—will make your studying fun and productive. Our commitment is to build the kind of learning tools that will allow you to study the way you want to, whenever you want to.

Visit ExamCram.com now to enhance your study program.

Help us continue to provide the very best certification study materials possible. Write us or email us at **learn@examcram.com** and let us know how our study products have helped you study. Tell us about new features that you'd like us to add. Send us a story about how we've helped you. We're listening!

Good luck with your certification exam and your career. Thank you for allowing us to help you achieve your goals.

Keith Weiskamp

Keith Weiskamp
President and CEO

Look for these other products from The Coriolis Group:

LPI General Linux II Exam Cram
By Emmett Dulaney

Sair Linux/GNU Installation and Configuration Exam Cram
by Michael Jang

Sair Linux/GNU Security, Ethics, and Privacy Exam Cram
By Dee-Ann LeBlanc

General Linux I Exam Prep
By Dee-Ann LeBlanc

Linux System Administration Black Book
By Dee-Ann LeBlanc

Real World Linux Deployment Black Book
By Dee-Ann LeBlanc

For Karen

❧

About the Author

Emmett Dulaney, MCT, MCSE, Network+, A+, i-Net+, is the co-owner of D S Technical Solutions and an instructor for the Continuing Education department of Indiana University/Purdue University of Fort Wayne. He has been working with Unix for more than 15 years and with Linux almost since its inception. He is the author of more than a dozen certification titles, as well as being the StudyGuides editor for *Certification Magazine*. Emmett can be reached at **edulaney@iquest.net**.

Acknowledgments

I would like to thank the entire Coriolis team for helping to make this book a reality. A special thanks is due to Sharon Linsenbach, Sally Scott, Kristine Simmons, and Bart Reed for all of their contributions and diligence. Thanks as well are due to Julian Laredo for verifying the facts and figures.

Last of all, an enormous amount of gratitude is owed to the entire Linux community for proving that the impossible is possible through organized collaboration.

Contents at a Glance

Table of Contents

Introduction

Welcome to *LPI General Linux I Exam Cram*! This book aims to help you get ready to take—and pass—the LPI certification 101 exam. This Introduction explains LPI's certification programs in general and talks about how the *Exam Cram* series can help you prepare for LPI's certification exams.

Exam Cram books help you understand and appreciate the subjects and materials you need to pass LPI certification exams. *Exam Cram* books are aimed strictly at test preparation and review. In this book, I do not teach you everything you need to know about a topic (such as the ins and outs of building your own servers). Instead, I present and dissect the questions and problems I've found that you're likely to encounter on a test. I've worked from LPI's own objectives, preparation guides, and tests. My aim is to bring together as much information as possible about LPI certification exams.

Nevertheless, to prepare yourself completely for any LPI test, you should begin by taking the Self-Assessment included in this book (immediately following this Introduction). This tool will help you evaluate your knowledge base against the requirements for the actual exam under both ideal and real circumstances.

Based on what you learn from that exercise, you might decide to begin your studies with some classroom training, or you might pick up and read one of the many Linux guides available from third-party vendors. I strongly recommend that you also install and configure the software and tools that you'll be tested on, because nothing beats hands-on experience and familiarity when it comes to understanding the questions you're likely to encounter on a certification test. Book learning is essential, but hands-on experience is the best teacher of all.

The Linux Professional Institute Certification (LPIC) Program

LPI certification is made up of three levels, with each level consisting of two exams. There is no time limit upon when the exams must be taken or an order in which they must be taken, but you must pass both of the exams within each level to be certified at that level.

Many of the higher-level exams are currently under development, and the best place to keep tabs on the program and its various certifications is the LPI Web site. The current URL for the LPI program is **www.lpi.org**. Before undertaking any certification venture, you should make certain you have the latest and most accurate information about the organization's certification programs.

Taking a Certification Exam

Alas, testing is not free. The current cost (always subject to change) per exam is $100, and the exams are offered through VUE (Virtual University) testing centers (**www.vue.com**).

Although VUE is flexible in scheduling, it is best to call at least 10 days in advance. Exam seats are limited and might be booked solid around the time you realize you are ready for the test. To cancel or reschedule an exam, you should call at least 2 days before the scheduled test time in order to receive any sort of refund. When calling to schedule, have the following information ready for the staff member who handles your call:

- Your name, social security number (if applicable), organization, and mailing address.
- A method of payment. (The most convenient approach is to supply a valid credit card number with sufficient available credit. Otherwise, payments by check, money order, or purchase order must be received before a test can be scheduled. If the latter methods are required, ask your order taker for more details.)

On the day of the test, arrive at least 15 minutes before your scheduled time slot. You must bring and supply two forms of identification, one of which must be a photo ID.

All exams are completely closed book. In fact, you will be required to stow anything you brought with you under your desk. You will be furnished with a blank sheet of paper, a pencil, and any other tools you might need for your exam. I suggest that you immediately write down on that sheet of paper all the information you've memorized for the test.

When you complete an exam, you will get an immediate printout of your results and you'll know whether you passed. All exam components are scored on a percentage basis.

How to Prepare for an Exam

Preparing for any Linux exam requires that you obtain and study materials designed to provide comprehensive information about Linux and the specific exam for which you are preparing. The following list of materials will help you study and prepare:

- A vendor's Linux manuals (or online documentation found on the vendor's Web site). This should be available for the vendor's version you are running (be it OpenLinux from Caldera, Red Hat, Debian, or any other).
- The Linux Documentation Project (online resource found at **www.linuxdoc.org**).
- Study guides. Several publishers—including The Coriolis Group—offer Linux titles. The Coriolis Group series includes the following:
  - *The Exam Cram series*—These books give you information about the material you need to know to pass the tests.
  - *The Exam Prep series*—These books provide a greater level of detail than the *Exam Cram* books and are designed to teach you everything you need to know from an exam perspective. Each book comes with a CD that contains interactive practice exams in a variety of testing formats.

  Together, the two series make a perfect pair. Check **ExamCram.com** for additional products from Coriolis.

You'll find that this book will complement your studying and preparation for the exam, either on your own or with the aid of the previously mentioned study programs. In the section that follows, I'll explain how this book works and why it counts as a member of the required and recommended materials list.

About This Book

Each topical *Exam Cram* chapter follows a regular structure, along with graphical cues about important or useful information. Here's the structure of a typical chapter:

- *Opening hotlists*—Each chapter begins with a list of the terms, tools, and techniques that you must learn and understand before you can be fully conversant with that chapter's subject matter. The hotlists are followed by one or two introductory paragraphs to set the stage for the rest of the chapter.

- *Topical coverage*—After the opening hotlist, each chapter covers a series of topics related to its subject. Throughout this section, I highlight important topics or concepts as Exam Alerts, like this:

This is what an Exam Alert looks like. Normally, an Exam Alert stresses concepts, terms, software, or activities that are likely to relate to one or more certification test questions. For that reason, any information found offset in Exam Alert format is worthy of unusual attentiveness on your part. Indeed, most of the information that appears on the Cram Sheet appears as Exam Alerts within the text.

Pay close attention to material flagged as an Exam Alert. Although all the information in this book pertains to what you need to know to pass the exam, I flag certain items that are really important. You'll find what appears in the meat of each chapter to be worth knowing, too, when preparing for the test. Because this book's material is very condensed, I recommend that you use this book along with other resources to achieve the maximum benefit.

In addition to the Exam Alerts, I have provided occasional notes that will help you build a better foundation for Linux knowledge. Although the information might not be on the exam, it is certainly related and will help you become a better test taker.

This is how tips are formatted. Keep your eyes open for these, and you'll become a Linux guru in no time.

- *Practice questions*—This section presents a series of mock test questions and explanations of both correct and incorrect answers.

- *Details and resources*—Every chapter ends with a section titled "Need to Know More?" These sections provide direct pointers to third-party resources offering more details on the chapters' subjects. If you find a resource you like in this collection, use it, but don't feel compelled to use all the resources. On the other hand, I recommend only those resources that I use on a regular basis, so none of my recommendations will be a waste of your time or money. (However, purchasing the recommended books all at once probably represents an expense to many network administrators and would be hard to justify.)

The bulk of the book follows this chapter structure slavishly, but there are a few other elements that I'd like to point out. Chapter 12 dwells on what your next step should be after you read this book, and it offers some suggestions for what moves you might want to plot out next. Chapter 13 includes a sample written test that provides a good review of the material presented throughout the book to ensure that you're ready for the exam. Chapter 14 is an answer key to the sample test that appears in Chapter 13. Additionally, you'll find a Glossary that explains important terms and an Index that you can use to track down terms as they appear in the text.

Finally, the tear-out Cram Sheet attached next to the inside front cover of this book represents a condensed and compiled collection of facts and tips that I think you should memorize before taking the test. Because you can dump this information out of your head onto a piece of paper before answering any exam questions, you can master this information by brute force—you need to remember it only long enough to write it down when you walk into the test room. You might even want to look at it in the car or in the lobby of the testing center just before you walk in to take the test.

How to Use This Book

If you're prepping for a first-time test, keep in mind that I've structured the topics in this book to build on one another. Therefore, some topics in later chapters make more sense after you've read earlier chapters. That's why I suggest you read this book from front to back for your initial test preparation. If you need to brush up on a topic or have to bone up for a second try, use the Index or Table of Contents to go straight to the topics and questions that you need to study. Beyond the tests, I think you'll find this book useful as a tightly focused reference to some of the most important aspects of Linux.

Given all the book's elements and its specialized focus, I've tried to create a tool that will help you prepare for—and pass—LPI's 101 exam. Please share your feedback on the book with me, especially if you have ideas about how I can improve it for future test takers.

Send your questions or comments to The Coriolis Group at **learn@examcram.com**. Please remember to include the title of the book in your message. Also, be sure to check out the Web page at **www.examcram.com**, where you'll find information updates, commentary, and clarifications on documents for each book. Thanks, and enjoy this book!

Self-Assessment

I have included a self-assessment in this *Exam Cram* to help you evaluate your readiness to tackle the LPI 101 exam. It should also help you understand which topics you need to master from this book and which you need to study in greater detail. But before you tackle this self-assessment, let's talk about concerns you might face when pursuing the LPI certification and what an ideal Level 1 candidate might look like.

Level I in the Real World

In the next section, I describe the ideal LPIC Level I candidate, knowing full well that not all candidates will meet this ideal. In fact, my description of that ideal candidate might seem downright scary. But take heart—many who have once been in the same position as you are already certified, so Level I certification is obviously an attainable goal. You can get all the real-world motivation you need from knowing that many others have gone before, so you will be able to follow in their footsteps. If you're willing to tackle the process seriously and do what it takes to obtain the necessary experience and knowledge, you can take—and pass—the certification tests involved in obtaining Level I certification. In fact, I've designed this *Exam Cram* (and its companion for the 102 exam) to make it as easy as possible for you to prepare for the exam. But prepare you must!

The Ideal LPIC Level I Candidate

Just to give you some idea of what an ideal candidate is like, here is a list of suitable tasks that should be in the candidate's job duties, as listed by the Linux Professional Institute (taken verbatim from LPI's Web site). Don't worry if you don't meet all these qualifications or don't even come that close—this is a far-from-ideal world, and where you fall short is simply where you'll have more work to do. Here are the tasks that the candidate should be able to do:

- Can work at the Unix command line.
- Performs easy maintenance tasks: help out users, add users to a larger system, backup and restore, shutdown and reboot.

- Can install and configure a workstation (including X) and connect it to the LAN, or a stand-alone PC via modem to the Internet.

I believe that well under half of all certification candidates meet these requirements and that, in fact, most meet less than half of these requirements—at least, when they begin the certification process. But because others who already have been certified have survived this ordeal, you can survive it, too—especially if you heed what this self-assessment can tell you about what you already know and what you need to learn.

Put Yourself to the Test

The following series of questions and observations is designed to help you figure out how much work you must do to pursue LPI certification and what kinds of resources you may consult on your quest. Be absolutely honest in your answers; otherwise, you'll end up wasting money on an exam you're not yet ready to take. There are no right or wrong answers, only steps along the path to certification. Only you can decide where you really belong in the broad spectrum of aspiring candidates.

Two things should be clear from the outset, however:

- Even a modest background in computer science will be helpful.
- Hands-on experience in Linux and Internet-related technologies is an essential ingredient to certification success.

The most important key to success on the 101 test is hands-on experience. If I leave you with only one realization after taking this self-assessment, it should be that there's no substitute for time spent installing, configuring, developing, and using the various Linux-related commands and technologies upon which you'll be tested repeatedly and in depth. If you have never worked with any of the technologies mentioned earlier, you would be well advised to purchase a couple systems upon which you can install and reinstall Linux as well as run through all the administrative aspects of Linux needed for the exam.

Testing Your Exam Readiness

Whether you attend a formal class on a specific topic to get ready for the exam or use written materials to study on your own, some preparation for the LPI certification exam is essential. At $100 a try (always subject to change), pass or fail, you want to do everything you can to pass on your first try. That's where studying comes in.

For any given subject, consider taking a class if you've tackled self-study materials, taken the test, and failed anyway. The opportunity to interact with an instructor and fellow students can make all the difference in the world, if you can afford that privilege.

If you can't afford to take a class, you should still invest in some low-cost practice exams from commercial vendors, because they can help you assess your readiness to pass a test better than any other tool.

I have included practice questions at the end of each chapter, plus a practice exam in Chapter 13 of this book. Therefore, if you don't score too well on the chapter tests, you can study more and then tackle the test in Chapter 13.

Have you taken a practice exam? If you have, and you scored 80 percent or better, you're probably ready to tackle the real thing. If your score isn't above that crucial threshold, obtain all the free and low-budget practice tests you can find (this is a new certification, so practice tests may be hard to find) and get to work. Keep at it until you can break the passing threshold comfortably.

When it comes to assessing your test readiness, there is no better way than to take a good-quality practice exam and pass with a score of 80 percent or better. When I'm preparing myself, I shoot for 90-plus percent, just to leave room for the "ambiguity factor" that sometimes shows up on LPI exams.

You should also cruise the Web looking for *braindumps* (recollections of test topics and experiences recorded by others) to help you anticipate topics you're likely to encounter on the test.

When using any braindump, it's okay to pay attention to information about questions. However, you can't always be sure that a braindump's author will also be able to provide correct answers. Therefore, use the questions to guide your studies but *never* rely on the answers in a braindump to lead you to the truth. Double-check everything you find in any braindump.

One last note: It might seem counterintuitive to talk about hands-on experience in the context of the mostly multiple-choice exam, but as you review the material for this exam, you'll realize that hands-on experience with Linux features is invaluable. Surprisingly, you'll also benefit from hands-on administrative experience with Windows NT, NetWare, and network hardware, as well as just playing around on the Internet.

Onward, through the Fog!

Once you've assessed your readiness, undertaken the right background studies, obtained the hands-on experience that will help you understand the technologies at work, and reviewed the many sources of information to help you prepare for a test, you'll be ready to take a round of practice tests. When your scores come back positive enough to get you through the exam, you're ready to go after the real thing. If you follow my assessment regime, you'll know not only what you need to study but also when you're ready to make a test date at VUE (Virtual University). Good luck!

LPI Certification Exams

Terms you'll need to understand:

- ✓ Radio button
- ✓ Checkbox
- ✓ Multiple-choice question formats
- ✓ Fill-in-the-blank question format
- ✓ Careful reading
- ✓ Process of elimination

Techniques you'll need to master:

- ✓ Preparing to take a certification exam
- ✓ Practicing (to make perfect)
- ✓ Making the best use of the testing software
- ✓ Budgeting your time
- ✓ Saving the hardest questions until last
- ✓ Guessing (as a last resort)

Exam taking is not something that most people anticipate eagerly, no matter how well prepared they might be. In most cases, familiarity helps to lessen test anxiety. In plain English, this means you probably won't be as nervous when you take your fourth or fifth certification exam as you'll be when you take your first one.

Whether it's your first exam or your tenth, understanding the details of exam taking (how much time to spend on questions, the environment you'll be in, and so on) and the exam software will help you concentrate on the material rather than on the setting. Likewise, mastering a few basic exam-taking skills should help you recognize—and perhaps even outfox—some of the tricks and gotchas you're bound to find in some of the exam questions.

This chapter, besides explaining the exam environment and software, describes some proven exam-taking strategies that you should be able to use to your advantage.

The Exam Situation

When you arrive at the testing center where you scheduled your exam, you'll sign in with an exam coordinator. He or she will ask you to show two forms of identification, one of which must be a photo ID, and both should have your signature. After you've signed in and your time slot arrives, you'll be asked to deposit any books, pagers, cell phones, bags, and other items you brought with you. Then, you'll be escorted into a closed room. Typically, the room will be furnished with anywhere from one to half a dozen computers, and each workstation will be separated from the others by dividers designed to keep you from seeing what's happening on someone else's computer.

You'll be furnished with a pen or pencil and a blank sheet of paper or, in some cases, an erasable plastic sheet and an erasable felt-tip pen. You're allowed to write down any information you want on both sides of this sheet. Before the exam, you should memorize as much of the material that appears on the Cram Sheet (inside the front cover of this book) as you can so you can write that information on the blank sheet as soon as you are seated in front of the computer. You can refer to your rendition of the Cram Sheet anytime you like during the test, but you'll have to surrender the sheet when you leave the room.

Most test rooms feature a wall with a large picture window. This permits the exam coordinator standing behind it to monitor the room, to prevent exam takers from talking to one another, and to observe anything out of the ordinary that might happen. The exam coordinator will have preloaded the appropriate Linux Professional Institute (LPI) certification exam—for this book, that's the LPI 101 Certification Exam—and you'll be permitted to start as soon as you're seated in front of the computer.

All LPI certification exams allow a certain maximum amount of time in which to complete your work. (This time is indicated on the exam by an on-screen counter/clock, so you can check the time remaining whenever you like.) The exam consists of randomly selected questions, and you may take up to 90 minutes to complete the exam.

The LPI 101 Certification Exam is computer generated and uses a combination of multiple-choice and short-answer (fill-in-the-blank) formats. Although this might sound simple, the questions are constructed not only to check your mastery of basic facts and figures about Linux technologies, but also to require you to evaluate one or more sets of circumstances or requirements. You might be asked to select the best or most effective solution to a problem from a range of choices, all of which technically are correct. Taking the exam is quite an adventure, and it involves real thinking. This book shows you what to expect and how to deal with the potential problems, puzzles, and predicaments.

Exam Layout and Design

Some exam questions require you to select a single answer, whereas others ask you to select multiple correct answers. The following multiple-choice question requires you to select a single correct answer. Following the question is a brief summary of each potential answer and why it is either right or wrong.

Question 1

Which command can be used with the appropriate parameters or switches to count the number of lines in a text file?

❍ a. **grep**

❍ b. **wcl**

❍ c. **lc**

❍ d. **cat**

The correct answer to this question is b. The command **wc -l** will count the number of lines within a file. **grep** can be used to find strings, **lc** does not exist, and **cat** is used to display files. Therefore, all answers except b are incorrect.

This sample question format corresponds closely to the LPI Certification Exam format; the only difference on the exam is that questions are not followed by answer keys. To select an answer, position the cursor over the radio button next to the answer. Then click the mouse button to select the answer.

Let's examine a question that requires choosing multiple answers. This type of question provides checkboxes rather than radio buttons for marking all appropriate selections.

Question 2

Which of the following are valid parameters for use with the **umount** command? [Check all correct answers]

- ❑ a. **-a**
- ❑ b. **-b**
- ❑ c. **-n**
- ❑ d. **-m**

The correct answers to this question are a and c. **umount -a** will unmount all filesystems within /etc/mtab, and **umount -n** will unmount a specified filesystem. The other two parameters are not valid for use with the **umount** utility.

For this type of question, more than one answer is required. Such questions are scored as wrong unless all the required selections are chosen. In other words, a partially correct answer does not result in partial credit when the test is scored. If you are required to provide multiple answers and you do not provide the number of answers that the question asks for, the testing software will mark the question for you and indicate at the end of the test that you did not complete that question. To the best of our knowledge, these questions are scored wrong unless all the required selections are chosen. For Question 2, you have to check the boxes next to items a and c to obtain credit for a correct answer. Notice that picking the right answers also means knowing why the other answers are wrong!

Let's examine a question that requires filling in the blank. On the test itself, you will see that this type of question provides an input box into which you type an answer; here, we've inserted a blank line for your answer.

Question 3

What is the numerical representation of a file's permissions if they are equal to **-rwxr-xr-x**? [Fill in the blank]

____

The correct answer to this question is 755. Any other value is incorrect.

Although these three basic types of questions can appear in many forms, they constitute the foundation on which all the LPI Certification Exam questions rest. At any time, LPI can choose to include other questions involving exhibits, charts, or network diagrams to help document a Web site scenario that you'll be asked to troubleshoot or configure. Paying careful attention to such exhibits is the key to success.

Using LPI's Exam Software Effectively

A well-known principle when taking exams is to first read over the entire exam from start to finish while answering only those questions you feel absolutely sure of. On subsequent passes, you can dive into more complex questions more deeply, knowing how many such questions you have left.

Fortunately, LPI's exam software makes this approach easy to implement. At the top-left corner of each question is a checkbox that permits you to mark that question for a later visit.

Note: Marking questions makes review easier, but you can return to any question if you are willing to click the Forward or Back button repeatedly.

As you read each question, if you answer only those you're sure of and mark for review those you're not sure of, you can keep working through a decreasing list of questions as you answer the trickier ones in order.

There's at least one potential benefit to reading the exam completely before answering the trickier questions: Sometimes, information supplied in later questions sheds more light on earlier questions. Other times, information you read in later questions might jog your memory about networking facts, figures, or behavior that will help with earlier questions. Either way, you'll come out ahead if you defer those questions about which you're not absolutely sure.

Keep working on the questions until you're certain of all your answers or until you know you'll run out of time. If questions remain unanswered, you'll want to zip through them and guess. Not answering a question guarantees you won't receive credit for it, and a guess has at least a chance of being correct.

At the very end of your exam period, you're better off guessing than leaving questions unanswered.

Exam-Taking Basics

The most important advice about taking any exam is this: Read each question carefully. Some questions are deliberately ambiguous, some use double negatives, and others use terminology in incredibly precise ways. I have taken numerous exams—both practice and live—and in nearly every one I have missed at least one question because I didn't read it closely or carefully enough.

Here are some suggestions on how to deal with the tendency to jump to an answer too quickly:

- Make sure you read every word in the question. If you find yourself jumping ahead impatiently, go back and start over.
- As you read, try to restate the question in your own terms. If you can do this, you should be able to pick the correct answers more easily.
- When returning to a question after your initial read-through, read every word again; otherwise, your mind can quickly fall into a rut. Sometimes, revisiting a question after turning your attention elsewhere lets you see something you missed, but the strong tendency is to see what you've seen before. Avoid that tendency at all costs.
- If you return to a question more than twice, try to articulate to yourself what you don't understand about the question, why the answers don't appear to make sense, or what appears to be missing. If you chew on the subject for a while, your subconscious might provide the details that are lacking or you might notice a "trick" that will point to the right answer.

Above all, deal with each question by thinking through what you know about networking essentials—the characteristics, behaviors, facts, and figures involved. By reviewing what you know (and what you've written down on your information sheet), you'll often recall or understand things sufficiently to determine the answer to the question.

Question-Handling Strategies

Based on exams I've taken, some interesting trends have become apparent. For those questions that take only a single answer, usually two or three of the answers will be obviously incorrect, and two of the answers will be plausible; of course, only one can be correct. Unless the answer leaps out at you (if it does, reread the question to look for a trick; sometimes those are the ones you're likely to get wrong), begin the process of answering by eliminating those answers that are most obviously wrong.

Things to look for in obviously wrong answers include nonexistent commands, incorrect utility names, inconsistent conditions, and terminology you've never seen. If you've done your homework for an exam, no valid information should be completely new to you. In that case, unfamiliar or bizarre terminology probably indicates a totally bogus answer.

Numerous questions assume that you understand the inner workings of Linux utilities inside and out. If your knowledge in these areas is well grounded, it will help you cut through many otherwise confusing questions.

As you work your way through the exam, another counter that LPI graciously provides will come in handy—the number of questions completed and questions outstanding. Budget your time by making sure you've completed one-quarter of the questions one-quarter of the way through the exam period and three-quarters of them three-quarters of the way through.

If you're not finished when 85 minutes have elapsed, use the last 5 minutes to guess your way through the remaining questions. Remember, guessing is potentially more valuable than not answering because blank answers are always wrong, but a guess can turn out to be right. If you don't have a clue about any of the remaining questions, pick answers at random, or choose all a's, b's, and so on. The important thing is to submit an exam for scoring that has an answer for every question.

Mastering the Inner Game

In the final analysis, knowledge breeds confidence, and confidence breeds success. If you study the materials in this book carefully and review all the practice questions at the end of each chapter, you should become aware of those areas where additional learning and study are required.

Next, follow up by reading some or all of the materials recommended in the "Need to Know More?" section at the end of each chapter. The idea is to become familiar enough with the concepts and situations you find in the sample questions that you can reason your way through similar situations on a real exam. If you know the material, you have every right to be confident that you can pass the exam.

After you've worked your way through the book, take the practice exam in Chapter 13. This will provide a reality check and help you identify areas you need to study further. Make sure you follow up and review materials related to the questions you miss on the practice exam before scheduling a real exam. Only when you've covered all the ground and feel comfortable with the whole scope of the practice exam should you take a real one.

If you take the practice exam and don't score at least 75 percent correct, you'll want to practice further. If you need more practice, you might want to purchase the *General Linux I Exam Prep* (Scottsdale, AZ: The Coriolis Group, 2000), which contains additional tests, or download self-study software from various Web sites.

Armed with the information in this book and with the determination to augment your knowledge, you should be able to pass the certification exam. However, you need to work at it, or you'll spend the exam fee more than once before you finally pass. If you prepare seriously, you should do well. Good luck!

Additional Resources

A good source of information about LPI certification exams comes from the Linux Professional Institute itself, and the best place to go for exam-related information is online. If you haven't already visited the LPI Web site, do so right now at **www.lpi.org** (see Figure 1.1).

Note: This page might not be there by the time you read this, or it might have been replaced by something new and different. Should this happen, please read the sidebar "Coping with Change on the Web."

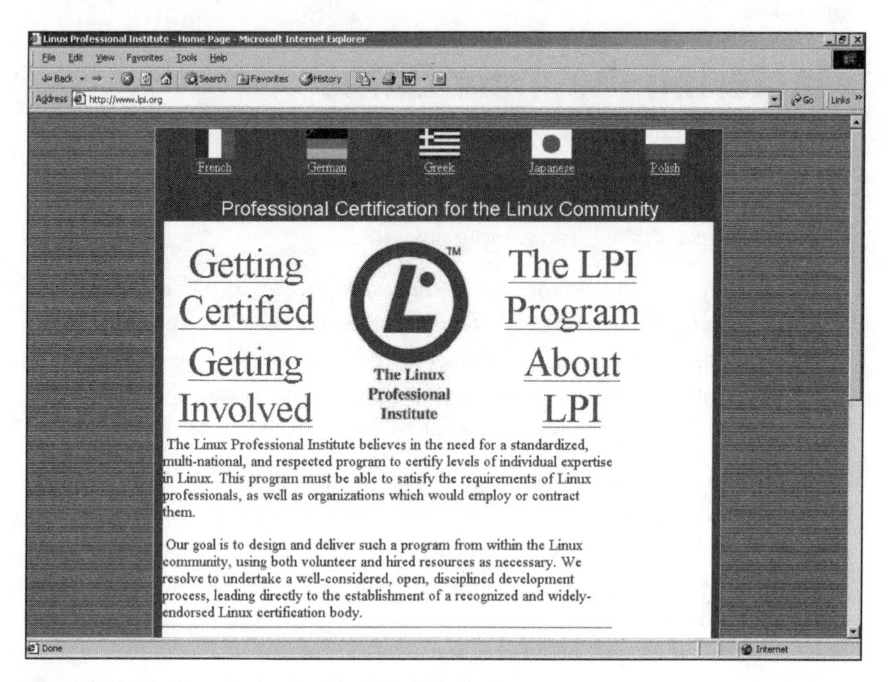

Figure 1.1 The Linux Professional Institute Web site.

The menu options at the bottom of the home page point to the most important sources of information in the Web pages. Here's what to check out, in order of importance:

- *Getting Certified*—Use this menu entry to review the skills and knowledge that will be tested on the exam, as well as find links to register.
- *Getting Involved*—This area discusses how to join LPI, get on the mailing lists, and see what upcoming events are planned.
- *The LPI Program*—This page fully explains the certification process and holds links to objectives, sample questions, and a glossary of terms used in the exams.
- *About LPI*—This page holds the FAQ (frequently asked questions) and links to the Board of Directors, Advisory Board, and meeting minutes.

These are just the high points of what's available in the LPI pages. As you browse through them—and I strongly recommend that you do—you'll probably find other informational tidbits mentioned that are every bit as interesting.

Coping with Change on the Web

Sooner or later, all the information I've shared with you about the LPI pages and the other Web-based resources mentioned throughout the rest of this book will go stale or be replaced by newer information. In some cases, the URLs you find here might lead you to their replacements; in other cases, the URLs will go nowhere, leaving you with the dreaded "404 File not found" error message. When that happens, don't give up.

There's always a way to find what you want on the Web if you're willing to invest some time and energy. Most large or complex Web sites offer a search engine. Feel free to use general search tools—such as **www.search.com**, **www.altavista.com**, and **www.excite.com**—to search for related information. Although LPI offers the best information about its certification exams online, plenty of third-party sources offer information, training, and assistance in this area. The bottom line is this: If you can't find something where the book says it lives, start looking around. If worse comes to worst, you can always email us at Coriolis. We just might have a clue.

The Command Line

Terms you'll need to understand:

✓ Shell

✓ Wildcard

✓ **PATH**

✓ Environmental variables

✓ Standard output

✓ Standard input

✓ Command history

✓ Aliases

Techniques you'll need to master:

✓ Understanding the basic concepts of shells within Linux

✓ Recognizing the differences between many basic shell commands

In this chapter, you'll learn the basics of the Linux command line and walk through an overview of operations and features. The main concepts to know for the real world, as well as for exam preparation, are addressed in detail.

Shell Basics

Within Linux, the shell is the command interpreter. It takes commands that a user gives, processes them (or sends them to the appropriate utility or interacts with the kernel), and formats the finished results for the user. The shell, therefore, is the mediator between the operating system and the user. Not only can it interpret commands, but it can also handle redirection (input and output), filename generation, some programming capabilities, variable substitution, piping, and a host of other services.

A number of different shells (interpreters) are available, and different vendors include different combinations of choices with their operating systems. The simplest of all is the Bourne shell (sh), which is one of the earliest ones created for the Unix platform, and it offers the smallest number of features. The Korn shell (ksh) was one of the first to expand upon, and deviate from, sh, and it includes a larger number of options. The Bourne Again shell (bash) took many of the features from Korn, and some new ones, and combined them with sh, while trying to reduce deviations. The Z shell (zsh) is the largest shell of all, and it adds a whole new set of features to the Korn shell.

Not to be overlooked are shells created to make the environment more friendly to those familiar with the C programming language. The first of these was the C shell (csh), which added C-like features to the interpreter and deviated greatly from the Bourne shell. It has been expanded upon by Tom's C shell (tcsh).

In general, every vendor includes more than one shell for the user to choose from, but rarely do vendors include all the available shells. Within Caldera, for example, are three shells:

- bash
- tcsh
- zsh

Additionally, two links within Caldera's operating system dictate that if users attempt to use sh, they are really given bash; and if they attempt to use csh, they are really given tcsh.

For the exam, remember that all the shells reside in the /bin directory, and the default can be specified for users in their /etc/passwd file entry.

Slight deviations exist in the way each shell carries out its tasks, but all perform a core set of functions. Throughout the rest of this chapter, we look at the core functions for all shells and discuss differences as they apply.

Command-Line Interaction

When a command is entered, the shell must determine if the command is for it (internal) or not (external). If the command is internal, it does the processing and sends the output back without further interaction. If the command cannot be found within the shell itself, then it is assumed to be external (such as **ls**, **cat**, **cal**, and so on). The command syntax for external commands is always assumed to be:

```
{program name} {option(s)} {argument(s)}
```

Although it is always assumed that the command has three components, it need not include all three. The simplest command to give is the name of the utility, such as:

```
ls
```

which returns an output similar to:

```
Desktop    sample    snapshot01.gif    snapshot02.gif
```

In this case, we gave only the program name with no options. This results in a list of all files within the present directory in the default format. We can specify an option to include or exclude information or to change the format of the display. An example is:

```
ls -l
```

which changes the output to:

```
total 34
drwx------  5  root  root  1024   Jul 19 16:34 Desktop
-rw-r--r--  1  root  root  155    Jul 19 16:48 sample
-rw-r--r--  1  root  root  12497  Jul 19 16:39 snapshot01.gif
-rw-r--r--  1  root  root  17257  Jul 19 16:50 snapshot02.gif
```

This example specified the program name (**ls**) as well as an option to use with it (-l) to change the list to the "long" format.

Note: It is important to understand that you must always use white space to separate the parameters. White space can be either a space character or a tab character.

*Typing the command as **ls-l** would generate an error message because there is no utility with the name **ls-l**, and the interpreter would not be able to distinguish the program name from the option.*

The options, as well as the arguments, are optional and never required. To complete the example, we can also use an argument with the command, such as:

```
ls -l *.gif
```

which results in a display of:

```
-rw-r--r--  1  root  root  12497  Jul 19 16:39 snapshot01.gif
-rw-r--r--  1  root  root  17257  Jul 19 16:50 snapshot02.gif
```

Or we can use the argument without the options, as in **ls *.gif**.

The number of arguments is not limited to one. Although an individual utility might place limitations on the number of parameters it will accept, typically you can string together multiple requests. For example, you could specify:

```
ls -l sa*
```

as one command and then follow it with:

```
ls -l *.gif
```

You can accomplish the same operation, however, with:

```
ls -l sa* *.gif
```

The result of the operation becomes:

```
-rw-r--r--  1  root  root  155    Jul 19 16:48 sample
-rw-r--r--  1  root  root  12497  Jul 19 16:39 snapshot01.gif
-rw-r--r--  1  root  root  17257  Jul 19 16:50 snapshot02.gif
```

If the number of arguments becomes too long to be easily readable on the command line, or if you simply want to break up the entry a bit, you can use the backslash character to signify that you are continuing from one line to the next:

```
ls -l sa* \
*.gif
```

If you give hundreds of such arguments, you can use the back slash to separate each entry. This makes the entry easier to view, and the command does not execute until you press the Enter key without preceding it with a back slash:

```
ls -l sa* \
*.gif \
*.ead \
*.txt \
*.doc
```

Connecting Commands

In all the examples thus far, we used the Enter key to inform the shell that a command needs to be processed. You are not, however, limited to giving the shell only one command at a time.

You can provide multiple commands, not connected to one another in any way, on the same line as long as you use the semicolon (;) to connect them. For example, it is possible to see all the files in the current directory and the current date by giving the following two commands in succession:

```
ls
date
```

Because these commands are unrelated in that the output of the second has absolutely nothing to do with the output of the first, you can combine them on a single command line with a semicolon and get the same result:

```
ls ; date
```

The semicolon is a special character that always means multiple commands are on the same line. Because it has this global meaning, you can break the white-space rule on both sides (**ls;date**) and get the same result.

If the commands *do* have something in common—the output of one is to become the input of the next—then you connect them using a pipe (|). For example, if a list of files within a directory is too long to fit on one screen, you can view one screen at a time by using the command:

```
ls -l | more
```

Here the output of the **ls -l** command becomes the input of the **more** command. If the first part of the entire command line fails, the second part cannot possibly be executed.

Wildcards

Wildcards are characters used to signify other characters that the shell fills in. The two most common wildcard characters are the asterisk (*) and question mark (?). Although often confused, their meanings are different and can lead to completely different results.

The asterisk is used to signify any and all, anything and nothing, alpha and omega:

```
ls s*
```

This example finds all entries (files and directories) within the current directory starting with the letter "s" and having any number of characters following—including none. Possible results it could generate in the display include:

```
s   sa   sam   samp   sampl   sample   samples   samples.gif
```

Note that it finds "s" alone and "s" with any number of characters following it. In contrast, the question mark is a placeholder for one thing and only one thing. Using the same file possibilities, the command:

```
ls s?
```

finds entries (files and directories) only within the current directory starting with the letter "s" and containing only one more character. The resulting display is:

```
sa
```

If you want to find only five-letter entries beginning with "s", the command to use is:

```
ls s????
```

To recap, the asterisk means all or none, and the question mark always means one. These two wildcards are not mutually exclusive, so you can use them in combination as the need arises. For example, to find only files with three-letter extensions, regardless of the file name, the command is:

```
ls *.???
```

To muddy the waters a bit, you can also use brackets ([]) to specify possible values. All the possible values must reside within the brackets, and the shell finds them individually:

```
ls [de]*
```

This example finds all entries that start with either "d" or "e" and contain an unlimited number of characters. To find only three-character entries that start with "d" or "e", the command becomes:

```
ls [de]??
```

The number of characters you can supply within the brackets is virtually unlimited. Therefore, if you want to find all entries that start with a lowercase letter instead of a number (or other character), you can use **[abcdefghijklmnopqrstuvwxyz]**. Because this is a range, a much simpler way to signify it is **[a-z]**, as in:

```
ls [a-z]*
```

The ranges need not be a complete set of all numbers or all characters (although they are easier to specify) and can include only a subset if need be. For example, if you want to look for only entries that fall within the range from "d" to "t", you can use either **[defghijklmnopqrst]** or **[d-t]**. If the entry can be between the two values uppercase and lowercase, you can either use **[DEFGHIJKLMNOPQRSTdefghijklmnopqrst]** or **[D-Td-t]**.

Some more examples include:

- All letters (uppercase and lowercase): [A-z]

[A-z] is the same as saying **[A-Z]** and **[a-z]**.

- All numbers: [0-9]
- All letters and numbers: [A-z0-9]
- Not a number: [!0-9]
- Not a letter: [!A-z]

The PATH Statement and Other Variables

When you enter a command at the command prompt and the shell cannot find it internally, it must look for a utility by that name externally. It does this by searching directories specified in the **PATH** variable, in the order they are listed, until it finds the first match. If the shell finds no match after searching all listed directories, then the result is an error message ("command not found").

The following list outlines several important things to know about the path:

- You can view your path by using the command:

```
echo $PATH
```

- The path does not, by default, include the present directory. Thus, you can create an executable file in your home directory, see it right before you (with **ls**), and, when you type its name, be told that the command cannot be found. To circumvent this, you can give the full path to the file, add your home directory to your **PATH** variable, move the file to a directory in the path statement, or add the present directory variable (.) to the **PATH** variable.
- Entries within the path are separated by colons (:).
- The order of the **PATH** search should always include the most common directories where executables can be found first (the bin directories) and the user-specific directories (if any) at the end.

To add another directory to your path, you can redefine the entire statement or simply append the new directory with the command:

```
PATH=$PATH:{new directory}
```

Thus, to add the directory /home/edulaney to the path, the command is:

```
PATH=$PATH:/home/edulaney
```

To add a variable that signifies you always want the directory you are currently working in to be searched for the utility, type:

```
PATH=$PATH:./
```

For security reasons, we always recommend that you not include the current directory in your path. If you must do so, however, it should appear at the end of the **PATH** statement—as shown previously—and not at the beginning.

Common Variables

Any variable that exists can display its values using the syntax:

```
echo ${variable name}
```

Thus, the command:

```
echo $MAIL
```

shows the mail directory, $HOME, the home directory, and so on. To see a complete list of defined environmental variables, you can use two commands—**env** and **set**. Although the displays can differ slightly (environmental variables only versus local variables), for the most part the output of **env** is a subset of the output of **set**. Some of the variables that can display include:

- HOME—The directory where you begin and where you end up when you type **cd** without any other parameters
- LINES—The number of lines within the display before pausing (more)
- LOGNAME—The name the user logged in as
- PWD—The present working directory, or where you are now
- SHELL—The interpreter you are using
- TERM—The type of terminal, or emulation, in use
- USER—Rarely differs from LOGNAME

As a general rule, predefined system variables always appear in all uppercase letters.

You can change the value of variables as needed or add your own to be referenced in programs or at the command prompt. For example, to create a new variable called TODAY, use the syntax:

```
TODAY=Wednesday
```

You can now see the value of the variable by using the command:

```
echo $TODAY
```

The result is **Wednesday**. If you now use the command:

```
set
```

the variable appears there. If you use the command:

```
env
```

however, it does not. The variable has been created locally and can only be referenced locally. For it to be accessible in subroutines and child processes, you must move it from local status into the environment, via the **export** command:

```
export TODAY
```

This moves the variable to where it can be found in the environment, as well as locally, and accessed by subroutines and child processes. The variable, and its value, will be available for the duration of the session and lost once you log out. To make the value permanent, you must add the entry to a profile (discussed in Chapter 8).

To change the value of the variable, simply define its new value:

```
TODAY=Monday
```

Because it has already been exported, this need not be done again, and the new value will apply locally as well as in the environment. Should it be necessary to remove a variable, you can use the **unset** command.

Among those variables present, and definable, are those that set the prompt. The prompt is the visual message from the shell that indicates it is ready for input. The default prompts include:

- $—The last character for sh, bash, and ksh
- %—The last character for csh and zsh
- >—The last character for tcsh

The primary prompt is either the variable **PS1** or **prompt**, based upon which shell you are using. In bash, a typical value for **PS1** is:

```
[\u@\h \W]\$
```

Dissected into its components, **PS1** is equal to the following:

- The left bracket ([)
- The name of the current user
- The at symbol (@)

- The name of the current host
- A space
- The present working directory
- The right bracket (])
- The dollar sign ($)

An example of this prompt is:

```
[edulaney@server7 home]$
```

The back-slash (\) character signifies that a special value should be used. Different values you can use for the prompt include those shown in Table 2.1.

Looking at the variables on the system, you will find that more than **PS1** exists. For example, earlier in this chapter we discussed ending a line with a back slash to signify that you are not finished entering input. If we look at the sequence of events and include prompts, it resembles:

```
[edulaney@server7 home]$ ls -l *.gif \
> *.fig \
> *.bmp
```

Note that the prompt changed from **PS1** to a greater-than sign (>). If it had stayed **PS1**, you would not know that it was still accepting input, so it changed from the primary prompt to a secondary prompt to signify the change in mode. The prompt represented (by default) by the greater-than sign is **PS2**. Its value can change from the default to any value you want, including all the special values in Table 2.1. Most shells have three to four layers of prompts.

Other Variables

By now you've realized that the dollar sign ($) is used to signify a variable; when you have a variable named **EXAMPLE**, you view its contents by examining **$EXAMPLE**. Three other variables can be useful in determining your environment.

The first—**$$**—shows the process ID number of the shell now running:

```
echo $$
```

The second—**$?**—shows the results of the last command you ran in terms of whether it was successful (**0**) or not (**1**). For example, the **ls** utility accepts an option of **-F** that will differentiate between directories and files by putting a slash

Table 2.1 Parameters that can be used for creating a prompt.

Value	Result
\d	Current date
\h	Name of host to first period
\n	New line
\s	Shell
\t	Time
\u	Username
\W	Current directory
\!	History number (discussed later in this chapter)
\#	Command number
\$	Default prompt—$ for standard users and # for root
\\	An actual back slash should appear (literal)
ABC	ABC (the value of that text)

behind the name of directories. The **ls** utility does not have a **-z** option. Given this knowledge, the following sequence shows how $? can be utilized and includes the prompts and output of each operation:

```
[edulaney@server7 home]$ ls -F
Desktop\    sample    snapshot01.gif    snapshot02.gif
[edulaney@server7 home]$ echo $?
0
[edulaney@server7 home]$ ls -z
ls: invalid option — z
[edulaney@server7 home]$ echo $?
1
```

The third variable—$!—shows the process ID number of the last child process started in the background. If no child processes have been started in the background, then the result is empty. Processes are covered in great detail in Chapter 6, but for this discussion it is useful to know that placing an ampersand (&) at the end of the command executes the command in the background:

```
[edulaney@server7 home]$ echo $!

[edulaney@server7 home]$ ls -F &
[edulaney@server7 home]$ echo $!
19321
[edulaney@server7 home]$
```

In the first instance, no job had been sent to the background, so the returned value was empty. We then sent a job to the background, and we found its process ID number by echoing **$!**.

Quoting

One of the most difficult shell components to understand is often the use of quotes. You can remember a few rules to make the concept easier to understand:

- The three types of quotes are double quotes ("), single quotes ('), and back quotes (`). Each has a different and distinct meaning. Double quotes disable all characters except ', \, and $. Single quotes disable all characters except the back quote. The back quote substitutes the value for a command.
- Quotes must always appear in even numbers. If you give an odd number, the shell believes that you have not finished with input and waits for more.
- You can mix and match different types of quotes and embed them within one another.

If you have a file named "sample of the worlds best cigars" and give the command:

```
cat sample of the worlds best cigars
```

the **cat** utility first tries to open a file named "sample", then one named "of", followed by four other files: "the", "worlds", "best", "cigars". The white space between the words is interpreted as delimiters between different files. To access the file, you must change the command to:

```
cat "sample of the worlds best cigars"
```

The double quotes cancel the default meaning of the white space and allow the value between them to be interpreted as a single entry. The double quotes cancel the meaning of most special characters, but not all. For example, if a variable named **EXAMPLE** is equal to 25, then:

```
echo $EXAMPLE
```

returns "**25**". Likewise:

```
echo "$EXAMPLE"
```

also returns "**25**", and:

```
echo '$EXAMPLE'
```

returns **"$EXAMPLE"**. The single quotes go above and beyond the double quotes and also cancel the meaning of the dollar sign.

Moving in another direction, the next example:

```
echo 'date'
```

returns "**date**", but substituting the single quotes for back quotes has a different result:

```
echo `date`
```

returns the results of the **date** command. An alternative to using the back quotes in the newer shells is placing the command within parentheses and treating it as a variable. Thus, you can echo the date as shown earlier with the command:

```
echo $(date)
```

If you fail to use an even number of any quote set, **PS1** is replaced by **PS2** and continues to do so until the total number of quotes used (each set) equals an even number. This feature can be useful when you want to break a lengthy entry into lines while typing it. The following example includes the prompts and also shows the use of one set of quotes (back quotes) within another (double quotes):

```
[edulaney@server7 home]$ EXAMPLE="Hi, the date
> and time now
> are `date`."
[edulaney@server7 home]$ echo $EXAMPLE
Hi, the date and time now are Thu Aug 10 11:12:37 EDT 2000
[edulaney@server7 home]$
```

In many instances, you need to mix and match quotes. One of the biggest problems you will encounter, however, is that special characters are difficult to display as output. For example, assume the end result of an echo operation is:

```
Karen says "Hi"
```

If you use the command:

```
echo Karen says "Hi"
```

The result is:

```
Karen says Hi
```

The shell lets the quotation marks indicate that the text within them should be a single entry. The shell performs the operation given it and loses the quotes in the process. To get around this, you must use the back-slash (\) character to override the default meaning of the quotes:

```
echo Karen says \"Hi\"
```

Note that the back-quote—literal—character must precede each incident of the quotes, and it is always only good for the character immediately following it.

Standard Output and Input

Standard output is where displays usually go—to your screen. When you give the command:

```
ls -F
```

a list of the subdirectories and files beneath the current directory displays on your screen. The default location for standard output, therefore, is to your screen. If you do not want the results displayed on your screen, you can redirect them to another location, such as a file. Redirection of standard output is possible through the use of the greater-than sign (>). For example, to send the results to a file, the command is:

```
ls -F > myfile
```

When given this command, the shell first creates a file named "myfile" with a size of zero. It then allows the **ls** utility to run and places the output within the newly created file rather than on your screen. It is important to note the order of operations because if you give a nonexistent command such as:

```
ls -z > myfile
```

the file named "myfile" is still created with a size of zero that then stays at zero. The error appears on your screen, but it occurs after the file is created. This point is important because if you attempt to add more information to the file, the file is overwritten first. To add more information, you must append to the file using two greater-than signs (>>):

```
ls -l >> myfile
```

This step adds the new information to the end of the existing file and keeps the original contents intact. In some situations, you want a command to run but don't care at all about the results. For example, I might want a database to compile, so

I run a utility. I don't care about the messages generated because I just want the utility to run. When this is the case, you can send the results to nowhere by specifying /dev/null, as in:

```
ls -F > /dev/null
```

The results are sent to this device—also known as the trashcan—never to be saved or displayed.

Standard input is typically the keyboard or expected to be among the arguments given on the command line. You can, however, specify the redirection of standard input using the less-than sign (<). Rarely is there ever a need for this sign, but it is available. For example:

```
cat myfile
```

gives the same results as:

```
cat < myfile
```

In the world of Linux, numerical values exist for these items as well. Standard input (abbreviated stdin) is 0, and standard output (abbreviated stdout) is 1. You can use these numbers with the redirection, but that move is rare. An example is:

```
ls -F 1> myfile
```

which states that standard output is to be redirected to the file named "myfile". The numbers are important for one reason only—because a third possibility exists as well. Standard error (abbreviated stderr) has a value of 2. For an example of standard error, think of the **ls -z** command discussed earlier. Even though the output was sent to a file, the command was nonexistent, and the error message appeared on the screen. You can send the error to the file with the command:

```
ls -z 2> myfile
```

The problem is that the error is sent to the file, but the output (in the absence of an error) appears on the screen. To send both output and errors to the same file, the command becomes:

```
ls -z > myfile 2>&1
```

This states that the output is to go to a file named "myfile" and further that standard error (2) is to go to the same location as standard output (1). Another alternative is to send errors to one location and output to another, as in:

```
ls -z > myfile 2>errors
```

In the order of operations here, the shell first creates two files ("myfile" and "errors") with zero sizes (whether or not they existed before). If the command is successful, the output goes to "myfile." If the command is unsuccessful, the errors go to "errors." If these were truly log files, the only other modification might be to append versus zero (empty, or write over) each time the operation is run:

```
ls -z >> myfile 2>>errors
```

Command History

The bash shell keeps a list of commands that you give it and allows you to reuse those commands from the list rather than retype them each time. From the command line, you can use the up and down arrows to scroll through recent commands. You can also enter two bangs (!!) to rerun the very last command you gave.

Typing **history** shows all the commands that are stored with an incrementing number on the left. Type a single bang, and one of those command numbers will rerun that command, as in **!205**.

Instead of seeing the entire history list, you can choose to see only the most recent entries by following the **history** command with the number of lines you want to see; for example:

```
history 5
history 10
```

You can also type a bang followed by a set of characters, and the shell reruns the most recent command starting with those characters:

```
!ls
```

This example reruns the most recent command that started with **ls**.

Important variables for history are:

- HISTFILE—Points to the file holding the history of commands. By default, it is .bash_history within each user's home directory.
- HISTSIZE—The number of entries to keep each session.

Note: You can use an internal alias for history, fc, to recall and rerun commands as well.

Command Aliasing

Although the operating system and shell offer a plethora of commands and utilities, you can create aliases that make more sense to you or that shorten the number of characters you have to type. For example, if you are familiar with the command line of Windows-based operating systems, you are accustomed to typing **dir** to see what files are there. A similar operation in Linux is possible with **ls -l**. You can create an alias so you can type **dir** to run **ls -l** by using the following syntax:

```
alias dir="ls -l"
```

The syntax is always the alias followed by the actual command that runs when the alias is entered, separated by the equal sign (=). In rare instances, you can get away with not using the quotation marks around the aliased entry; as a general rule, however, you should always include them.

Always remember that, for aliases to survive a session, they should be added to the .bashrc file within a user's home directory.

Other Features and Notes

You should not overlook a number of other features of the Linux command line. Although they are not complicated enough to warrant sections of their own, it is useful to know of their existence:

- When typing a command, you can press the Tab key after entering a few characters to make the shell attempt to complete the name of the command you are typing.
- You can edit the command-line history to alter commands before running them again. The default editor in bash is **emacs**, and in zsh it is **vi**. Editors are discussed later in this book.
- When you press the Enter key, the shell first scans the command line and determines what elements it has been given by looking for white space. It next replaces wildcards with any relevant file names. Following that, it strips all quotes and substitutes variables. Finally, it substitutes any embedded commands and then executes the entry.

➤ You can use the **test** utility in conjunction with $? to test almost anything. For example, to see whether a file exists and is readable, use the combination:

```
test -r snapshot01.gif
echo $?
```

Find the complete syntax for all the **test** options by typing **man test**.

➤ We talked about >, >>, and < in this chapter, but not <<. The two less-than signs are known simply as “here” and signify that processing is to wait until the string following them is given as a **PS2** prompt on a line to itself. For example:

```
cat << litter
```

accepts input at a **PS2** prompt until the string “litter” is entered on a line by itself.

Metacharacter Summation

We have discussed a great many special characters in this chapter. Table 2.2 lists them and their purposes as given within this chapter.

Table 2.2 Shell characters with special meanings.

Metacharacter	Meaning
‘ ‘	Cancels the special meaning of anything but the back quote.
“ “	Cancels the special meaning of most characters.
$	Treats the next string as a variable.
$()	Allows a command to be treated as a variable.
*	Substitutes any number of characters.
;	Treats as dissimilar commands.
?	Substitutes any single character.
[ ]	Substitutes any of the enclosed characters.
\	Treats the next character literally.
‘ ‘	Executes the enclosed command.
|	Allows one command’s output to be the next command’s input.
<	Uses input redirection.
<<	Treats as “Here” document.
>	Redirects output.
>>	Appends output.

Practice Questions

Question 1

What is the correct syntax to use so that each time you enter the command **cls**, the shell executes the **clear** command? [Fill in the blank]

____

The correct answer to this question is **alias cls="clear"**.

Question 2

You want to see all the files on your system in long format (using the **-l** option), including any hidden files (which requires the **-a** option). Which command should you use?

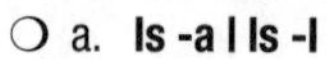

- ❍ a. **ls -a | ls -l**
- ❍ b. **ls -a ; ls -l**
- ❍ c. **ls -la**
- ❍ d. **ls -a \ls -l**

The correct answer to this question is c, which will show all files (including hidden ones) in long-listing format. Answer a will take the output of the first command and try to input it into the second command—which will fail because **ls** is not written to accept input. Answer b will run two separate commands, but the first list will not be in long format and the second will not include hidden files. Answer d will try to list the hidden files named **ls -l** and will fail as well.

Question 3

You have just created a variable using the command **RITE=20**. You need to echo the value of the variable as a monetary sum in the sentence "You owe me $20." Which of the following will accomplish this result? [Check all correct answers]

- ❑ a. **echo You owe me $RITE**
- ❑ b. **echo You owe me "$RITE"**
- ❑ c. **echo You owe me $$RITE**
- ❑ d. **echo You owe me \$RITE**
- ❑ e. **echo You owe me \$$RITE**
- ❑ f. **echo You owe me "$"$RITE**
- ❑ g. **echo You owe me '$'$RITE**

The correct answers to this question are e, f, and g. The other answers will not display the dollar sign or the value of the variable.

Question 4

You want to find all the files in your current directory that begin with either "c", "r", "u", "s", or "h", and end with "G", "R", "A", "P", or "E". How can you best accomplish this?

- ❍ a. **ls crush*GRAPE**
- ❍ b. **ls c*G c*R c*A c*P c*E r*G r*R r*A r*P r*E u*G u*R u*A u*P u*E s*G s*R s*A s*P s*E h*G h*R h*A h*P h*E**
- ❍ c. **ls [crush]?[GRAPE]**
- ❍ d. **ls [crush]*[GRAPE]**

The correct answer to this question is d, because it will find all characters from the first and second character sets, with any text between. Answer a will find only files that begin with "crush" and end with "GRAPE" and won't include any variations at all. Answer b will work, and it is a solution, but it's not a good solution unless you want carpal tunnel syndrome. Answer c will not work because it will find only three-letter combinations.

Question 5

You want to obtain a long list of all the files in your current directory that do not have an uppercase character as the second letter of the name. How can you accomplish this?

- ❍ a. **ls -l *[A-Z]***
- ❍ b. **ls -l ?[A-Z]***
- ❍ c. **ls -l *[!A-Z]***
- ❍ d. **ls -l ?[!A-Z]***

The correct answer to this question is d. It specifies that the first character can be anything (?) and that you are specifically looking at the second character, which cannot (!) be uppercase (A-Z). Answer a will look for uppercase (and allow it) anywhere in the name. Answer b wants an uppercase character as the second letter—the exact opposite of what the question calls for. Answer c will disallow an uppercase character anywhere (in theory) but is overruled by the use of the asterisks on both ends.

tion 6

What is the command to add the directory /crush/grape to the end of the current path statement while maintaining the rest of the statement? [Fill in the blank]

____

The correct answer to this question is **PATH=$PATH:/crush/grape.** Remember always to add the colon as a delimiter within the path and always to append to the end of the existing entries.

Question 7

Mary has been tinkering with her variables on the System9 computer and changed the default setting for **PS1** using the command:

```
PS1="Monday Monday"
```

What does her prompt now resemble?

❍ a. Monday Monday

❍ b. Monday Monday$

❍ c. [Mary@System9 Monday Monday]$

❍ d. $

The correct answer to this question is a. If you set **PS1** to a string value, the prompt will be equal to that string value alone. To have the dollar sign appear on the end (answer b), she would need to add that as a string or use the **\$** variable. To get the other information shown in answer c, she would need to add **\u**, **\h**, the brackets, and the dollar sign. Answer d could be obtained with either **PS1="$"** or **PS1="\$"**.

Question 8

You have inadvertently started a process in the background that you suspect will bring the system to its knees. You want to stop it quickly before havoc breaks out. What variable can you echo to see the process ID of the job you just started?

❍ a. **$$**

❍ b. **$?**

❍ c. **$!**

❍ d. **!!**

The correct answer to this question is c. The **$!** variable will show the process ID of the last job started in the background. The **$$** variable (answer a) shows the current processes ID, and **$?** (answer b) shows the return status of the last operation. To be avoided at all costs in this situation is answer d (!!), which will start another instance of the job by rerunning the last command given from history.

Question 9

Kristin is starting a long job that will run in the background while she goes to lunch. She does not want to know any of the details of the job because she will not be present to interact with it. She wants any good data that can be accumulated to go into a temporary file with the extension ".good" and any errors to go into a temporary file with the extension ".errors". How can she best create these unique files and fulfill her wishes with a job named "chex"?

❍ a. **chex >> good errors**

❍ b. **chex > $$.good 2>&1**

❍ c. **chex >$$.good 2>$$.errors**

❍ d. **chex 2<>1 $$.[goodlerrors]**

The correct answer to this question is c. It will create the two unique files and send output to one and errors to the other. In answer a, the output of chex is appended to the file good (errors is ignored), and standard errors are displayed on the screen. Answer b will create a unique file based on the process ID number with the extension of .good, but both standard output and standard errors are sent to the same location. Answer d will not work at all.

Question 10

Evan feels this has been the most productive day of his life. He wants to show his history file to his manager while suggesting a 10 percent raise in his salary. If Evan is running the bash shell and has kept defaults, what file must he attach to his email to send the history file?

❍ a. bash_history

❍ b. bashrc

❍ c. .bashrc

❍ d. .bash_history

The correct answer to this question is d. The hidden file (.bash_history) within his home directory contains his history.

Need to Know More?

Hare, Chris, and Emmett Dulaney, et al. *Inside Unix*. Indianapolis, IN: New Riders Publishing, 1994. ISBN: 1-56205-401-5. Chapter 5 covers the basics of the shell and its functions.

LeBlanc, Dee-Ann. *General Linux I Exam Prep*. Scottsdale, AZ: The Coriolis Group, 2000. ISBN: 1-57610-567-9. Chapter 5, "Shells, Scripting, Programming, and Compiling," gives more information about the topics discussed within this chapter.

http://daffy.robelle.com/smugbook/shell.html is Robelle's Guide to Shells in UNIX, which contains information specific to sh, csh, and ksh.

www.linuxcare.com/products/prodmore.ep?PRODUCT_ GROUP =Shells offers a comparing of shells and user-contributed comments on each.

http://metalagb.unc.edu/mdw/index.html is The Linux Documentation Project, which includes FAQs, how-tos, and individual man pages.

Text-Processing Basics

Terms you'll need to understand:

- ✓ cat
- ✓ tac
- ✓ nl
- ✓ head
- ✓ tail
- ✓ cut
- ✓ paste
- ✓ join
- ✓ sort
- ✓ wc
- ✓ fmt
- ✓ tr

Techniques you'll need to master:

- ✓ Understanding the basic concepts of working with Linux text utilities
- ✓ Recognizing the differences between ASCII text operations

In this chapter, you'll learn the basic utilities used to create and modify text and text files within the Linux operating system. We expand upon many of the redirection concepts and command-line basics from Chapter 2.

The Irrepressible cat

The simplest text-processing utility of all is **cat**, a derivative from the word "concatenate." By default, it displays the entire contents of a file on the screen (standard output). **cat** also has a number of useful options:

- **-b**—Numbers lines
- **-E**—Shows a dollar sign ($) at the end of each line (carriage return)
- **-T**—Shows all tabs as ^I
- **-v**—Shows nonprinting characters except tabs and carriage returns
- **-A**—Does the same as **-v** combined with **-E** and **-T**

To illustrate **cat**'s uses, assume a four-line file named "example" has the following contents:

```
How much wood
could a woodchuck chuck
if a woodchuck
could chuck wood?
```

To view the contents of the file on the screen, exactly as they appear here, the command is:

```
cat example
```

To view the file with lines numbered, the command, and the output generated, becomes:

```
cat -b example
     1     How much wood
     2     could a woodchuck chuck
     3     if a woodchuck
     4     could chuck wood?
```

Note the inclusion of the spaces, inserted by tabs, that were not present before but were added by the numbering process. They are not truly in the file, but appear only in the display, as can be witnessed with the command:

```
cat -Ab example
```

```
     1      How much wood$
     2      could a woodchuck chuck$
     3      if a woodchuck$
     4      could chuck wood?$
```

The only nonprintable characters within the file are the carriage returns at the end, which appear as dollar signs.

One of the most common uses of the **cat** utility is to create a text file quickly. From the command line, you can specify no file at all to display and redirect the output to a given file name. **cat** accepts keyboard input and places it in the new file until it receives the end-of-file character (Ctrl+D, by default).

The following example includes a dollar sign ($) prompt to show this operation in process:

```
$ cat > example
Peter Piper picked a peck of pickled peppers
A peck of pickled peppers Peter Piper picked.
If Peter Piper picked a peck of pickled peppers,
Where's the peck of pickled peppers Peter Piper picked?
{press Ctrl+D}
$
```

You enter the Ctrl+D sequence on a line by itself to signify the end of the file. Viewing the contents of the directory (via the **ls** utility) shows the file has been created, and you can view its contents with:

```
cat example
```

Note that the single redirection (>) creates a file named "example" if it did not exist before, and overwrites it if it did, as discussed in Chapter 2. To add to an existing file, use the append character (>>).

The Ctrl+D keyboard sequence is the typical default for specifying an end-of-file operation. Like almost everything in Linux, this sequence can be changed, customized, and so on. To see the settings for your session, use the command:

```
stty -a
```

and look for **eof =**.

A utility of use in limited circumstances—**tac**—displays the contents of files in reverse order (**tac** is **cat** in reverse). Instead of displaying a file from line 1 to the end of the file, it shows the file from the end of the file to line 1, as illustrated here:

```
$ tac example
Where's the peck of pickled peppers Peter Piper picked?
If Peter Piper picked a peck of pickled peppers,
A peck of pickled peppers Peter Piper picked.
Peter Piper picked a peck of pickled peppers
$
```

nl, head, and tail

Three simple commands can be used to view all or parts of files: **nl**, **head**, and **tail**. The first, **nl**, used to number the lines, is similar to **cat -b**. Both number the lines of display, and by default neither number blank lines. **nl** can use certain options to alter the display:

- **-i**—Allows you to change the increment (default is 1)
- **-v**—Allows you to change the starting number (default is 1)
- **-n**—Changes the alignment of the display:
  - **-nln**—Aligns the display on the left
  - **-nrn**—Aligns the display on the right
  - **-nrz**—Uses leading zeros
- **-s**—Uses a specified character between the line number and the text (default is a space)

The second utility to examine is **head**. As the name implies, this utility looks at the top portion of a file: by default, the first 10 lines. You can change the number of lines displayed by using a dash followed by the number of lines to display. The following examples assume that a text file named "numbers" has 200 lines in it counting from "one" to "two hundred":

```
$ head numbers
one
two
three
four
five
six
seven
eight
```

```
nine
ten
$
$ head -3 numbers
one
two
three
$
$ head -50 numbers
one
two
three
{skipping for space purposes}
forty-eight
forty-nine
fifty
$
```

When printing multiple files, **head** places a header before each list identifying what file it is displaying. The **-q** option suppresses the headers.

The **tail** command has several modes in which it can operate. By default, it is the opposite of **head** and shows the end of a file rather than the beginning. Once again, it defaults to the number 10 to display, but you can change that by using the dash and a number:

```
$ tail numbers
one hundred ninety-one
one hundred ninety-two
one hundred ninety-three
one hundred ninety-four
one hundred ninety-five
one hundred ninety-six
one hundred ninety-seven
one hundred ninety-eight
one hundred ninety-nine
two hundred
$
$ tail -3 numbers
one hundred ninety-eight
one hundred ninety-nine
two hundred
$
```

```
$ tail -50 numbers
one hundred fifty-one
one hundred fifty-two
one hundred fifty-three
{skipping for space purposes}
one hundred ninety-eight
one hundred ninety-nine
two hundred
$
```

The **tail** utility goes beyond this functionality, however, by including a plus (+) option. This allows you to specify a starting point, beyond which you see the entire file. For example:

```
$ tail +50 numbers
```

starts with line 50 (skipping the first 49) and displays all the rest of the file—151 lines in this case. Another useful option is **-f**, which allows you to *follow* a file. The command:

```
$ tail -f numbers
```

displays the last 10 lines of the file but then stays open—following the file—and displays any new lines that are appended to the file. To break out of the endless monitoring loop, you must press the *interrupt* key sequence, which is Ctrl+C by default on most systems.

Note: To find the interrupt key sequence for your session, use the command:

```
stty -a
```

*and look for **intr** =.*

cut, paste, and join

There are another three important utilities, **cut**, **paste**, and **join**.

cut

The ability to separate columns that could constitute data fields from a file is provided by the **cut** utility. The default delimiter used is the tab, and the **-f** option specifies the desired field. For example, for a text file named "august" with three columns, resembling:

```
one      two       three
four     five      six
```

```
seven    eight    nine
ten      eleven   twelve
```

the command:

```
cut -f2 august
```

returns:

```
two
five
eight
eleven
```

and the command:

```
cut -f1,3 august
```

returns the opposite:

```
one      three
four     six
seven    nine
ten      twelve
```

Of a number of options available with this command, the two to recognize (besides **-f**) are:

- **-c**—Allows you to specify characters instead of fields
- **-d**—Allows you to specify a delimiter other than the tab

To illustrate how to use the other options, the **ls -l** command shows permissions, number of links, owner, group, size, date, and file name—all separated by white space, with two characters between the permissions and links. If you want to see only who is saving files in the directory, and you are not interested in the other data, you can use:

```
ls -l | cut -d" " -f5
```

This example ignores the permissions (first field), two sets of white space (second and third fields), and number of links (fourth field), and it displays the owner (fifth field), ignoring everything following. Another way to look at this is that with **ls -l**, the permissions always take up 10 characters, there is white space of 3 characters, and the number of links and white space follow. The owner always begins with the 16th character and continues for the length of the name. The command:

```
ls -l | cut -c16
```

returns the 16th character—the first letter of the owner's name.

Note: If your output differs from the standard display, due to differences in terminal types or other causes, you can tweak the number of characters to be cut in order to get the correct return value.

If you assume that most users will use eight characters or fewer for their names, the command:

```
ls -l | cut -c16-24
```

returns those entries in the name field.

The name of the file begins with the 55th character, but it can be impossible to determine how many characters to take after that because some file names will be considerably longer than others. A solution is to begin with the 55th character and not specify an ending character (meaning that you take the entire rest of the line), as in:

```
ls -l | cut -c55-
```

paste

Whereas the **cut** utility extracts fields from a file, you can combine fields using either **paste** or **join**. The simpler of the two is **paste**; it has no great feature set and merely takes one line from one source and combines it with another line from another source. For example, if the contents of fileone are:

```
Indianapolis
Columbus
Peoria
Livingston
Scottsdale
```

And the contents of filetwo are:

```
Indiana
Ohio
Illinois
Montana
Arizona
```

Then the following (including prompts) is the display generated:

```
$ paste fileone filetwo
Indianapolis    Indiana
Columbus    Ohio
Peoria    Illinois
Livingston    Montana
Scottsdale    Arizona
$
```

If fileone had more lines than filetwo, then the pasting would continue with blank entries following the tab. The tab character is always the default delimiter, but you can change it to anything by using the **-d** option:

```
$ paste -d"," fileone filetwo
Indianapolis,Indiana
Columbus,Ohio
Peoria,Illinois
Livingston,Montana
Scottsdale,Arizona
$
```

You can also use the **-s** option to output all of fileone on a line, followed by a carriage return and then filetwo:

```
$ paste -s fileone filetwo
Indianapolis    Columbus    Peoria    Livingston    Scottsdale
Indiana    Ohio    Illinois    Montana    Arizona
$
```

join

You can think of the **join** utility as a greatly enhanced version of **paste**. It is critically important, however, to know that **join** can work only if the files being joined share a common field. For example, if you use **join** in the same example as **paste** was used earlier, the result is:

```
$ join fileone filetwo
$
```

In other words, there is no display. **join** must find a common field between the files in question, and by default it expects that common field to be the first. For example, assume that fileone now contains these entries:

```
11111    Indianapolis
22222    Columbus
```

```
33333    Peoria
44444    Livingston
55555    Scottsdale
```

And the contents of filetwo are:

```
11111    Indiana    500 race
22222    Ohio    Buckeye State
33333    Illinois    Wrigley Field
44444    Montana    Yellowstone Park
55555    Arizona    Grand Canyon
```

Then the following (including prompts) is the display generated:

```
$ join fileone filetwo
11111    Indianapolis    Indiana    500 race
22222    Columbus    Ohio    Buckeye State
33333    Peoria    Illinois    Wrigley Field
44444    Livingston    Montana    Yellowstone Park
55555    Scottsdale    Arizona    Grand Canyon
$
```

The **join** utility identified the commonality of the first field and combined the matching entries. Whereas **paste** blindly takes from each file to create the display, **join** only combines lines that match, and—of critical importance—**join** must find an exact match with the corresponding line in the other file. We cannot illustrate this point enough; for example, suppose filetwo had an additional line in the middle:

```
11111    Indiana    500 race
22222    Ohio    Buckeye State
66666    Tennessee    Smoky Mountains
33333    Illinois    Wrigley Field
44444    Montana    Yellowstone Park
55555    Arizona    Grand Canyon
```

Then the following (including prompts) is the display generated:

```
$ join fileone filetwo
11111    Indianapolis    Indiana    500 race
22222    Columbus    Ohio    Buckeye State
$
```

As soon as the files no longer match, **join** can perform no further operations. **join** checks each line with the same—and only the same—line in the opposite file for a match on the default field. If matches are found, they are incorporated in the display; otherwise, they are not. To illustrate one more time—use the original filetwo:

```
$ tac filetwo > filethree
$ join fileone filethree
55555    Scottsdale    Arizona    Grand Canyon
$
```

Even though a match exists for every line in both files, only one match is found.

I highly recommend that you overcome problems with **join** by first sorting each file to arrange them in like order.

You don't have to keep **join**'s default behaviors of looking at only the first fields for matches or of outputting all columns. The **-1** option lets you specify what field to use as the matching field in fileone, and the **-2** option lets you specify what field to use as the matching field in filetwo. For example, if the second field of fileone matches with the third field of filetwo, then the syntax is:

```
$ join -1 2 -2 3 fileone filethree
```

You use the **-o** option to specify output fields in the format {file.field}. Thus, to print only the second field of fileone and the third field of filetwo on matching lines, the syntax is:

```
$ join -o 1.2 2.3 fileone filethree
Indianapolis    500
Columbus    Buckeye
Peoria    Wrigley
Livingston    Yellowstone
Scottsdale    Grand
$
```

Sorting, Counting, Formatting, and Translating

Often you will want not only to display text, but also to manipulate and modify it a bit before the output is shown or simply gather information on it. This section explains four utilities: **sort**, **wc**, **fmt**, and **tr**.

sort

The **sort** utility sorts the lines of a file in alphabetical order and displays the output. We cannot overstate the importance of alphabetical order versus any other. For example, assume the fileone file contains the following lines:

```
Indianapolis Indiana
Columbus
Peoria
Livingston
Scottsdale
1
2
3
4
5
6
7
8
9
10
11
12
```

When you perform a sort on the file, the result becomes:

```
$ sort fileone
1
10
11
12
2
3
4
5
6
7
8
9
Columbus
Indianapolis Indiana
Livingston
Peoria
Scottsdale
$
```

The cities are correctly sorted in alphabetical order. The numbers, however, are sorted so that every number starting with "1" appears before every number starting with "2"; then every number starting with "2" appears before every number starting with "3", and so on.

The **sort** utility includes some options to add a great deal of flexibility to the output. Among those options are the following:

- **-d**—Sorts in phone-directory order (the same as that shown earlier)
- **-f**—Sorts lowercase letters in the same manner as uppercase letters
- **-i**—Ignores any characters outside the ASCII range
- **-n**—Sorts in numerical order instead of alphabetical
- **-r**—Reverses the order of the output

Thus, you can change the display to:

```
$ sort -n fileone
Columbus
Indianapolis Indiana
Livingston
Peoria
Scottsdale
1
2
3
4
5
6
7
8
9
10
11
12
$
```

The **sort** utility assumes all blank lines to be a part of the display and always places them at the beginning of the output. To prevent blank lines from being sorted, use the **-b** option.

wc

The **wc** utility (named for "word count") displays information about the file in terms of three values: number of lines, words, and characters. The last entry in the output is the name of the file, so the output is:

```
$ wc fileone
    17    18    86    fileone
$
```

You can choose to see only some of the output by using the following options:

- -c—Shows only the number of bytes or characters
- -l—Shows only the number of lines
- -w—Shows only the number of words

In all cases, the name of the file still appears:

```
$ wc -l fileone
    17    fileone
$
```

The only way to keep the name from appearing is to use the standard input redirection:

```
$ wc -l < fileone
    17
$
```

fmt

The **fmt** utility formats the text by creating output to a specific width. The default width is 75 characters, but you can specify a different value with the -w option. Short lines are combined to create longer ones unless you use the -s option, and spacing is justified unless you use **-u**. The **-u** option enforces uniformity and places one space between words and two spaces at the end of each sentence.

The following example shows how the fileone lines are combined to create a 75-character display:

```
$ fmt fileone
Indianapolis Indiana Columbus Peoria Livingston Scottsdale
   1 2 3 4 5 6
7 8 9 10 11 12
$
```

To change the output to 60 characters:

```
$ fmt -w60 fileone
Indianapolis Indiana Columbus Peoria Livingston Scottsdale
   1 2 3 4 5 6 7 8 9 10 11 12
$
```

Remember that the default for any option with **fmt** is **-w**, so **fmt -60 fileone** gives the same result as **fmt -w60 fileone**.

tr

The **tr** (translate) utility can convert one set of characters to another. For example, to change all lowercase characters to uppercase:

```
$ tr '[a-z]' '[A-Z]' < fileone
INDIANAPOLIS INDIANA
COLUMBUS
PEORIA
LIVINGSTON
SCOTTSDALE
$
```

It is extremely important to realize that the syntax of **tr** accepts only two character sets and not the name of the file. You must feed the name of the file into the utility by directing input (as in the example), by piping to it (**|**), or by using a similar operation.

Not only can you give character sets as string options, but you can also specify a number of unique values:

- **lower**—All lowercase characters
- **upper**—All uppercase characters
- **print**—All printable characters
- **punct**—Punctuation characters
- **space**—All white space (you can use **blank** for horizontal white space only)
- **alnum**—Alpha characters and numbers
- **digit**—Numbers only
- **cntrl**—Character control
- **alpha**—Letters only
- **graph**—Printable characters but not white space

For example, you can obtain the output shown earlier with:

```
$ tr '[:lower:]' '[:upper:]' < fileone
INDIANAPOLIS INDIANA
```

```
COLUMBUS
PEORIA
LIVINGSTON
SCOTTSDALE
$
```

Utility Summation

We discussed a great many text utilities in this chapter. Table 3.1 lists them and their purposes.

Associated Utilities

Linux includes a number of other useful text utilities. Some of these have limited usefulness and are intended only for a specific purpose. Some of these are not on Exam 101, but we discuss them because knowing of their existence and purpose can make your life with Linux considerably easier.

In alphabetical order, the additional utilities are:

- **expand**—Allows you to expand tab characters into spaces. The default number of spaces per tab is eight, but you can change that using the **-t** option.
- **file**—Looks at an entry's signature and reports what type of file it is—ASCII text, GIF image, and so on. The definitions it returns (and thus the files it can correctly identify) appear in a file called "magic". This file typically resides in /usr/share/misc or /etc.

Table 3.1 Utilities addressed in this chapter.

Utility	Default Purpose
cat	Displays the contents of a file.
cut	Extracts a field from each line of a file.
fmt	Formats the output to fit the desired display.
head	Displays the beginning lines of a file.
join	Combines columns from two files into a single display.
nl	Numbers the lines of a file.
paste	Puts the contents of two files in a single display.
sort	Sorts the lines of the file.
stty	Shows the settings for the terminal.
tac	Displays the contents of a file in reverse order.
tail	Displays the last lines of a file.
tr	Translates one set of characters into another.
wc	Counts the number of words, lines, and characters or bytes within a file.

- **more**—Displays only one screen of output at a time.
- **od**—Performs an octal dump to show the contents of files other than ASCII text files. Used with the **-x** option, it performs a hexadecimal dump, and with the **-c** option, it shows only recognizable ASCII characters.
- **pr**—Converts the file into a format suitable for printed pages—including a default header with the date and time of last modification, file name, and page numbers. You can overwrite the default header with the **-h** option, and the **-l** option allows you to specify the number of lines to include on each page—with the default being 66. Default page width is 72 characters, but you can specify a different value with the **-w** option. Use the **-d** option to double-space the output and **-m** to print numerous files in column format.
- **split**—Chops a single file into multiple files. The default is that a new file is created for every 1,000 lines of the original file. Using the **-b** option, you can avoid the 1,000-line splitting and specify a number of bytes to be put into each output file, or you can use **-l** to specify a number of lines.
- **uniq**—Examines entries in a file, comparing the current line with the one directly preceding it, to find lines that are unique.
- **vi**—One of the greatest file editors, it allows you to create files as well as modify their contents. Alternative editors include **ed** (very difficult to use) and **emacs** (another good editor).

Practice Questions

Question 1

The /etc/passwd file contains usernames, passwords, and related information and has fields delimited by colons. What is the correct syntax to use to look only at the seventh field to see what shells users are using on your system? [Fill in the blank]

____

The correct answer to this question is:

```
cut -d: -f7 /etc/passwd
```

Question 2

You want to combine two files so that fileone's content is followed by filetwo's content in a single file. Which of the following commands allows you to perform this operation? [Check all correct answers]

- ❑ a. **cat fileone filetwo > fileone**
- ❑ b. **cat filetwo >> fileone**
- ❑ c. **cat fileone filetwo > filethree**
- ❑ d. **cat fileone >> filetwo**

The correct answers to this question are b and c. Answer b will append the existing filetwo to the existing fileone and meet the criteria of the question. Answer c will create a brand new file—filethree—containing the contents of fileone with the contents of filetwo appended and thus meet the criteria of the question. Answer a will see the shell first, create a zero-size file named fileone (thus emptying the contents of the existing file), copy the empty file into itself, and then copy the contents of filetwo; thus, the result is a mirror of filetwo, and all of fileone's data will be lost. Answer d will append fileone to the end of filetwo, and the data will appear in the opposite order of what the question required.

Question 3

You have a log file named OUTPUT that is written to every time a widget is produced. Your company is about to produce its 1,000th widget, and you want to know the moment it happens. Which of the following commands will you use to monitor the log file?

- ❍ a. **nl OUTPUT**
- ❍ b. **tail +1000 OUTPUT**
- ❍ c. **cat -A OUTPUT**
- ❍ d. **tail -f OUTPUT**

The correct answer to this question is d because the key is that not only do you want to see the file, but you also want to monitor it. This answer will show the last 10 lines of the file and keep the monitoring open. Answer a will number the existing file but not monitor it. Answer b will display the entire file, beginning with line 1,000 and going to the end, and then finish—with no monitoring. Answer c will show the entire file and display nonprintable characters.

Question 4

You have a log file named USRS that has three lines appended to it each time a user logs in or out of your system. The file has grown to 30,000 lines in length, and you want to lose the oldest two-thirds of the file. You have copied the file to OLDUSRS; what should you do next?

- ❍ a. **head -10000 OLDUSRS > USRS**
- ❍ b. **tail +10000 OLDUSRS > USRS**
- ❍ c. **tail -10000 OLDUSRS > USRS**
- ❍ d. **cut -f10000 OLDUSRS > USRS**

The correct answer to this question is c. It will take the last 10,000 lines—the newest one-third of the file—and keep it. Answer a will keep the first third of the file—the oldest information. Answer b will begin with line 10,000 and copy the remainder of the file (20,001 lines) to the new file—keeping the newest two-thirds of the file. Answer d will look for the 10,000th field in each line (not an item it would find) to save and fail immediately.

Question 5

You want to combine the contents of FILEA with the contents of FILEB and use a single quotation mark (') as a delimiter between the two fields. Which command will allow you to create the desired display?

- ❍ a. **paste -d' FILEA FILEB**
- ❍ b. **cut -s' FILEA FILEB**
- ❍ c. **join -o' FILEA FILEB**
- ❍ d. **paste -d\' FILEA FILEB**

The correct answer to this question is d. Answer d will identify the delimiter (**-d**) as a special character to be used literally (\). Answer a is very close but will not work because the shell will go into input mode and wait for a second quotation mark. Answer b will use the wrong utility: **cut** pulls from files and does not put them together. Answer c will incorrectly use the **-o** parameter, which specifies which fields to use, not what delimiter to use.

Question 6

What is the command to use to translate all numbers in the FILEA file to the letter "z"? [Fill in the blank]

____

The correct utility to use is **tr**. There are a number of correct ways to specify the requested result:

- tr '[0-9]' z < FILEA
- tr '[:digit:]' z < FILEA
- tr '0123456789' z < FILEA

All work correctly.

Question 7

Which command can you use to sort FILEC in alphabetical order?

- ❍ a. **sort -a FILEC**
- ❍ b. **sort -n FILEC**
- ❍ c. **sort -r FILEC**
- ❍ d. **sort FILEC**

The correct answer to this question is d. The default operation of **sort** is to display the file in alphabetical order. If you need to sort in another order, then—and only then—must you specify an option. Answer a will fail because there is no **-a** option. Answer b will sort in numeric order with the **-n** option. Answer c will sort in reverse order with the **-r** option.

Question 8

Which command can you use to determine how many files are in your current directory?

- ❍ a. **ls | fmt -w**
- ❍ b. **ls | wc -l**
- ❍ c. **ls | wc -w**
- ❍ d. **ls | tac**

The correct answer to this question is b, which will create a list of the files within the directory and then count the number of lines in the list. Answer a will use the **fmt** utility to format the display but cannot count the number of entries. Answer c will count the number of words, rather than the number of lines; if a file name has more than one word, the count will be incorrect. Answer d will reverse the display with the **tac** utility but will not count the number of entries.

Question 9

Spencer wants to use the **tr** utility to look for specific characters. Which of the following is not a valid specification?

❍ a. **cntrl**—For control characters

❍ b. **lower**—For lowercase characters

❍ c. **clear**—For white space

❍ d. **alnum**—For digits and letters

The correct answer to this question is c. You can specify white space with **blank** or **space,** but not **clear** (which is an invalid option). All other answers are wrong for this question because their specifications are correct.

Question 10

Karen wants to print a text file on her printer. She wants it to look like a report and print a header that includes page numbers. The name of the file is BeeThree. Which command should she use for this task?

❍ a. **pr BeeThree**

❍ b. **file BeeThree**

❍ c. **od BeeThree**

❍ d. **expand BeeThree**

The correct answer to this question is a. The **pr** utility will format a file for printing. Answer b will use the **file** utility merely to report what type of file the entry is. Answer c will do an octal dump but will not print. Answer d (**expand**) will convert tabs to white space but will not format for printing.

Need to Know More?

Hare, Chris, Emmett Dulaney, et al. *Inside Unix*. Indianapolis, IN: New Riders Publishing, 1994. ISBN: 1-56205-401-5. Chapter 6 covers the basics of creating files and manipulating files and directories.

Siever, Ellen, Stephen Spainhour, et al. *Linux in a Nutshell, 3rd Edition*. Sebastopol, CA: O'Reilly and Associates, 2000. ISBN: 0-59600-025-1. Chapter 3 is an alphabetical overview of Linux commands.

Welsh, Matt, et al. *Running Linux, 3rd Edition*. Sebastopol, CA: O'Reilly and Associates, 1999. ISBN: 1-56592-469-X. Chapter 4 covers basic commands and concepts.

Working with grep and sed

Terms you'll need to understand:

- ✓ **grep**
- ✓ **fgrep**
- ✓ **egrep**
- ✓ **sed**

Techniques you'll need to master:

- ✓ Understanding the basic concepts of working with the **grep** and **sed** utilities
- ✓ Recognizing the differences between regular expressions and how to interact with them

In this chapter, you'll learn about two important utilities used for working with files and output. The **grep** family of utilities finds values, and the **sed** utility can change the value of strings. In the examples here, we use many of the utilities discussed in Chapter 3, and we expand upon the concept of redirection, previously introduced in Chapter 2.

The grep Family

The utility with the funny name (something common in Linux) is really an acronym for the function that it performs: Globally look for Regular Expressions and then Print the results. To put it another way, it is one of the most advanced search utilities you can use. To be proficient with it, however, you must understand what a regular expression is and how to use it in searching for matches to a query.

We can give a number of rules for regular expressions, and the eight listed here constitute the most important:

- Any nonspecial character is equal to itself.
- Any special character is equal to itself if preceded by a back slash (\).
- Indicate the beginning of the line with an up caret (^) and the end of the line with a dollar sign ($).
- Express a range within brackets ([]).
- Typing an up caret (^) as the first character within a bracket finds values that do not match entries within the brackets.
- A period (.) can signify any single character.
- An asterisk (*) stands for anything and everything.
- Quotation marks are not always needed around search strings, but they might be needed, so you should use them as a general rule.

Table 4.1 offers some examples and elaborates on each of these rules.

To illustrate some of these operations using **grep**, assume that a small file named "garbage" has the following contents:

```
I heard about the cats last night
and particularly the one cat that
ran away with all the catnip
```

If you want to find all occurrences of the word "cat", the syntax becomes:

```
$ grep "cat" garbage
I heard about the cats last night
```

```
and particularly the one cat that
ran away with all the catnip
$
```

In this instance, that three-letter sequence "cat" appears in every line. Not only does "cat" appear in the second line, but also "cats" in the first, and "catnip" in the third—all matching the character sequence specified. If you are interested in "cat" but not "cats", the syntax becomes:

```
$ grep "cat[^s]" garbage
and particularly the one cat that
ran away with all the catnip
$
```

Table 4.1 Regular expression examples.

Rule	Characters	Search Result
1	**c** (any character without a special purpose)	Matches "c" anywhere within the line.
1	**apple**	Matches "apple" anywhere within the line.
2	**$**	Every line that has a carriage return (every line).
2	**\$**	Every line that contains a dollar sign.
3	**^c**	Every line that begins with the character "c".
3	**c$**	Every line that ends with the character "c".
4	**[apple]**	Every line that has an "a", "p", "l", or "e" (because the brackets are interpreted as a range, the second occurrence of the "p" is completely ignored.
4	**[a-z]**	Any lowercase letter.
4	**[:lower:]**	Any lowercase letter. Other special values that you can use, introduced in Chapter 3, include [:alnum;], [:alpha:], [:digit:], and [:upper:].
5	**[^a-z]**	Everything but lowercase letters.
5	**[^0-9]**	Anything but digits.
6	**c.**	Two-letter words beginning with "c".
6	**c..$**	Three-letter words at the end of the line that begin with "c".
7	**c***	Any word beginning with "c" (and including just "c").
8	**"c*"**	Any word beginning with "c" (and including just "c").
8	**"c apple"**	The letter "c" followed by a space and the word "apple".

This specifically removes a four-letter sequence of "cats" while finding all other three-letter sequences of "cat". If you truly were interested only in "cat" and no deviations thereof, you can explore a couple other possibilities. The first method is to include a space at the end of the word and within the quotation mark:

```
$ grep "cat " garbage
and particularly the one cat that
$
```

This finds four-letter combinations equal to that given—meaning that nothing must follow. The only problem (and it is a big one) is that if the word given is the last entry in a line of a large file, it might not be followed by a space, and thus it would not be returned in the display. Another possibility is to eliminate "s" and "n" from the return display:

```
$ grep "cat[^sn]" garbage
and particularly the one cat that
$
```

This accomplishes the task but does not catch other words where the fourth character differs from an "s" or "n". To eliminate all fourth characters, it is better to use:

```
$ grep "cat[^A-z]" garbage
I heard about the cats last night
and particularly the one cat that
ran away with all the catnip
$
```

which removes both the uppercase and lowercase character sets.

Options for grep

The default action for **grep** is for it to find matches within lines to strings specified and then to print them. This action can be useful for pulling out key data from a large display; for example, to find what port user karen is on, use the following:

```
$ who | grep "karen"
karen    pts/2    Aug 21 13:42
$
```

From all the output of the **who** command, only those having the string "karen" are displayed. As useful as this is, sometimes the actual output is not as important as other items surrounding it. For example, if you don't care where karen is logged on, but you want to know how many concurrent sessions she has, you can use the **-c** option:

```
$ who | grep -c "karen"
1
$
```

You can also modify it to use a logical OR (||) to tell you whether the user has not come in yet if the operation fails:

```
who | grep "karen" || echo "She has not come in yet"
```

The **-c** option is used to *count* the number of lines that would be displayed, but the display itself is suppressed. The **-c** option is basically performing the same task as:

```
$ who | grep "karen" | wc -l
1
$
```

It is quicker and more efficient, however, to shave an additional operation from the process. Other options that can be used with **grep** are:

- **-f**—Uses a file to find the strings to search for.
- **-H**—Includes in the display a default header of the file name from which the match comes (if applicable), which appears at the beginning of each line, but **-h** prevents the header from appearing (the default).
- **-i**—Ignores case. If this option did not exist, you would conceivably have to search a text file for "karen", "Karen", "KAREN", and all deviations thereof to find all matches.
- **-L**—Prints file names that do not contain matches, but **-l** prints file names that do contain matches.
- **-n**—Shows line numbers in the display. This differs from numbering the lines (which **nl** can do) because the numbers that appear denote the numbering of the lines in the existing file and not the output.
- **-q**—Quiets all output and is usually used for testing return conditions.
- **-s**—Prevents any errors that occur from displaying error messages. This option is useful if you do not want errors stating that you have inadequate permissions to view something when scanning all directories for a match.

- -v—Serves as the "not" option. It produces the opposite display of what not using it would produce. For example, **who | grep -v karen** shows all users who are not karen.
- -w—Forces the found display to match the whole word. This provides the best solution to the earlier discussion of finding "cat" but no derivatives thereof.
- -x—Forces the found display to match the whole line.

You can mix and match the options, as desired, as long as one parameter does not cancel another. For example, it is possible to search for whole words and include header information by using either **-wH** or **-Hw**. You cannot, however, indicate that you want to see line numbers and see only a final count, **-nc**, because the two options cancel each other out.

Some examples follow to show how you can use these options. For the first, assume that we want to get a long list (**ls -l**) of the subdirectories beneath the current directory and have no interest in actual file names. Within the output of **ls -l**, the first field shows the permissions of the entry. If the entry is a file, the first character is -; if it is a directory, it is **d**. You use the command:

```
ls -l | grep "^d"
```

If you want to know how many words are in the spelling dictionary, you can find out using a number of methods:

```
wc -l /usr/dict/words
```

Or you can use:

```
grep -c "." /usr/dict/words
```

Both of these generate a number based on the number of lines within the file. Suppose, however, you want to find out only how many words start with the letter "c" (uppercase or lowercase):

```
grep -ic "^c" /usr/dict/words
```

If you want to learn how many words appear in the last half of the alphabet:

```
grep -ic "^[n-z]" /usr/dict/words
```

Within Linux, you can often get the same results while using different methods. For example:

```
grep -ic "^[^a-m]" /usr/dict/words
```

can also be expressed as:

```
grep -ci "^[^a-m]" /usr/dict/words
```

or

```
grep -vci "^[a-m]" /usr/dict/words
```

Suppose you want to find a number of different strings, not just one. You can search for them individually, requiring a number of operations, or you can place the search criteria within a text file and input it into **grep** using the -f option:

```
$ cat wishlist
dog
cat
fish
$
$ grep -if wishlist /usr/dict/words
```

Approximately 450 lines display, because all matches of all combinations of the three words are displayed. You can also continue one line to another to input multiple search sequences by using an uneven number of quotation marks to put the shell into input mode (**PS2** prompt):

```
$ grep -ic "dog
> cat
> fish" /usr/dict/words
457
$
```

fgrep

The first attempt to greatly enhance **grep** was **fgrep**—as in either "file grep" or "fast grep." This utility was created in the days of Unix, prior to Linux. It enhanced **grep** by adding the ability to search for more than one item at a time (something that **grep** has since gained with the -f option). The tradeoff for gaining the ability to search for multiple items was an inability to use regular expressions—never mind what the acronym stood for.

Adding this functionality to **grep**, and facing the inability to use regular expressions here, **fgrep** still exists but is rarely used in place of **grep**. In fact, one of the options added to **grep** is **-F**, which forces it to interpret the string as a simple string and work as **fgrep** does (the default action is **-G** for basic regular expressions).

For exam purposes, **grep -F** is identical to **fgrep**.

egrep

The second attempt to enhance **grep** was **egrep**—as in "extended grep." This utility combined the features of **grep** with those of **fgrep**—keeping the use of regular expressions. You can specify multiple values that you want to look for within a file (**-f**) on separate lines (using uneven numbers of quotation marks) or by separating with the pipe symbol (|). For example:

```
$ cat names
Jan May
Bob Mays
Shannon Harris
Richard Harriss
William Harrisson
Jim Buck
$
$ egrep "Jim|Jan" names
Jan May
Jim Buck
$
```

It also added two new variables:

- ?—Means zero or one.
- +—Means one or more.

Assume you can't recall how Jan spells her last name; is it May or Mays? Not knowing whether there really is an "s" on the end, you can ask for zero or one occurrences of this character:

```
$ egrep "Mays?" names
Jan May
Bob Mays
$
```

Even though there was no "s", Jan's entry was found—as were those that contained the character in question. With the plus sign (+), you know that at least one iteration of the character exists, but you are not certain whether there are more. For example, does Shannon spell her last name with one or two "s"s?

```
$ egrep "Harris+" names
Shannon Harris
Richard Harriss
William Harrisson
$
```

To look for values of greater length than one character, you can enclose text within parentheses. For example, if you want to find Harriss and Harrisson (not Harris), the "on" becomes an entity with zero or more occurrences:

```
$ egrep "Harriss(on)?" names
Richard Harriss
William Harrisson
$
```

Since the creation of **egrep**—again in the days of Unix—most of the features have been worked into the version of **grep** included with Linux. Using the -E option with **grep**, you can get most of the functionality of **egrep**.

For exam purposes, **grep -E** is identical to **egrep**.

sed

The name "sed" is an acronym for "stream editor," which is as accurate a description as any. The utility accepts input (text) to flow through it like a river or stream. It edits that text and makes changes to it based upon the parameters it has been given. The syntax for **sed** is:

```
sed {options} {commands} filename
```

The number of options is limited, but the commands are numerous. Accepted options are:

- **-e**—Specifies a command to execute.
- **-f**—Specifies a file in which to find commands to execute.
- **-n**—Runs in quiet mode.

The best way to understand the commands is to examine a few examples. One of the simplest commands to give **sed**, or any editor, is to substitute one string for another. You accomplish this with the **s** (for substitute) command, followed by a slash, the string to find, a slash, the string to replace the first value with, and another slash. The entire entry should appear within single quotes:

```
's/old value/new value/'
```

An example is:

```
$ echo I think the new neighbors are getting a new
   air pump | sed 's/air/heat/'
```

And the output displayed becomes:

```
I think the new neighbors are getting a new heat pump
```

The string "air" was replaced by the string "heat". One of its simplest features, text substitution is how **sed** is used most of the time because it is here that its power and features truly excel.

It is important to recognize that **sed** is not an interactive editor. Once you give it the commands to execute, it does so without further action on the user's part.

By default, **sed** works by scanning each line in successive order. If it does not find a match after searching the entire line, it moves to the next. If it finds a match for the search text within the line, it makes the change and immediately moves on to examine the next line. This can provide some unexpected results. For example, suppose you want to change the word "new" to "old":

```
$ echo I think the new neighbors are getting a new
   air pump | sed 's/new/old/'
```

The output becomes:

```
I think the old neighbors are getting a new air pump
```

The second occurrence of the search phrase is not changed because **sed** finished with the line after finding the first match. If you want all occurrences within the line to be changed, you must make the search *global* by using a **g** at the end of the command:

```
$ echo I think the new neighbors are getting a new
   air pump | sed 's/new/old/g'
```

The output becomes:

```
I think the old neighbors are getting a old air pump
```

The global parameter makes **sed** continue to search the remainder of the line, after finding a match, until the end of the line is reached. This handles multiple occurrences of the same phrase, but you must go in a different direction if you want to change more than one value.

You use the **-e** option on the command line to flag every command:

```
$ echo this line is shorter | sed -e 's/line/phrase/' -e 's/
   short/long/'
```

The output becomes:

```
this phrase is longer
```

The second method is to place all the substitution criteria in a file and then summon the file with the **-f** option:

```
$ cat wishlist
s/line/phrase/
s/short/long/
$
$ echo this line is shorter | sed -f wishlist
this phrase is longer
$
```

Both produce the same results, but using a file to hold your commands makes it easier to change criteria, keep track of the operations, and rerun the commands at a later time.

It is important to understand that for multiple operations, **sed** completes all of the first operation before starting the second. It completes all of the second—for the entire file, line, and so on—before starting the third and so on.

Technically (but not recommended), you could also complete the same operation by using semicolons after each substitution, or by going into input mode through an uneven number of single quotes:

```
$ echo this line is shorter | sed 's/line/phrase/; s/short/long/'
```

Or you can use:

```
$ echo this line is shorter | sed '
> s/line/phrase/
> s/short/long/'
```

Restricting Lines

If you have a large file, you might want to edit not the entire file but only selected lines. As with everything, you can address this issue in a number of ways. The first method is to specify a search clause and make substitutions only when the search phrase is found. The search phrase must precede the operation and be enclosed within slashes:

```
/search phrase/ {operation}
```

For example, assume you have the following file named "tuesday":

```
one     1
two     1
three     1
three     1
two     1
one     1
```

You want the end result displayed to be:

```
one     1
two     2
three     3
three     3
two     2
one     1
```

In this case, the search should target the word "two". Then, any "1"s following the word "two" should be converted to "2"s. Likewise, a search for the word "three" should then convert any "1"s to "3"s:

```
$ cat wishlist
/two/ s/1/2/
/three/ s/1/3/
$
$ sed -f wishlist tuesday
one 1
```

```
two 2
three 3
three 3
two 2
one 1
$
```

By design, **sed** changes only the values displayed and not the values in the original file. To keep the results of the change, you must redirect output to a file, as in:

```
sed -f wishlist tuesday > wednesday
```

Sometimes the actions specified should take place not on the basis of a search, but purely on the basis of the line number. For example, you might want to change only the first line of a file, the first 10 lines, or any other combination. You can specify a range of lines using the syntax:

```
First line,last line
```

For example, to change all non "one"s to that value in the first five lines:

```
$ cat wishlist
1,5 s/two/one/
1,5 s/three/one/$
$ sed -f wishlist tuesday
one 1
one 1
one 1
one 1
one 1
one 1
$
```

Printing

The default operation for **sed** is simply to print. If you give no parameters at all, an entire file is displayed without any editing occurring. The one caveat is that **sed** must always have an option or command. If you simply give the name of a file following **sed** and nothing more, it misinterprets the file name as a command.

You can give a number of lines for **sed** to display, followed with the **q** command (for quit), and see the contents of any file:

```
sed 75000q /usr/dict/words
```

This example displays all of the words in the file because the number of lines within the file is far less than 75,000. If you want to see only the first 60, you can use:

```
sed 60q /usr/dict/words
```

The antithesis, or opposite, of the default action is the **-n** option. This prevents lines from displaying that normally would:

```
sed -n 75000q /usr/dict/words
```

This example displays nothing. Although it might seem foolish to let a tool designed to display data include an option that prevents displaying data, it can actually be a marvelous feature. To put it into perspective, however, you must know that the **p** command is used to force a print (the default action).

In an earlier example, the file "tuesday" had numbers changed to match their alpha counterpart. Some of the lines in the file were already correct and did not need to be changed. If the lines aren't being changed, do you really need to see their output—or are you interested only in the lines being changed? For the latter case, the following example displays only those entries:

```
$ cat wishlist
/two/ s/1/2/p
/three/ s/1/3/p
$
$ sed -nf wishlist tuesday
two 2
three 3
three 3
two 2
$
```

To print only lines 200 to 300 of a file (no actual editing taking place), the command becomes:

```
sed -n '200,300p' /usr/dict/words
```

Deleting

You use the **d** command to specify deletion. As with all **sed** operations, the line is deleted from the display only and not from the original file. The syntax is always:

```
{the specification} d
```

To delete all lines that have the string "three":

```
$ sed '/three/ d' tuesday
one 1
two 1
two 1
one 1
$
```

Or to delete lines 1 through 3:

```
$ sed '1,3 d' tuesday
three 1
two 1
one 1
$
```

In all cases, the **d** command forces the deletion of the entire line. You cannot use this command to delete a portion of a line or a word. If you want to delete a word, substitute the word with nothing:

```
sed 's/word//'
```

Appending Text

You can append to strings in a display using the **a** command. Append always places the string at the end of the specification—after the other lines. For example, to place a string equal to "The End" as the last line of the display, the command is:

```
$ sed '$a\
> The End\' tuesday
one 1
two 1
three 1
three 1
two 1
one 1
The End
$
```

You use the dollar sign ($) to specify the end of the file and the \s to add a carriage return. If you leave the dollar sign out of the command, the text is appended after every line:

```
$ sed 'a\
> The End\' tuesday
one 1
The End
two 1
The End
three 1
The End
three 1
The End
two 1
The End
one 1
The End
$
```

If you want the string appended following a certain line number, add the line number to the command:

```
$ sed '3a\
> Not The End\' tuesday
one 1
two 1
three 1
Not The End
three 1
two 1
one 1
$
```

In place of the append, you can use the insert (i) command to place strings before the given line, rather than after:

```
$ sed '3i\
> Not The End\' tuesday
one 1
two 1
Not The End
three 1
three 1
two 1
one 1
$
```

Other Commands

You can use a few other commands with **sed** to add functionality:

- **b**—Branches execution to another part of the file specifying what commands to carry out.
- **c**—Changes one line to another. Whereas **s** substitutes one string for another, **c** changes the entire line:

```
$ sed '/three/ c\
> four 4' tuesday
one 1
two 1
four 4
four 4
two 1
one 1
$
```

- **r**—Reads additional files and appends text from a second file into the display of the first.
- **w** —Writes to a file. Instead of using the redirection (> **filename**), you can use **w filename**:

```
$ cat wishlist
/two/ s/two/one/
/three/ s/three/one/
w friday
$
sed -f wishlist tuesday
one 1
one 1
one 1
one 1
one 1
one 1
$
$ cat friday
one 1
one 1
one 1
one 1
one 1
one 1
$
```

- **y**—Translates one character space into another.

A Word to the Wise

When working with **sed** and performing more than one change, substitution, or deletion operation, you must be *very* careful about the order you specify for operations to take place. Using the example of the tuesday file, assume that the numbering is off. You want to change all "one"s to "two", all "two"s to "three", and all "three"s to "four". One way to approach it, and the results it generates, follow:

```
$ cat wishlist
s/one/two/
s/two/three/
s/three/four/
$
$ sed -f wishlist tuesday
four 1
four 1
four 1
four 1
four 1
four 1
$
```

The results are not what was expected or wanted. Because **sed** goes through the entire file and performs the first operation, it first changes the file to:

```
two 1
two 1
three 1
three 1
two 1
two 1
```

After that, **sed** goes through the file again, to perform the second operation. The file changes to:

```
three 1
three 1
three 1
three 1
three 1
three 1
```

When it comes time for the third iteration through the file, every line is the same and gets the change—completely defeating the purpose. This example is one of the reasons that **sed**'s style of changing the display only and not the original file is a blessing.

To solve the problem, you need only realize what is transpiring and then arrange the order of operations to prevent it:

```
$ cat wishlist
s/three/four/
s/two/three/
s/one/two/
$
$ sed -f wishlist tuesday
two 1
three 1
four 1
four 1
three 1
one 1
$
```

Utility Summation

We discussed only a few utilities in this chapter. Table 4.2 lists them and their purposes.

Associated Utilities

Linux includes a number of other useful text utilities. Some of these have limited usefulness and are intended only for a specific purpose. Some of these are not included on Exam 101, but knowing of their existence and purpose can make your life with Linux considerably easier.

Table 4.2 Utilities discussed in this chapter.

Utility	Default Purpose
grep	Displays lines that contain the given string.
fgrep	Originally offered features not found in **grep** but can now be emulated with **grep -F**.
egrep	Originally combined features of **grep** and **fgrep** with new possibilities. Can now be emulated with **grep -E**.
sed	Allows text to be changed before being displayed.

In alphabetical order, the additional utilities (and one programming language) follow:

- **awk**—Often used in conjunction with **sed, awk** is a utility, language, and tool with an enormous amount of flexibility for manipulating text. Examining **awk** is beyond the scope of this LPI exam, but it is worth investing time in learning **awk** to simplify administrative tasks. The GNU implementation of the utility is called **gawk** (as in GNU **awk**) but is truly the same.
- **cmp**—Compares two files and reports if they are the same or where the first difference occurs in terms of line number and character.
- **comm**—Looks at two files and reports what they have in common.
- **diff**—Allows you to see the differences between two files.
- **diff3**—Similar to **diff** but works with more than two files.
- Perl—A programming language useful for working with text.

Practice Questions

Question 1

Give the correct syntax to use the **sed** utility to change the line:

```
I think the new neighbors are getting a new
heat pump
```

to:

```
I think the old neighbors are getting a
reconditioned heat pump
```

[Fill in the blank]

____

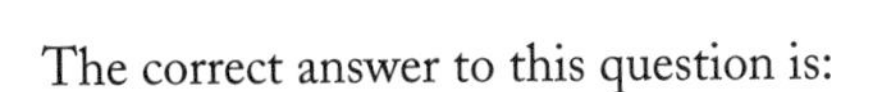

The correct answer to this question is:

```
echo I think the new neighbors are getting a new heat pump | sed
   -e 's/new/old/' -e 's/new/reconditioned/'
```

Because the same word is being substituted for two different values, you can leave off the global (**g**) parameter. This will allow **sed** to quit after the first substitution and then come back and change the second match to the other value on the second iteration through the line.

Question 2

Which of the following commands can you use to view the first 300 lines of a file named "flashlight"? [Check all correct answers]

❑ a. **sed 300q flashlight**

❑ b. **sed 300p flashlight**

❑ c. **head -300 flashlight**

❑ d. **tail +300 flashlight**

The correct answers to this question are a and c, both of which will print the first 300 lines and then quit. Answer b is the incorrect usage of the print **p** command and will not work. Answer d will show all but the first 300 lines of the file—the opposite of the desired result.

Question 3

Using the **grep** utility, you want to view the entire contents of a file named "savedmail", except the blank lines. Which one of the following commands will accomplish this?

❍ a. **grep "^" savedmail**

❍ b. **grep -v "\" savedmail**

❍ c. **grep -n " " savedmail**

❍ d. **grep -v "^$" savedmail**

The correct answer to this question is d. Looking for the beginning of a line immediately followed by the end of the line (^$) will find blank lines. The -v option will show all lines that do not match what you are searching for, so it will display all nonblank lines. Answer a will look for the beginning of a line that is a blank character, answer b will look for lines that do not contain a space, and answer c will number lines and look for lines that contain a space.

Question 4

Which regular expression character is used to signify a single character?

- ❍ a. **.**
- ❍ b. **?**
- ❍ c. **+**
- ❍ d. **#**

The correct answer to this question is a: A period (.) is used to denote any single character. Answer b (?) is used with **egrep** to denote zero or one occurrences of an entity. Answer c (+) is used with **egrep** to denote one or more occurrences of an entity. Answer d (#) is a Linux global character used to indicate that remarks follow.

Question 5

Which of the following commands can you use to determine who, besides the root user, is logged into a system?

- ❍ a. **who | grep -i "root"**
- ❍ b. **who | grep -v "root"**
- ❍ c. **who | grep -n "root"**
- ❍ d. **grep -n "root" | who**

The correct answer to this question is b, which will show all users except **-v** the root user. Answer a will ignore case and still print only entries matching "root" and not those of other users. Answer c will pull out only "root" entries and then number the lines. Answer d will not work because the order of operations is completely reversed.

Question 6

You can use the command **date +%d** to extract today's date only. Write a command that—in one line—will create a file named "fileone" that has the correct syntax to be fed into **sed** to substitute the value of today's date with "XX". [Fill in the blank]

____

The correct answer to this question is:

```
echo "s/`date +%d`/XX/" > fileone
```

If today's date is the 22nd, the resulting contents of fileone will become

```
S/22/XX/
```

You can use this with commands such as **cal** (which creates calendars) to mark today's date.

Question 7

Which of the following commands must you use with **sed** to issue more than one command at a time on the command line?

- ❍ a. **-i**
- ❍ b. **-a**
- ❍ c. **-e**
- ❍ d. **-f**

The correct answer to this question is c. You must use the **-e** option in front of each operation to correctly identify the commands. Answer d signifies that a file containing commands is to be used. Answers a and b are not valid options.

Question 8

Evan is trying to create a file that can be used to convert dates to modified Julian values. To do this, he must convert months in a log file from the syntax "10-10-01" to the syntax "273-10-01". Which **sed** command should he use?

❍ a. **sed 's/10/273/'**

❍ b. **sed 's/10/273/g'**

❍ c. **sed '/10/ s/10/273/'**

❍ d. **sed '/^10/ s/10/273/'**

The correct answer to this question is d. This will look for 10 in the month field and change it; lacking the global option, it changes only the month field. Answer a will change all "10"s to "273"s, even if they are not in the right location for the month—so "9-10-01" will become "9-273-01". Answer b will change all "10"s to "273"s throughout each line (globally)—not just the month. Answer c looks for "10"s and then performs the changes—the same thing that would happen without first searching for it. Again, it is not limited to the month field.

Question 9

You can use the command **sed -n** to prevent most lines from displaying. You want, however, to change the value "abc" globally to "def" and you want to print those lines. Which of the following is the correct specification?

❍ a. **s/def/abc/g p**

❍ b. **s/abc/def/gp**

❍ c. **s/def/abc/pg**

❍ d. **s/abc/def/g p**

The correct answer to this question is b, which will globally (**g**) change all "abc"s to "def"s and print (**p**) the results. Answers a and c have the substitution in the wrong order (and a does not have the commands together, **gp**). Answer d does not have the commands together (**gp**).

Question 10

Which command can you use with **sed** to write the output to a file as well as to the screen, which is the default for standard output?

- ❍ a. **w**
- ❍ b. **c**
- ❍ c. **r**
- ❍ d. **d**

The correct answer to this question is a. The **w** command will take as a parameter the name of the file to write the contents to. The **c** command (answer b) will allow you to change entire lines. The **r** command (answer c) will read in from another file. The **d** command (answer d) will delete lines.

Need to Know More?

Dougherty, Dale, and Arnold Robbins. *sed & awk, 2nd Edition.* Sebastopol, CA: O'Reilly & Associates, 1997. ISBN: 1-56592-225-5. This book is an excellent reference to the two powerful utilities—both GNU and POSIX versions.

Friedl, Jeffrey. *Mastering Regular Expressions.* Sebastopol, CA: O'Reilly & Associates, 1997. ISBN: 1-56592-257-3. Chapter 3 covers basic **grep** commands and concepts.

www.ptug.org/sed/sedfaq.htm contains the FAQ for the **sed** utility and its operations. It provides great detail on the different versions currently available and where to find them.

www.wollery.demon.co.uk/sedtut10.txt is an excellent tutorial on the use of **sed**.

File Management

Terms you'll need to understand:

- ✓ **cd**
- ✓ **pwd**
- ✓ Absolute addresses
- ✓ Relative addresses
- ✓ **ls**
- ✓ **touch**
- ✓ **cp**
- ✓ **mv**
- ✓ **dd**
- ✓ **rm**
- ✓ **rmdir**
- ✓ **mkdir**

Techniques you'll need to master:

- ✓ Understanding how to manage files with a core set of utilities provided by the Linux filesystem
- ✓ Recognizing the differences between various utilities and address methods

In this chapter, you'll learn about a number of utilities used for managing files and directories. Some of these utilities—such as **cd** and **ls**—are of such importance that it was impossible to get this far in the book without using them in some of the examples. Here, I expand upon them and explore their functions and uses in greater detail.

Working with cd and pwd

You use the **cd** command to change the directory in which you are working. Entering the command with no parameters moves you to whatever directory is defined by the **HOME** variable. Specifying any parameter with it is seen as denoting the directory you want to change to.

Some characters that can be of great use with **cd** are the single period (.) and double period (..). The former represents whatever directory you are currently in, and the latter is the parent directory of the current one.

The **pwd** utility shows the present working directory—the one you are currently in. The same value it returns is contained in the environmental variable **PWD**.

Always remember that more than one item can have the same name in Linux. As a general rule, all uppercase entries represent variables and are not executables; all lowercase entries are files or utilities and are rarely variables.

Following are some examples of how you can use these two utilities:

```
$ pwd
/usr/bin
$ echo $HOME
/home/edulaney
$ cd
$ pwd
/home/edulaney
$
```

This sequence showed the present working directory to be "/usr/bin" and the **HOME** variable to be equal to "/home/edulaney". Entering **cd** without any parameters changed to that directory.

In the following sequence, the first change is to the root directory (/):

```
$ pwd
/home/edulaney
$ cd /
$ pwd
```

```
/
$ cd /home/edulaney
$ pwd
/home/edulaney
$ cd ..
$ pwd
/home
$
```

The second change was to "/home/edulaney". Using the shortcut for the parent of this directory, it was then possible to move back one directory.

Absolute and Relative Addressing

The two methods of specifying paths to anything—files, directories, and so on—are absolute and relative. When you give an absolute path, you assume nothing, and you give a value that is always true. When you give a relative path, you take into account where you are currently, and you give a path relative to that location.

To use an analogy, suppose two people live in the same city and state: Muncie, Indiana. The first person lives at 1909 Rosewood, and the second person lives at 4104 Peachtree Lane. If the first person wants to find and visit the second person, she can find out where he is via an absolute path known as the mailing address: 4104 Peachtree Lane, Muncie, IN 47304.

This address says she should:

1. Find Indiana.
2. Within Indiana, find Muncie.
3. Within Muncie, find the section of the city within the 47304 zip code.
4. Within all earlier confines, find Peachtree Lane.
5. On Peachtree Lane, go to house number 4104.

Be sure to remember that absolute addresses never change and point to the entity regardless of where you are coming from.

The absolute address is the same whether the person coming to visit lives in Muncie or Alaska. Because the first person does live in Muncie, however, you can also tell her how to reach her destination using relative addressing:

1. Take Rosewood to Bethel, and turn left.

2. Take Bethel to Jackson, and turn right.
3. Take Jackson across the railroad tracks to the stop sign at Hawthorne.
4. Turn left on Hawthorne, and go to the next stop, which is Peachtree Lane.
5. Turn right on Peachtree Lane; go to the first house on the right.

Relative addresses always change and are relative to where you are coming from.

Table 5.1 illustrates a few examples you can use with the **cd** command.

Working with ls

The ability to list files and directories is one of the most essential to any operating system, and the **ls** utility performs this function for Linux. As shown in earlier chapters, when given by itself, **ls** lists the names of files and directories beneath the current directory in a column-style format. Entries are always—by default—given in alphabetical order, and nothing differentiates names of directories from names of files. An example follows:

```
Desktop  emmett    filethree  junk2     questions
TestPro  errors    filetwo    mischief  sample
brio     example   Friday     myfile    sample of the world
dulaney  example2  garbage    numbers   simplesimon
eRRors   fileone   junk1      pull      snapshot01.gif
```

Table 5.1 Addressing examples.

Present Working Directory	New Location	Absolute Address	Relative Address
/usr/home/edulaney/docs /proposals	/usr/home/ edulaney/docs	/usr/home/ edulaney/docs	..
/usr/home/edulaney/docs /proposals	/usr/home/edulaney	/usr/home/edulaney	../..
/usr/home/edulaney/docs /proposals	/usr/home/edulaney/ docs/proposals/ law_order	/usr/home/edulaney/ docs/proposals/ law_order	law_order
/usr/home/edulaney/docs /proposals	/	/	../../../..

The listings are always in alphabetical order by default, with all uppercase entries coming before lowercase entries.

You can use a slew of options with this command, and one of the most useful is **-F**, which indicates what type of entry is being displayed:

```
Desktop/  emmett    filethree  junk2      questions
TestPro   errors    filetwo    mischief*  sample
brio      example   Friday     myfile     sample of the world*
dulaney   example2  garbage    numbers    simplesimon
eRRors    fileone   junk1      pull       snapshot01.gif
```

Entries without any trailing characters are standard files. Entries with a "/" on the end—such as **Desktop/**—are directories. Those entries with a trailing asterisk ("*") are executable.

Another useful option is **-a**, which shows all files. By default, hidden files are not displayed by **ls**. A hidden file is any file that has a period (.) as its first character:

```
.              Desktop  emmett    filethree  junk2     questions
..             TestPro  errors    filetwo    mischief  sample
.bash_history  brio     example   Friday     myfile    sample of_
                                                       the world
.bash_logout   dulaney  example2  garbage    numbers   simple_
                                                       simon
.fileone.swp   eRRors   fileone   junk1      pull      snapshot_
                                                       01.gif
```

You should know that periods can appear anywhere within a file name as many times as you want. The only time a period has any special significance is when it is the first character of the name.

Using **-A** in place of **-a** leaves off the first two entries ("." and ".."). Undoubtedly, however, the most useful option of all is **-l**, which displays a long list of the files. Entries resemble the following:

```
drwx------   5  root  root  1024  Aug 30 11:12  Desktop
-rw-r--r--   1  root  root  548   Aug 23 22:01  TestPro
-rw-r--r--   1  root  root  28    Aug 22 10:26  brio
```

The seven columns here can be broken out as follows:

- The permissions on the entry. Permissions are fully discussed in Chapter 8, but for now it is important to realize that the first character identifies what type of entry it is. A "-" indicates a file, and a **d** is a directory. Other possibilities for the first character are **c** for a character special file (such as a terminal), **b** for a block special device (such as a tape drive), **l** for a symbolic link (covered in Chapter 7), or **p** for a named pipe.
- The number of links. If this is a directory, it is equal to the number of entries beneath it. If it is a file, it is equal to the number of ways to reference it.
- The name of the owner who created (or now owns) the entity
- The name of the group owning the file
- The size of the file
- The date of creation or modification into the format it is currently in
- The name

Table 5.2 describes some other options for **ls**.

Applying a touch

Essentially, three dates are associated with each file or entry: creation, modification, and access. Using the **touch** utility, you can change the access and modification time associated with a file:

Table 5.2 Options for the ls command.

Option	Purpose
-c	Lists in order of time of last change or modification instead of alphabetical.
-d	Lists directories.
-G	When used with **-l**, doesn't show the group.
-i	Shows the inode number (pointer) to each entry.
-n	Shows the owner and group by their numeric values instead of name.
-o	Same as **-lG**.
-r	Reverses the order of the display.
-R	Recursively shows entries in subdirectories as well.
-S	Sorts.
-u	Sorts by last access time.
-w	Specifies screen width.
-x	Shows lines instead of columns.
-X	Alphabetizes by extension.

```
$
ls -l brio
-rw-r--r--    1    root    root    28    Aug 22 10:26    brio
$ touch brio
$ ls -l brio
-rw-r--r--    1    root    root    28    Aug 30 16:01    brio
$
```

A few options can be used with the **touch** utility as well, as summarized in Table 5.3.

An example using the last option in Table 5.3 follows:

```
$
ls -l tuesday wednesday
-rw-r--r--    1    root    root    85    Aug 22 10:26    tuesday
-rw-r--r--    1    root    root    85    Aug 29 13:08    wednesday
$ touch tuesday -r wednesday
ls -l tuesday wednesday
-rw-r--r--    1    root    root    85    Aug 29 13:08    tuesday
-rw-r--r--    1    root    root    85    Aug 29 13:08    wednesday
$
```

Be sure to remember that if you use the **touch** utility with the name of a file that does not exist, it creates the file—with the current date and time and a size of zero.

Copying and Moving

System administration would be so much easier if nothing ever moved or changed. Unfortunately, it is rare for anything to stay static, and changes take place at a nonstop pace. Linux offers two powerful utilities for copying and moving files—**cp** and **mv**, respectively—and a third utility—**dd**—that combines features of both.

Table 5.3 Options for the touch command.

Option	Purpose
-a	Changes only the access time.
-m	Changes only the modification time.
-r	Uses the time/date associated with a reference file to make the change instead of the current time/date.

cp

cp works with both files and directories and can move multiple entities at a time using wildcards. After the utility, you must specify the source, followed by the target. The simplest use of all can be illustrated as the following:

```
$ ls -l fileone onefile
ls: onefile: No such file or directory
-rw-r--r--   1   root   root   85   Aug 22 10:26   fileone
$
$ cp fileone onefile
$ ls -l fileone onefile
-rw-r--r--   1   root       root    85   Aug 22 10:26   fileone
-rw-r--r--   1   edulaney   users   85   Aug 30 16:18   onefile
$
```

Notice that the original entry (source) remains unchanged, but now there is a second entry (target) as well. On the second entry, the contents are identical, but the date and time are those of the present (when **cp** was executed) and not those of the source. Notice as well that the owner and group of the new file became those of the user executing the command. This same action would take place if you were creating the target file completely from scratch.

To be able to copy a file—to create a new entity equal in content to another—you need only read permission to the source.

You can use the **-p** option to force as many of the old variables as possible to remain the same. It preserves what it can in terms of attributes:

```
$ ls -l fileone nextfile
ls: nextfile: No such file or directory
-rw-r--r--   1   root   root   85   Aug 22 10:26   fileone
$
$ cp -p fileone nextfile
$ ls -l fileone nextfile
-rw-r--r--   1   root       root    85   Aug 22 10:26   fileone
-rw-r--r--   1   edulaney   users   85   Aug 22 10:26   nextfile
$
```

Notice that the date and time associated with the source were kept, but the owner and group still must change.

When you do a copy operation, the utility first checks whether the source file exists. If it does, then whatever file is specified as the target is created (with a size of zero), and the contents of the source are copied. The emphasis here is on the fact that the target is always created—regardless of whether it existed before. To illustrate:

```
$ ls -l fileone filetwo
-rw-r--r--   1   root   root   85      Aug 22 10:26   fileone
-rw-r--r--   1   root   root   16432   Aug 28 13:43   filetwo
$
$ cp fileone filetwo
$ ls -l fileone filetwo
-rw-r--r--   1   root       root    85   Aug 22 10:26   fileone
-rw-r--r--   1   edulaney   users   85   Aug 30 16:18   filetwo
$
```

The original contents of filetwo have been lost, save for any backup tape versions, because filetwo is *created* to be a copy of fileone. You can use an **-i** (as in inquiry or interactive) option to always ask whether you really want to erase the contents of the target file if it already exists:

```
$ ls -l fileone filetwo
-rw-r--r--   1   root   root   85      Aug 22 10:26   fileone
-rw-r--r--   1   root   root   16432   Aug 28 13:43   filetwo
$
$ cp -i fileone filetwo
cp: overwrite 'filetwo'?
```

At the prompt, you can enter **y** to perform the operation or anything else to stop it.

You can copy a number of files from one directory to another as long as the last item on the command line is a valid directory path into which the files will be copied:

```
$ ls -l /home/sdulaney
-rw-r--r--   1   root   root   85   Aug 22 10:26   exit
$
$ cd /home/examples
$ ls -l s* q*
-rw-r--r--   1   root   root   585    Aug 23 12:16   questions
-rw-r--r--   1   root   root   1985   Aug 24 15:17   samples
-rw-r--r--   1   root   root   8501   Aug 25 18:30
   snapshot01.gif
$ cp s* q* /home/sdulaney
$ cd ../sdulaney
$ ls -l
-rw-r--r--   1   root   root   85     Aug 22 10:26   exit
-rw-r--r--   1   root   root   585    Aug 31 22:50   questions
-rw-r--r--   1   root   root   1985   Aug 31 22:50   samples
```

```
-rw-r--r--   1   root   root   8501   Aug 31 22:50
   snapshot01.gif
$
```

To move an entire directory from one location to another, use the **-r** or **-R** option to move the directory recursively as well as any subdirectories and files beneath it. Other options you can use include **-f** to force a copy without any prompting (the opposite, so to speak, of **-i**); **-u** to copy only when the source file is more recent (updated) than the target; and **-v** for verbose mode (show all operations, rather than silently perform them).

Lastly, the **-P** option reproduces the entire path to a file in another location—creating directories and subdirectories as needed to do so.

mv

You can use the move utility (**mv**) for several operations. At the risk of being overly simplistic, it includes the ability to:

- Rename a file
- Rename a directory
- Move a file from one directory to another
- Move a subdirectory from one directory to another
- Move an entity to another partition or media

The simplest operation is to rename a file in its current directory, as follows:

```
$ ls -l file*
-rw-r--r--   1   root   root   85      Aug 22 10:26   fileone
-rw-r--r--   1   root   root   16432   Aug 28 13:43   filetwo
$
$ mv fileone filethree
$ ls -l file*
-rw-r--r--   1   root   root   85      Aug 22 10:26   filethree
-rw-r--r--   1   root   root   16432   Aug 28 13:43   filetwo
$
```

The dates, permissions, and everything else associated with fileone stay with filethree. When a file is moved within the same directory (or even on the same partition), all that changes is the information about the name. No physical operation takes place; only the descriptor is changed. The move has become a simple rename operation.

As simplistic as it sounds, always remember that when you copy a file, you leave the original intact and create something that did not exist before; thus a new set of attributes are created for the new entity. When you move a file, however, the default action is a rename; you are changing only the name of the original entity and not creating anything new.

One way to put it in perspective is that copying a file that is 9MB in size takes longer than copying a file that is 9 bytes in size. With move being used as a rename, it takes the same amount of time to do the operation regardless of the size of the file.

You will need to know this for the exam.

As with the copy operation, if you attempt to move a file to a name that already exists, the contents of the target are lost. To illustrate:

```
$ ls -l file*
-rw-r--r--    1    root    root    85       Aug 22 10:26    fileone
-rw-r--r--    1    root    root    16432    Aug 28 13:43    filetwo
$ mv fileone filetwo
$ ls -l file*
-rw-r--r--    1    root    root    85       Aug 22 10:26    filetwo
$
```

You can use the **-i** option (as in inquiry or interactive) to prompt before overwriting, and the opposite of it is **-f** (for force), which is the default operation. The **-u** option does the move only if the source file is newer, and **-v** turns on verbose mode. The **-b** option makes a backup of the target file, if it exists, with a tilde (~) as the last character—essentially performing a pseudo-copy operation:

```
$ ls -l help*
-rw-r--r--    1    root    root    85    Aug 22 10:26    helpfile
$ mv -b helpfile helpfiletwo
$ ls -l help*
-rw-r--r--    1    root    root    85    Aug 22 10:26    helpfiletwo
$
$ ls -l file*
-rw-r--r--    1    root    root    85       Aug 22 10:26    fileone
-rw-r--r--    1    root    root    16432    Aug 28 13:43    filetwo
$ mv -b fileone filetwo
$ ls -l file*
-rw-r--r--    1    root    root    85       Aug 22 10:26    filetwo
-rw-r--r--    1    root    root    16432    Aug 28 13:43    filetwo~
$
```

The first instance did not have an existing file with the target name, so the **-b** option was ignored. The second instance had a file by the name of the target, so the original target file was renamed with a tilde as the last character.

You can also use the **-b** option with **cp** to perform the same action during a copy, as it does here.

dd

You use the device-to-device (**dd**) utility to copy a file from one device to another. It goes beyond that in functionality, however, because it can convert a file during the copy process from one format to another. It can convert from EBCDIC to ASCII (and reverse), change uppercase to lowercase (and reverse as well), and work with bytes, blocks, or keywords.

The most common use for **dd** is copying files to and from removable media, and you must use arguments, which can include:

- **bs**—Block file size
- **if**—Input file
- **of**—Output file

Removing Files and Directories

You can remove files you no longer need from the system with the **rm** (remove) command. Be careful using this command because Linux offers no undelete command or function like those found in other operating systems. The following example illustrates how the **rm** command is used:

```
$ ls -l file*
-rw-r--r--    1    root    root    85       Aug 22 10:26    fileone
-rw-r--r--    1    root    root    16432    Aug 28 13:43    filetwo
$ rm fileone
$ ls -l file*
-rw-r--r--    1    root    root    16432    Aug 28 13:43    filetwo
$
```

With the **-i** option, a prompt appears before each file to be deleted. Pressing Y deletes the file, and pressing any other character skips the file. The following example illustrates the use of the **–i** option:

```
$ ls -l t*
-rw-r--r--    1    root    root    85       Aug 22 10:26    today
-rw-r--r--    1    root    root    16432    Aug 28 13:43    tuesday
```

```
$ rm -i t*
rm: remove 'today'?
```

The **-f** option forces deletion, and **-v** puts the utility in verbose mode. The **-r** or **-R** option recursively deletes directories (including subdirectories and files beneath). To delete a file, you must have write permissions within the directory where it resides.

Be sure to remember that a write permission is required only on the directory from which you are deleting the file—not on the file itself.

You can use a safer utility, **rmdir**, to delete directories that have nothing beneath them. It deletes only empty directories, so you cannot use it for directories that have files or subdirectories beneath them. The only option you can use with **rmdir** is **-p** to remove parent directories (if they are empty). In the next example, you will see how an empty directory cannot be deleted in this manner:

```
$ ls -R kdulaney
kdulaney:
docs

kdulaney/docs:
attempt
$
$ rmdir kdulaney
rmdir: kdulaney: Directory not empty
$
```

Because there is a file ("attempt") within kdulaney/docs and a subdirectory ("docs") beneath kdulaney, you cannot delete the directory kdulaney with the **rmdir** utility. You have three possible ways to accomplish the task:

- Use the **rm -r** command.
- Delete "attempt" with **rm**, delete "docs" with **rmdir**, and—finally—delete "kdulaney" with **rmdir**.
- Delete "attempt" with **rm**, and then delete "kdulaney/docs" with **rmdir -p**.

Because **rmdir** can delete only empty directories, it is naturally a safer utility to use than **rm** for cleaning a system.

Making Directories

Because you've seen how to copy, move, and delete directories, the only order of business left is to make a directory: This is accomplished via the **mkdir** command. Used without options, it creates a child directory (subdirectory) in the current directory. Two options works with it as well:

- **-m**—Specifies permissions other than the default for the new directory (covered in Chapter 8).
- **-p**—Creates a parent and child in one command.

Some examples of the utility are:

```
$ pwd
/home
$ mkdir edulaney
$
```

This created the subdirectory edulaney beneath /home (/home/edulaney). The next example illustrates the limitation of not being able to make multiple directories without using **-p**:

```
$ pwd
/home
$ mkdir kdulaney/docs
mkdir: cannot make directory 'kdulaney/docs': No such file
   or directory
$
$ mkdir -p kdulaney/docs
$ cd kdulaney
$ cd docs
$
```

In the first attempt, the utility fails because you cannot create multiple directories by default. Using the **-p** option, however, the multiple directories are created.

Utility Summation

This chapter discussed several utilities. Table 5.4 lists them and their purposes.

Table 5.4 Utilities discussed in this chapter.

Utility	Default Purpose
cd	Changes from the current directory to another.
pwd	Displays the current directory—always in absolute format.
ls	Lists files and directories on the system.
touch	Changes the times associated with a file.
cp	Copies a file or directory.
mv	Renames or moves a file or directory.
dd	Copies files between media.
rm	Removes files and directories.
rmdir	Removes empty directories.
mkdir	Makes directories.

Practice Questions

Question 1

You are currently in the "/usr/home/spencer/lists/phone" directory. Your **HOME** variable is set to "/usr/home/spencer", and the **PATH** is set to "/usr/local/sbin:/sbin". The **OLDPWD** variable is set to "/root". When you give the command **pwd**, what directory will you be in when the command ends?

- ❍ a. /root
- ❍ b. /usr/local/sbin
- ❍ c. /usr/home/spencer
- ❍ d. /usr/home/spencer/lists/phone

The correct answer to this question is d. The **pwd** command shows the present working directory—where you currently are—but does not change anything. The other answers are invalid since they all reflect other directories.

Question 2

You are currently in the /usr/home/spencer/lists/phone directory, and you want to change to /usr/home/spencer. Using the **cd** command, give the correct syntax to change to the path in question using an absolute address. [Fill in the blank]

____

The correct answer to this question is:

```
cd /usr/home/spencer
```

You must always give the full path with absolute addresses.

Question 3

> You are currently in the "/usr/home/spencer/lists/phone" directory, and you want to change to "/usr/home/spencer". Using the **cd** command, give the correct syntax to change to the path in question using a relative address. [Fill in the blank]
>
> ____________

The correct answer to this question is:

```
cd ../..
```

You must give a path to the destination relative to where you currently are with relative addresses. In this case, you need move back only two directories, and two sets of double periods allow you to do so.

Question 4

> You are currently in a directory with a number of subdirectories beneath it. You want to see all files within the subdirectories using the **ls** utility. Which option should you use with the utility to accomplish this?
>
> ❍ a. **-r**
>
> ❍ b. **-d**
>
> ❍ c. **-l**
>
> ❍ d. **-R**

The correct answer to this question is d. The **-R** option will show the recursive listing—including subdirectories and files beneath the current directory. The **-r** option (answer a) will reverse the order of the display. The **-d** option (answer b) will show directories only. The **-l** option (answer c) will show a long list.

Question 5

You are in the empty directory "abcd", and you give the command **touch abcd**. What will the result of this command be?

- ❍ a. An error message will be returned.
- ❍ b. The times associated with the directory will be updated.
- ❍ c. A new file will be created.
- ❍ d. A new directory will be created.

The correct answer to this question is c. If you use **touch** with the name of a file that does not exist, it will create the file (with a size of zero). The directory (answer b), or any directory (answer d) will not be affected, and there will be no error message (answer a) to return.

Question 6

A user with the name of kevin copies a file from the home directory of sarah. Within sarah's home directory, the owner of the file was root. The directory that kevin copies the file into is evan's home directory, owned by evan. Who will appear as the owner of the file in evan's home directory?

- ❍ a. kevin
- ❍ b. sarah
- ❍ c. root
- ❍ d. evan

The correct answer to this question is a. Because kevin is creating the new file through the copy operation, he is the owner. If the file were moved, the original owner would be kept, but copy must always use the person performing the operation as the owner. The other choices are invalid because they represent users other than the one performing the operation.

Question 7

With the **ls -l** command, which field shows the name of the owner of each file or directory shown in the display?

❍ a. first

❍ b. second

❍ c. third

❍ d. fourth

The correct answer to this question is c; the third field shows the owner. Answer a is wrong because the first field shows the permissions on the file, and answer b is wrong because the second field shows the number of links. Answer d is wrong because the fourth field identifies the group.

Question 8

Kristin is doing a number of operations on her system as she attempts to clean up files and make the system more manageable. Which of the following operations will take the least amount of time to complete?

❍ a. **cp certification exam**

❍ b. **mv certification exam**

❍ c. **dd certification exam**

❍ d. **cp -i certification exam**

The correct answer to this question is b. **mv certification exam** will rename a pointer and will be finished in a fraction of a second, regardless of the file size. Answer a will copy one file to another, and the amount of time it takes to complete will depend upon the size of the certification exam file. Answer c is also a copy operation (missing some syntax). Answer d is a derivative of answer a but adds the user interaction that must take place if a file named "certification exam" exists.

Question 9

Kristin has been cleaning up files that are no longer used on her system. Inadvertently, she typed **rm -r *** when working in one directory further back than she thought she was. How can she restore the files that were accidentally deleted from all the subdirectories?

❍ a. **dd**

❍ b. **rm -i**

❍ c. Type Ctrl-Z

❍ d. Restore from backup

The correct answer to this question is d. The only way to restore deleted files in Linux is to break out the backup tapes and restore from there. Answer a is a utility to copy files to media. Answer b is another version of remove. Answer c is completely invalid.

Question 10

Karen wants to create a path consisting of several subdirectories that do not presently exist. Which command should she use for this purpose?

❍ a. **md**

❍ b. **md -p**

❍ c. **mkdir**

❍ d. **mkdir -p**

The correct answer to this question is d. You must use the **-p** option with **mkdir** to create a path that includes subdirectories. The **md** command (answers a and b) exists in the non-Linux world (DOS, Windows 2000, and so on) but is not a valid option here. By default, **mkdir** (answer c) will allow you to create only one file.

Need to Know More?

Hare, Chris, and Emmett Dulaney, et al. *Inside Unix*. Indianapolis, IN: New Riders Publishing, 1994. ISBN: 1-56205-401-5. Chapter 6 covers the basics of listing, copying, and moving files and directories.

Siever, Ellen, and Stephen Spainhour, et al. *Linux in a Nutshell, 3rd Edition*. Sebastopol, CA: O'Reilly & Associates, 2000. ISBN: 0-59600-025-1. Chapter 3 contains an alphabetical listing of Linux utilities.

Welsh, Matt, and Matthias Kalle Dalheimer, et al. *Running Linux, 3rd Edition*. Sebastopol, CA: O'Reilly & Associates, 1999. ISBN: 1-56592-469-X. Chapter 4 covers basic commands and concepts.

6

Working with Processes

Terms you'll need to understand:

- ✓ ps
- ✓ pstree
- ✓ top
- ✓ kill
- ✓ killall
- ✓ &
- ✓ wait
- ✓ jobs
- ✓ fg
- ✓ bg
- ✓ nice
- ✓ renice
- ✓ tee

Techniques you'll need to master:

- ✓ Understanding how processes are the building blocks of transactions within the Linux operating system
- ✓ Recognizing how to manage processes with a core set of utilities

In this chapter, you'll learn about utilities used to manage processes and you'll see how processes are utilized for all transactions. Previous chapters discussed many utilities and commands; each time one of them is issued, a process is started to carry out the request, as you will see in greater detail.

What Is a Process?

Crucial to understanding this chapter is knowing that a process is *any* instance, command, or utility in execution. When you issue the command **ls**, as discussed in Chapter 5, a process is started to run the utility and return the results.

Even the shell with which you are interacting is running as a process. When you give a command to be carried out, the shell checks whether it can do so without any outside help. (Assume the command is really just an empty line: No other utilities are needed to return another prompt.) If your shell cannot perform the command, then it calls another process to perform the action. The other process called is a child to your shell, which becomes a parent to the new process (see Figure 6.1).

When the child is finished performing its task, it returns its results to the parent and then goes away. Because Linux is a multitasking operating system, there can be more than one child for any given parent. If the child cannot perform all of the tasks on its own (think of compiling an annual report), then the child might need to call one or more additional processes. When it does this, it becomes the parent to those child processes (see Figure 6.2).

For the exam, be sure to remember that, barring any restrictions coded into it, every process has the ability to be a parent or child.

On a system, at any given time, there are processes that you are running, there can be processes that others are running, and there are processes that the system itself is running. The latter are often *daemons*—services that are running without interaction to provide functionality to the operating system. Examples of services that daemons can perform include printing, running scheduled jobs, sending mail, monitoring run state, and so forth.

Working with ps

The **ps** command is key to any interaction with processes and is used to show process status. When run by itself (with no options), it shows the processes you currently have running, with the last line always noting itself (because it is a running process as well):

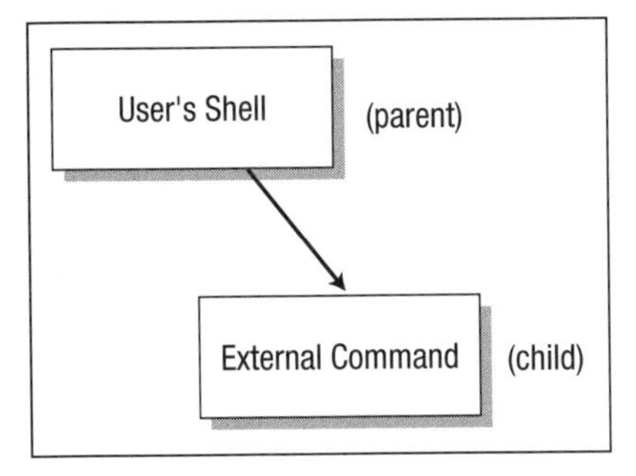

Figure 6.1 When one process calls another, it becomes a parent to that child.

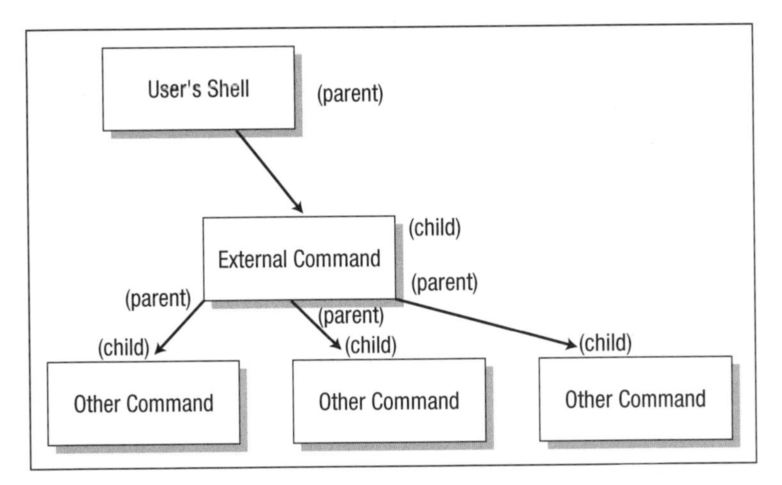

Figure 6.2 Every child has the ability to call other processes and be a parent to them.

```
$ ps
  PID      TTY          TIME     CMD
19605     pts/0      00:00:34    bash
30089     pts/0      00:00:00    vi
30425     pts/0      00:00:00    paste
32040     pts/0      00:00:00    cat
 1183     pts/0      00:00:00    awk
30679     pts/0      00:00:00    ps
$
```

The first column is the process ID number (PID), a unique number assigned to every process that executes. When the system is booted, the numbers begin incrementing until they reach a defined limit and then begin back through the numbering again, using only the numbers that are free.

The second column indicates the terminal upon which the user responsible for the process is associated. Because the list outlines processes only for the user issuing the command, all terminal listings should be the same.

The third column indicates the amount of processor time the process is utilizing. In most cases, processes can run quickly, sit idle, and so on and utilize very little time. A very high time reading can indicate a process that is dragging down the performance of the system.

The fourth column is the name of the process (command) itself. The first line mentions the user's shell—which must appear, or you would not have a user here at all: The user's shell is known as the *session leader*. The last line is the command just executed. Those entries in between are other processes the user is running.

The **ps** utility has a number of options to make it more flexible. The **-a** option removes obvious choices. For example, you know that you must have a shell running or you could not be interacting with the system, so it isn't really as important to see that item as the others. Using the **-a** option, the display changes just slightly:

```
$ ps -a
  PID     TTY         TIME     CMD
30089   pts/0   00:00:00     vi
30425   pts/0   00:00:00     paste
32040   pts/0   00:00:00     cat
 1183   pts/0   00:00:00     awk
30685   pts/0   00:00:00     ps
$
```

Be sure you remember that **ps -a** shows all processes associated with the current tty (terminal) *except* the session leader. Also note that the PID associated with **ps** increments every time it runs because each instance requires a new process. It does not increment by one, in this case, because several other processes ran (probably in the background) between the first and second running of **ps**.

Using either the **-A** or the **-e** option (all or everything), it is possible to see every process running and not just those linked to the current tty:

```
$ ps -e
PID TTY          TIME CMD
    1 ?          00:00:05 init
    2 ?          00:00:39 kflushd
    3 ?          00:00:00 kpiod
    4 ?          00:00:15 kswapd
    5 ?          00:00:00 mdrecoveryd
11635 ?          00:00:11 update
12046 ?          00:00:00 syslogd
12049 ?          00:00:00 klogd
```

```
12061 ?        00:00:00 inetd
12063 ?        00:00:00 rpc.portmap
12086 ?        00:00:00 amd
12092 ?        00:00:00 rpciod
12093 ?        00:00:00 lockd
12103 ?        00:00:00 cron
12109 ?        00:00:00 atd
12115 ?        00:00:00 sendmail
12129 ?        00:00:00 rpc.rstatd
12158 ?        00:00:00 httpd.apache
12164 ?        00:00:00 httpd.apache
12165 ?        00:00:00 httpd.apache
12228 tty1     00:00:00 getty
12229 tty2     00:00:00 getty
12230 tty3     00:00:00 getty
12231 tty4     00:00:00 getty
12232 tty5     00:00:00 getty
12233 tty6     00:00:00 getty
12234 ?        00:00:00 sh
12235 ?        00:00:00 rc.gui
12237 ?        00:00:00 kdm
12239 ?        00:07:26 X
14269 ?        00:00:02 kwmsound
29595 ?        00:00:00 kdm
29608 ?        00:00:18 kwm
29629 ?        00:00:01 kbgndwm
29658 ?        00:00:26 kfm
29659 ?        00:00:00 kaudioserver <defunct>
29660 ?        00:00:00 kwmsound <defunct>
29661 ?        00:00:02 krootwm
29662 ?        00:00:14 kpanel
29665 ?        00:00:02 kdewizard
19603 ?        00:01:02 kvt
19605 pts/0    00:00:34 bash
30089 pts/0    00:00:00 vi
30425 pts/0    00:00:00 paste
32040 pts/0    00:00:00 cat
 1183 pts/0    00:00:00 awk
30704 pts/0    00:00:00 ps
$
```

Notice the following items in the display:

- Processes started when the system came up have the lowest number PIDs (notice items 1 through 5). As a general rule, these are mission-critical processes; if they did not appear, some or all of the system would be unusable.

- Not all processes are tied to a terminal. A question mark (?) indicates that the process is running on the system without terminal interaction or without a terminal as the default standard output.
- Every terminal without a user runs a getty. This process sits and waits for a user to attempt to log on. Even though no user is using tty1 through tty6, it is easy to see that these represent six other terminals that can be used by users for interacting with this system.

Other options you can use to determine what information to display include:

- **l**—Displays a long listing (think of **ls -l**).
- **u**—Shows username and related stats.
- **f**—Displays the full listing (everything possible).

The last option is often used, and favored by administrators, for the additional columns it adds to the display:

```
$ ps -f
UID          PID   PPID  C STIME TTY      TIME CMD
root       19605  19603  0 Aug10 pts/0  00:00:34 bash
root       30089  19605  0 Aug20 pts/0  00:00:00 vi fileone
root       30425  19605  0 Aug20 pts/0  00:00:00 paste_
   -d fileone filetwo?
root       32040  19605  0 Aug22 pts/0  00:00:00 cat
root        1183  19605  0 Aug23 pts/0  00:00:00 awk -F: questions
root       30778  19605  0 14:25 pts/0  00:00:00 ps -f
$
```

Four new columns now exist that were not there before. The first column identifies the user ID associated with the process. The third column is the parent process ID—showing which process this one reports back to. (See Figure 6.3 for a graphical representation of these results.) The fourth column indicates whether scheduling is involved, and the fifth column is the time at which the process started.

Be sure to notice that, when using **f**, the **CMD** lists the entire command and not just the first portion, as in the other displays.

You can combine these options; the most common combination is **ef**, which displays all processes in a full format:

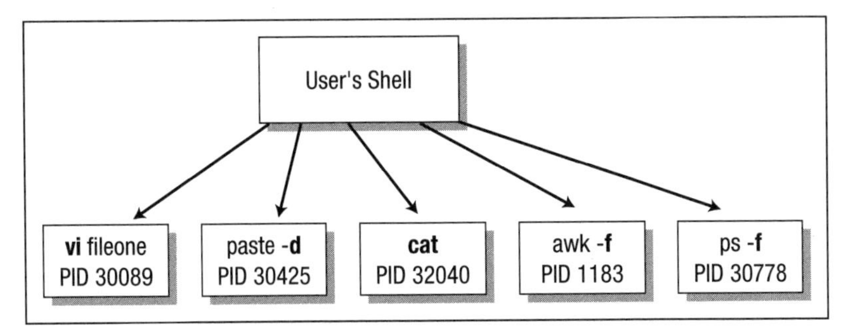

Figure 6.3 A graphic representation of the parent/child relationship **ps -f** insinuated.

```
$ ps -ef
UID        PID  PPID  C STIME TTY      TIME CMD
root         1     0  0 Jul06 ?        00:00:05 init [5]
root         2     1  0 Jul06 ?        00:00:39 [kflushd]
root         3     1  0 Jul06 ?        00:00:00 [kpiod]
root         4     1  0 Jul06 ?        00:00:15 [kswapd]
root         5     1  0 Jul06 ?        00:00:00 [mdrecoveryd]
root     11635     1  0 Jul06 ?        00:00:11 update (bdflush)
root     12046     1  0 Jul06 ?        00:00:00 syslogd
root     12049     1  0 Jul06 ?        00:00:00 klogd_
   -k /boot/System.map-2.2.10
root     12061     1  0 Jul06 ?        00:00:00 inetd
bin      12063     1  0 Jul06 ?        00:00:00 rpc.portmap
root     12086     1  0 Jul06 ?        00:00:00 amd -F /etc/am.d/
conf
root     12092     1  0 Jul06 ?        00:00:00 [rpciod]
root     12093     1  0 Jul06 ?        00:00:00 [lockd]
root     12103     1  0 Jul06 ?        00:00:00 cron
daemon   12109     1  0 Jul06 ?        00:00:00 atd
root     12115     1  0 Jul06 ?        00:00:00 sendmail:_
   accepting connections
root     12129     1  0 Jul06 ?        00:00:00 rpc.rstatd
root     12158     1  0 Jul06 ?        00:00:00 httpd_
   -f /etc/httpd/apache/conf/
nobody   12164 12158  0 Jul06 ?        00:00:00 httpd_
   -f /etc/httpd/apache/conf/
nobody   12165 12158  0 Jul06 ?        00:00:00 httpd_
   -f /etc/httpd/apache/conf/
root     12228     1  0 Jul06 tty1     00:00:00 /sbin/getty_
   tty1 VC linux
root     12229     1  0 Jul06 tty2     00:00:00 /sbin/getty_
   tty2 VC linux
root     12230     1  0 Jul06 tty3     00:00:00 /sbin/getty_
```

```
   tty3 VC linux
root      12231     1  0 Jul06 tty4     00:00:00 /sbin/getty_
   tty4 VC linux
root      12232     1  0 Jul06 tty5     00:00:00 /sbin/getty_
   tty5 VC linux
root      12233     1  0 Jul06 tty6     00:00:00 /sbin/getty_
   tty6 VC linux
root      12234     1  0 Jul06 ?        00:00:00 /bin/sh -c_
   C=/etc/rc.d/rc.gui;[
root      12235 12234  0 Jul06 ?        00:00:00 bash_
   /etc/rc.d/rc.gui
root      12237 12235  0 Jul06 ?        00:00:00_
   /opt/kde/bin/kdm -nodaemon
root      12239 12237  0 Jul06 ?        00:07:39_
   /usr/X11R6/bin/X -auth /etc/X11/
edulaney 14269     1  0 Jul06 ?        00:00:02 kwmsound
root      29595 12237  0 Jul19 ?        00:00:00 -:0
root      29608 29595  0 Jul19 ?        00:00:19 kwm -nosession
root      29629 29608  0 Jul19 ?        00:00:01_
   /opt/kde/bin/kbgndwm
root      29658 29608  0 Jul19 ?        00:00:29 kfm
root      29659 29608  0 Jul19 ?        00:00:00_
   [kaudioserver <defunct>]
root      29660 29608  0 Jul19 ?        00:00:00_
   [kwmsound <defunct>]
root      29661 29608  0 Jul19 ?        00:00:02 krootwm
root      29662 29608  0 Jul19 ?        00:00:15 kpanel
root      29665     1  0 Jul19 ?        00:00:02 kdewizard
root      19603 29658  0 Aug10 ?        00:01:03_
   kvt -T ption Terminal -icon kvt.
root      19605 19603  0 Aug10 pts/0    00:00:34 bash
root      30089 19605  0 Aug20 pts/0    00:00:00 vi fileone
root      30425 19605  0 Aug20 pts/0    00:00:00_
   paste -d fileone filetwo?
root      32040 19605  0 Aug22 pts/0    00:00:00 cat
root       1183 19605  0 Aug23 pts/0    00:00:00 awk -F: questions
root      30758 19605  0 14:21 pts/0    00:00:00 ps -ef
$
```

Working with pstree and top

Two commands closely related to **ps** offer slightly different views of the processes. The first of these is **pstree**, which graphically depicts the relationship between the processes:

```
$ pstree
init-+-amd
     |-atd
     |-cron
     |-6*[getty]
     |-httpd.apache—2*[httpd.apache]
     |-inetd
     |-kdewizard
     |-kflushd
     |-klogd
     |-kpiod
     |-kswapd
     |-kwmsound
     |-lockd
     |-mdrecoveryd
     |-rpc.portmap
     |-rpc.rstatd
     |-rpciod
     |-sendmail
     |-sh—rc.gui—kdm-+-X
     |               '-kdm—kwm-+-kaudioserver
     |                         |-kbgndwm
     |                         |-kfm—kvt—bash-+-awk
     |                         |              |-cat
     |                         |              |-paste
     |                         |              |-pstree
     |                         |              '-vi
     |                         |-kpanel
     |                         |-krootwm
     |                         '-kwmsound
     |-syslogd
     '-update
$
```

This graphically depicts the five children beneath the user's shell, as well as shows where the shell fits in—what process is the parent of it, and so on.

The second utility related to **ps** is **top**, shown in Figure 6.4. Not only does it show the current processes, but it also stays active and continually updates the display. Additionally, the top of the screen depicts information about the number of days the system has been up; the number of users, memory, and swap statistics; and so on.

When **top** is running, you can press any of the following keys to interact with it:

- **h**—Help
- **q**—Quit

```
Terminal
  3:08pm  up 62 days, 18 min,  4 users,  load average: 0.23, 0.10, 0.03
48 processes: 39 sleeping, 3 running, 2 zombie, 4 stopped
CPU states:  6.0% user,  1.9% system,  0.0% nice, 91.9% idle
Mem:   63168K av,  61572K used,   1596K free,  14376K shrd,  11504K buff
Swap:       0K av,      0K used,      0K free                 10288K cached

  PID USER     PRI  NI  SIZE  RSS SHARE STAT  LIB %CPU %MEM   TIME COMMAND
12239 root      11   0  5864 5864  1004 R       0  4.9  9.2   8:07 X
30813 root       5   0  1060 1060   852 R       0  1.9  1.6   0:33 top
29608 root       2   0  1992 1992   812 S       0  0.5  3.1   0:20 kwm
29662 root       1   0 14952  14M  2012 S       0  0.3 23.6   0:16 kpanel
30834 root       0   0  4076 4076  2768 S       0  0.1  6.4   0:00 ksnapshot
    1 root       0   0   112  112    48 S       0  0.0  0.1   0:05 init
    2 root       0   0     0    0     0 SW      0  0.0  0.0   0:39 kflushd
    3 root       0   0     0    0     0 SW      0  0.0  0.0   0:00 kpiod
    4 root       0   0     0    0     0 SW      0  0.0  0.0   0:15 kswapd
    5 root     -20 -20     0    0     0 SW<     0  0.0  0.0   0:00 mdrecoveryd
11635 root       0   0    80   80    24 S       0  0.0  0.1   0:11 update
12046 root       0   0   340  340   232 S       0  0.0  0.5   0:00 syslogd
12049 root       0   0   532  532   108 S       0  0.0  0.8   0:00 klogd
12061 root       0   0   100  100     0 S       0  0.0  0.1   0:00 inetd
12063 bin        0   0    76   76     0 S       0  0.0  0.1   0:00 rpc.portmap
12086 root       0   0   440  440   268 S       0  0.0  0.6   0:00 amd
12092 root       0   0     0    0     0 SW      0  0.0  0.0   0:00 rpciod
12093 root       0   0     0    0     0 SW      0  0.0  0.0   0:00 lockd
12103 root       0   0   176  176    68 S       0  0.0  0.2   0:00 cron
12109 daemon     0   0   164  164    68 S       0  0.0  0.2   0:00 atd
12115 root       0   0   500  500   216 S       0  0.0  0.7   0:00 sendmail
```

Figure 6.4 The **top** utility shows memory and usage statistics as well as processes, and it continually updates the display.

- s—Sets the delay between updates (the default is five seconds)
- *space*—Updates now rather than waits for renewal interval
- u—Displays a single user only

The columns show the standard **PID/CMD** information, as well as the amount of memory and CPU processes being utilized.

Ending a Process

Under normal circumstances, a child acts on behalf of, and reports to, a parent. When the child is no longer needed, it goes away on its own accord. Sometimes, however, processes become runaways; they are no longer needed, yet they continue to run and consume resources.

A parent process cannot (and should not) cease as long as child processes are associated with it. Given that, a child process that fails to cease can keep a number of unneeded processes on a system. To illustrate, assume that a user's shell calls another process (A), which cannot do everything needed, so it calls another (B), and it in turn starts another (C).

Under normal conditions, when Process C finishes, it reports back to Process B and goes away. Process B massages the data, reports back to Process A, and goes away. Process A does whatever it needs to do with the data, returns it to the user's shell, and goes away.

For a non-normal condition, assume that Process C has a glitch and does not end after reporting back to Process B. It continues to run. This prevents Process B from ending because it still has a child associated with it. We can assume that Process B returns its values to Process A, and Process A returns its values to the user's shell. Process A, like Process B, cannot end because it still has a child associated with it. Because there is a glitch in Process C, three processes that are no longer needed continue to run.

Yet another possibility for the glitch (and it depends on how applications are written) is that Process B could go ahead and end without Process C going away. Process A could do its task and go away as well. What happens in this instance is that only Process C remains a problem, but now it has nonexistent parents above it and has no idea who it reports to. It becomes a true runaway.

To solve problems with erratic processes, you use the **kill** command. This utility works with the syntax:

```
kill {option} PID
```

Thus, to get rid of the **cat** process, the sequence is:

```
$ ps -f
UID         PID  PPID  C STIME TTY       TIME CMD
root      19605 19603  0 Aug10 pts/0    00:00:34 bash
root      30089 19605  0 Aug20 pts/0    00:00:00 vi fileone
root      30425 19605  0 Aug20 pts/0    00:00:00_
   paste -d fileone filetwo?
root      32040 19605  0 Aug22 pts/0    00:00:00 cat
root       1183 19605  0 Aug23 pts/0    00:00:00 awk -F: questions
root      30900 19605  0 14:25 pts/0    00:00:00 ps -f
$
$ kill 32040
$
```

This "politely" asks the process to terminate. It is polite because, out of 32 different ways to kill a process (*signals* to send), this is the safest method of doing so. In a great many instances, the process simply ignores the request and continues on. When that happens, you can use one of the other 32 ways by specifying the number to use. Among the possibilities are:

- **-1**—On hangup/disconnect
- **-2**—Using an interrupt (Ctrl+C) sequence
- **-3**—Upon quit

- **-9**—Without regard—immediately
- **-15**—The default

To see a list of signals on your system, use the command **kill -l**.

Assuming the **cat** process does not go away politely, the sequence of operations then becomes:

```
$ ps -f
UID        PID  PPID  C STIME TTY      TIME CMD
root     19605 19603  0 Aug10 pts/0    00:00:34 bash
root     30089 19605  0 Aug20 pts/0    00:00:00 vi fileone
root     30425 19605  0 Aug20 pts/0    00:00:00_
   paste -d fileone filetwo?
root     32040 19605  0 Aug22 pts/0    00:00:00 cat
root      1183 19605  0 Aug23 pts/0    00:00:00 awk -F: questions
root     30996 19605  0 14:25 pts/0    00:00:00 ps -f
$
$ kill 32040
$ ps -f
UID        PID  PPID  C STIME TTY      TIME CMD
root     19605 19603  0 Aug10 pts/0    00:00:34 bash
root     30089 19605  0 Aug20 pts/0    00:00:00 vi fileone
root     30425 19605  0 Aug20 pts/0    00:00:00 paste_
   -d fileone filetwo?
root     32040 19605  0 Aug22 pts/0    00:00:00 cat
root      1183 19605  0 Aug23 pts/0    00:00:00 awk -F: questions
root     30998 19605  0 14:25 pts/0    00:00:00 ps -f
$
$ kill -9 32040
[3]- Killed
$ ps -f
UID        PID  PPID  C STIME TTY      TIME CMD
root     19605 19603  0 Aug10 pts/0    00:00:34 bash
root     30089 19605  0 Aug20 pts/0    00:00:00 vi fileone
root     30425 19605  0 Aug20 pts/0    00:00:00 paste_
   -d fileone filetwo?
root      1183 19605  0 Aug23 pts/0    00:00:00 awk -F: questions
root     31000 19605  0 14:25 pts/0    00:00:00 ps -f
$
```

I highly recommend that you always attempt signal **15** (terminate) before signal **9** (kill). I also highly recommend that you make certain a process has no child processes beneath it before you kill it. If child processes exist, you should remove them first, before proceeding further.

Just when you thought it couldn't get any more bloody, you can use another command—**killall**—to get rid of processes by name, versus PID. **killall** also has the ability (with the **-w** option) to wait for processes to die and to require confirmation (with the **-i** option) before killing.

Foreground and Background

When a process is started, the default behavior is for it to run in the foreground. In the foreground, it becomes the only job the user can work on, and interaction is based on completion of the job. For example, when a user runs **ls -l**, the display appears on her terminal, and she is unable to issue another command until **ls** has finished.

To run a process in the background, simply add an ampersand (&) to the end. This option allows you to run more than one command at the same time:

```
$ sleep 90 &
[5] 31168
$
```

The number that appears in the brackets is equal to the number of jobs you currently have running in the background. The number following it (31168, in this case) is the process ID number of this job.

Be sure to remember that the PID of the last job placed in the background can also be referenced as **$!**.

Placing the job in the background allows the user to continue working and starting other processes. If you must wait for a process to finish before starting another, the **wait** command, used with the PID of the process, can cease processing until the specified process finishes:

```
$ sleep 120 &
[5] 31175
$
$ wait 31175
```

The prompt does not return as long as 31175 remains a valid PID.

jobs

To see the jobs that you have running in the background, use the command **jobs**:

```
$ jobs
[1]   Stopped              vi fileone  (wd: ~)
[2]-  Stopped              paste -d' fileone filetwo ' (wd: ~)
[4]+  Stopped              awk -F: questions (wd: ~)
[5]   Done                 sleep 120
$
```

Jobs that were terminated [3] do not appear, and jobs that have finished [5] show up only one time. (The next time **jobs** is run, 5 does not appear.) A plus sign (+) follows the job number brackets for the most recent job that can run, or is running. The next most recent job is indicated by a minus sign (-). The **wd** information references the working directory.

The - option adds the PID numbers to the display, and you can use the **-p** option to show only the PID numbers of the processes. You can use the **-n** option to show only jobs that have been suspended.

fg

You can move a job running in the background to the foreground through the use of the **fg** command. The syntax for **fg** allows reference to a job using a percent sign (%) and the job number. For example, the following sequence starts a two-minute sleep sequence in the background and then moves it into the foreground:

```
$ sleep 120 &
[5] 31206
$
$ fg %5
sleep 120
```

Notice that the command being executed is echoed to the screen as it is brought to the foreground. Where **%5** was used, you can also reference the two most recent jobs with **%+** and **%-**, respectively. If you don't know the job number (and can't remember to use the **jobs** command), you can refer to a job by a portion of its name when using it after the percent sign and question mark (%?):

```
$ fg %?v
vi fileone
```

bg

The opposite of the foreground (**fg**) command is the background (**bg**) command, which allows you to move a job running in the foreground to the background. Before you can do so, however, you must suspend the job (to get the prompt back).

You suspend a job by pressing the keyboard sequence equal to the **susp** signal—Ctrl+Z, by default. When suspended, the job stops and does not start again until moved into the foreground or background:

```
$ sleep 180
{Ctrl+Z pressed}
[5]+   Stopped         sleep 180
$
```

Issuing the **bg** command now moves the job into the background and changes the status to running.

Changing Priorities

When a process starts, it does so at a default priority of zero. This puts it at an even keel with all other processes competing for attention from the CPU and other resources. You can change processes' priorities through the use of two utilities.

nice

You can start processes at different priorities using the **nice** utility. You can use **nice** with 40 different levels (half negative and half positive), including:

- **19** (lowest priority)
- **0** (default priority)
- **-20** (highest priority)

A normal user can use only the negative numbers, meaning he can only lower a process and not raise it. You can also specify an increment (the default is 10) with the **-n** option, and **nice** uses it to change the priority over time. The root user (superuser) has the ability to raise a priority (give a negative increment), but no other user can.

Keep in mind that only the superuser can give negative values.

If you give only the **nice** command, it shows the scheduling priority used by default.

renice

You can use the **nice** utility only when starting a process, not with a process already running. That is when the **renice** utility comes into play. The utility uses the same priorities available to **nice** and is followed by one of three options:

- -p—For PIDs
- -g—For a process group
- -u—For a group associated with a user

tee for Two

A miscellaneous utility that really stands alone, and does not fit well with any section, is **tee**. This utility, as the name implies, sends output in two directions. The default for most processes is to write their output to the screen. Using redirection (>), you can divert the output to a file, but what if you want to do both?

The **tee** utility lets you send output to the screen and to a file as well. The utility must always be followed by the name of the file that you want output to write to:

```
$ ps -f | tee example
UID         PID  PPID  C STIME TTY      TIME CMD
root      19605 19603  0 Aug10 pts/0    00:00:34 bash
root      30089 19605  0 Aug20 pts/0    00:00:00 vi fileone
root      30425 19605  0 Aug20 pts/0    00:00:00 paste_
   -d fileone filetwo?
root      32040 19605  0 Aug22 pts/0    00:00:00 cat
root       1183 19605  0 Aug23 pts/0    00:00:00 awk -F: questions
root      30778 19605  0 14:25 pts/0    00:00:00 ps -f
$
$ cat example
UID         PID  PPID  C STIME TTY      TIME CMD
root      19605 19603  0 Aug10 pts/0    00:00:34 bash
root      30089 19605  0 Aug20 pts/0    00:00:00 vi fileone
root      30425 19605  0 Aug20 pts/0    00:00:00 paste_
   -d fileone filetwo?
root      32040 19605  0 Aug22 pts/0    00:00:00 cat
root       1183 19605  0 Aug23 pts/0    00:00:00 awk -F: questions
root      30778 19605  0 14:25 pts/0    00:00:00 ps -f
$
```

As illustrated, the output appears on the screen and gets written to the file as well. This can be an extremely useful utility any time you need a file and you also want to view the output.

Utility Summation

This chapter discussed several utilities. Table 6.1 lists them and their purposes.

Associated Utilities

Several utilities not covered on the exam work in conjunction with those listed in this chapter. Table 6.2 lists those for purposes of real-world knowledge only.

Table 6.1 Utilities discussed in this chapter.

Utility	Purpose
ps	Shows the running processes.
pstree	Graphically depicts the relationship between processes.
top	Shows and monitors system information and processes.
kill	Ends a process.
killall	Ends several processes.
&	Starts a process in the background.
wait	Suspends further processing until another process completes.
jobs	Displays a list of running jobs.
fg	Moves a job to the foreground.
bg	Moves a job to the background.
nice	Starts a process at a priority other than the default.
renice	Changes the priority of a running process.
tee	Sends output to default (the screen) and to a file.

Table 6.2 Related utilities.

Utility	Purpose
free	Shows memory usage information similar to that shown in the heading of the **top** utility.
uptime	Displays statistics on how long the system has been up, similar to that shown in the heading of the **top** utility.
w	Shows information combining **uptime** and **who** information.

Practice Questions

Question 1

What will be the output of the command **ps -ae**?

❍ a. Only processes for the current user will be shown, minus the session leader.

❍ b. Only processes for the current user will be shown, with the session leader.

❍ c. All processes will be shown for all users.

❍ d. All processes will be shown for all users, minus any session leaders.

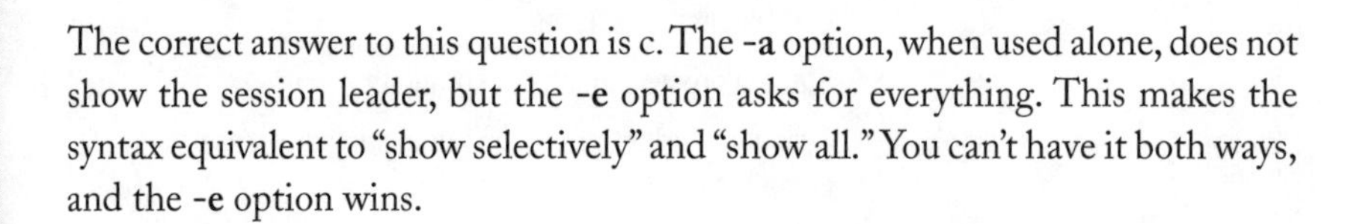

The correct answer to this question is c. The **-a** option, when used alone, does not show the session leader, but the **-e** option asks for everything. This makes the syntax equivalent to "show selectively" and "show all." You can't have it both ways, and the **-e** option wins.

Question 2

Which of the following will produce the same display as **ps -e**?

❍ a. **ps -f**

❍ b. **ps -A**

❍ c. **ps -l**

❍ d. **ps -u**

The correct answer to this question is b. The **-e** option asks for everything, and the **-A** option asks for all. The **-f** option (answer a) will give a full listing, but only for the current user. The **-l** option (answer c) will give a long listing; again, it will be only for the current user in this case. The **-u** option (answer d) will add user-related information.

Question 3

You suspect a runaway process is consuming resources on your machine. After investigating further, you find the process ID of the runaway process to be 79865. What is the command to end this process with a termination signal? [Fill in the blank]

____

The correct answer to this question is:

```
kill 79865
```

The default mode for the **kill** utility is the termination signal.

Question 4

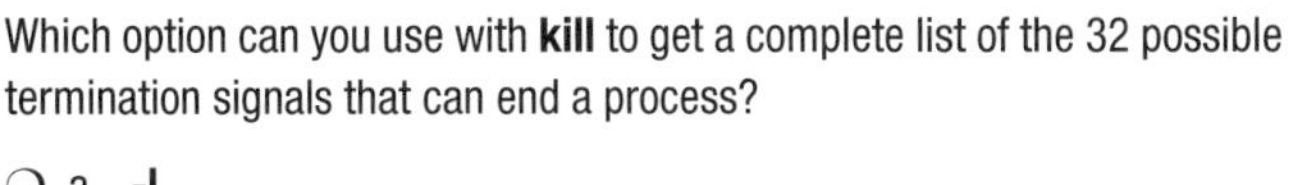

Which option can you use with **kill** to get a complete list of the 32 possible termination signals that can end a process?

- ❍ a. **-l**
- ❍ b. **-a**
- ❍ c. **-e**
- ❍ d. **-v**

The correct answer to this question is a: The **-l** option will list the signal possibilities that can be used with **kill**. The **-a** option (choice b) can be used to specify the signal to send, while the other two options are nonexistent.

Question 5

Which of the following represents the most powerful **kill** signal that you can use on a process or set of processes?

- ❍ a. **-1**
- ❍ b. **-9**
- ❍ c. **-15**
- ❍ d. **-31**

The correct answer to this question is b. **-9** is the most powerful **kill** signal you can use. The default signal is **-15** (answer c), the **-1** signal (choice a) will kill the process upon hangup, and **-31** (answer d) is available for a user/programmer to define (by default, it is undefined).

Question 6

Which of the following will start a job in the background?

- ❍ a. **-**
- ❍ b. **+**
- ❍ c. **%**
- ❍ d. **&**

The correct answer to this question is choice d. The ampersand (&) will start a job in the background. All other options will be ignored if used as trailing characters on the command line.

Question 7

You are getting ready to leave the office for the day. About a minute ago, you started a job in the background to compile a report that might run for hours. When the compilation ends, you need another process to run to print the results. Which of the following commands will accomplish this?

❍ a. **bg {process}**

❍ b. **fg {process}**

❍ c. **wait $! ; {process}**

❍ d. **sleep ; {process]**

The correct answer to this question is c. The dollar and bang signs ($!) represent the last process started in the background. When you use them with **wait**, the background process must end before the next process begins. All other choices are invalid for specifying a process to wait for another to complete.

Question 8

Which of the following will represent the most recent job started in the background, as displayed by the **jobs** command?

❍ a. **[1] Running {process}**

❍ b. **[1]- Running {process}**

❍ c. **[1]% Running {process}**

❍ d. **[1]+ Running {process}**

The correct answer to this question is d. The plus sign (+) to the right of the job number will indicate the most recent job placed in the background. The other choices are invalid as they have nothing to do with the most recent job placed in the background.

Question 9

You have accidentally started a job that consumes a great deal of resources. You feel that it has the possibility of negatively affecting how other jobs run on the system. Which command can you use to alter the priority level of this job?

❍ a. **nice**

❍ b. **start**

❍ c. **renice**

❍ d. **ps**

The correct answer to this question is c. Answer a will let you start a job at a priority other than the default but cannot be used once the job is running. Answer b is not a valid Linux utility. Answer d will show the processes that are running but will not allow you to make any changes.

Question 10

You want to view a full list of all the processes currently running and save a copy of it in the file named "archive." Which command, or set of commands, are best for this?

❍ a. **ps -f ; ps -f > archive**

❍ b. **ps -ef >> archive**

❍ c. **ps -ef I tee archive**

❍ d. **ps -ef ; tee archive**

The correct answer to this question is c. The **tee** command will take the input it receives and send it to standard output, as well as to the file named after it. Answer a will not show all processes and requires two processes, versus one. Answer b will append the output to a file but not display to standard output. Answer d uses the wrong syntax.

Need to Know More?

Hare, Chris, and Emmett Dulaney, et al. *Inside Unix*. Indianapolis, IN: New Riders Publishing, 1994. ISBN: 1-56205-401-5. Chapter 19 covers the basics of job control.

Siever, Ellen, and Stephen Spainhour, et al. *Linux in a Nutshell, 3rd Edition*. Sebastopol, CA: O'Reilly & Associates, 2000. ISBN: 0-59600-025-1. Chapter 3 contains an alphabetical list of Linux utilities.

Welsh, Matt, and Matthias Kalle Dalheimer, et al. *Running Linux, 3rd Edition*. Sebastopol, CA: O'Reilly & Associates, 1999. ISBN: 1-56592-469-X. Chapter 4 covers basic commands and concepts.

The Linux Filesystem

Terms you'll need to understand:

- ✓ **mknod**
- ✓ **fdisk**
- ✓ **mkfs**
- ✓ **df**
- ✓ **du**
- ✓ **fsck**
- ✓ Inode
- ✓ **ln**
- ✓ **mount**
- ✓ **umount**
- ✓ **quotaon**
- ✓ **quotaoff**
- ✓ **edquota**
- ✓ **repquota**
- ✓ Quota
- ✓ **quotacheck**
- ✓ **quotastats**
- ✓ **locate**
- ✓ **updatedb**
- ✓ **which**
- ✓ **find**
- ✓ **xargs**

Techniques you'll need to master:

- ✓ Understanding how the standard Linux directories are arranged and the purpose for each
- ✓ Recognizing the core utilities used for interaction with the disk

In this chapter, you'll learn about the standard disk layout and the utilities used to manage and alter disks. Directories, subdirectories, and files have been major topics throughout this book, and now it is time to elaborate on them by discussing the purpose and default content of each.

The Standard Disk Layout

The Linux installation created a number of directories to hold system files. Any normal installation, regardless of the vendor, creates the file structure depicted in Figure 7.1.

The following sections discuss each of the directories.

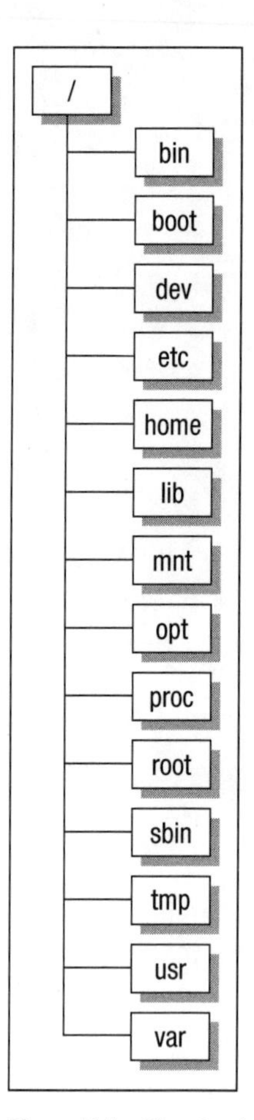

Figure 7.1 The standard directory layout in Linux.

The / Directory

Everything begins at the root directory (/). The root is the directory from which everything else becomes a subdirectory or subcomponent. When specifying locations using absolute addressing, you always begin with this directory because it is the ultimate origin, and it is impossible to move any further back since there is no directory above it.

The bin Directory

The bin directory holds the binaries (executables) that are essential to using the Linux operating system. Many of the utilities discussed so far are located in the bin directory, including:

- cat
- cp
- date
- ls
- mkdir
- mv
- ps
- sed

As a rule of thumb, the executable or binary files located within this directory are available to all users. Binary files that are not critical to the operation of the system, or that are needed by all users, commonly appear in /usr/bin instead of here.

The boot Directory

This directory houses the files needed to boot the system, minus configuration files, as well as the kernel. In some implementations, the kernel is stored in the / directory (a holdover from the days of Unix), but most newer versions of Linux use /boot.

The dev Directory

The dev directory holds the device definitions. Copying a file to a graphical icon of the floppy drive on the desktop is possible because a definition for the floppy appears within the /dev directory. A file is associated with every device, whether it is a terminal, drive, driver, and so on. The following listing shows a few of the files beneath the directory; I changed some of the names to make the entries more decipherable:

```
brw-rw-rw-   1 root   root       2,   4 Aug 10  1999 floppy
brw-r--      1 root   operator   3,   1 Aug 10  1999 hard drivel
crw-rw--     1 root   lp         6,   0 Aug 10  1999 lp0
crw-rw--     1 root   lp         6,   1 Aug 10  1999 lp1
crw-rw--     1 root   lp         6,   2 Aug 10  1999 lp2
brw-rw-r--   1 root   disk      23,   0 Aug 10  1999 cd
crw-r--      1 root   kmem       1,   1 Aug 10  1999 mem
crw-rw-rw-   1 root   root       1,   3 Aug 10  1999 null
crw-rw-rw-   1 root   root      10,   1 Sep 13 10:29 mouse
brw-------   1 root   root       1,   0 Aug 10  1999 ram0
brw-------   1 root   root       1,   1 Aug 10  1999 ram1
brw-------   1 root   root       1,   2 Aug 10  1999 ram2
brw-------   1 root   root       1,   3 Aug 10  1999 ram3
brw-------   1 root   root      31,   0 Aug 10  1999 rom0
brw-------   1 root   root      31,   1 Aug 10  1999 rom1
br--------   1 root   root      31,   8 Aug 10  1999 rrom0
br--------   1 root   root      31,   9 Aug 10  1999 rrom1
brw-rw-r--   1 root   disk      15,   0 Aug 10  1999 sonycd
crw-w-w-     1 root   root       4,   0 Aug 10  1999 tty0
crw-rw--     1 root   tty        4,   1 Jul  6 15:27 tty1
crw-rw--     1 root   tty        4,  10 Aug 10  1999 tty10
crw-rw--     1 root   tty        4,  11 Aug 10  1999 tty11
crw-rw--     1 root   tty        4,  12 Jul  6 15:27 tty12
crw-rw--     1 root   tty        4,  13 Aug 10  1999 tty13
crw-rw--     1 root   tty        4,  14 Aug 10  1999 tty14
crw-rw--     1 root   tty        4,  15 Aug 10  1999 tty15
```

The first thing to note is that the files do not resemble listings you have examined in previous chapters. The first character of the permissions is either **b** or **c** to indicate how data is read—by block or by character. Typically, devices that require constant interaction, such as a mouse or terminal (tty), are character based. Devices that do not require interaction once a process is started, such as floppy drives, memory (RAM and ROM), and CD drives, are block based.

The second item of note is that the sizes of the files are expressed not in bytes but in pairs of numbers separated by commas. Covering the creation of such special files is beyond the scope of either of the current LPI exams, but you should know that you must use the **mknod** utility to create device files.

The etc Directory

In everyday language, *etc.* means "and so on." In the Linux world, however, the etc directory holds files that are specific to the machine. For example, ABC Corporation and DEF Corporation can both install Caldera OpenLinux on Intel-based machines at their sites. When they do, both have root directories, both have /bin directories with matching sets of utilities in them, and so on.

One major difference between the two machines is the values in the /etc directory. The users who can log on at ABC are not the same as those who can log on at DEF; the user accounts are stored in /etc. The groups are not the same at the two organizations; those related files are stored in /etc. Other files include:

- *motd*—The Message of the Day file for displaying text when logging on
- *X11*—A folder holding X Window values
- *HOSTNAME*—The name of the machine
- *hosts*—A file mapping hostnames to IP addresses for other machines available through a network

In a nutshell, the /etc directory holds system configuration files specific to a machine.

The home Directory

As the name implies, the home directory holds subdirectories that are the home directories of users. For example, user edulaney, when entering the command cd, is placed in /home/edulaney, providing that that value (the default) is used when setting up the account.

Each user's home directory provides a location to store files, as well as a place to locate and access individual configuration files. Some services, such as FTP and HTTP, also create directories beneath home.

Keep in mind the fact that, for security reasons, there is no /home/root directory. The home directory for the root user is /root.

The lib Directory

Shared library files needed by binaries (such as those in the /bin directory) are located in the /lib directory and subdirectories beneath it. Generally, the libraries consist of executables written in the C language.

The mnt Directory

The mnt directory holds external filesystems that are mounted (discussed later in this chapter). The entities that appear within this directory are never on this filesystem, but rather they represent external resources that can be linked to and accessed from /mnt. The external resources can be other filesystems or devices.

The devices appear as directories with common names (cdrom, floppy, and so on). The tmp subdirectory within /mnt is intended to hold temporary files, but the use of /tmp is preferred.

The opt Directory

The opt directory holds optional (add-in) application software. Not all applications install themselves here; when they do, however, they each create a subdirectory for their variables using the application name. For example, an application named DEF creates the directory /opt/DEF.

No requirement dictates that third-party applications must write their values in /opt, but such behavior is traditional from the days of Unix. Some common subdirectories here include:

- *kde*—For the K Desktop Environment variables
- *netscape*—For the browser

The proc Directory

The proc directory is the virtual filesystem. It is dynamically generated and updated, and it holds information about processes, the kernel, and related system information.

Processes are depicted as folders, each having permissions and variables associated with them. Other system information is most commonly depicted as files, as shown here:

```
$ ps
  PID TTY        TIME CMD
15193 pts/0    00:00:00 bash
15220 pts/0    00:00:00 sleep
15222 pts/0    00:00:00 sleep
15236 pts/0    00:00:00 ps
$ ls -l
dr-xr-xr-x   3 root     root          0 Sep 20 08:34 15193
dr-xr-xr-x   3 root     root          0 Sep 20 08:34 15220
dr-xr-xr-x   3 root     root          0 Sep 20 08:34 15222
dr-xr-xr-x   4 root     root          0 Sep 20 08:34 bus
-r--r--r--   1 root     root          0 Sep 20 08:34 cmdline
-r--r--r--   1 root     root          0 Sep 20 08:34 cpuinfo
-r--r--r--   1 root     root          0 Sep 20 08:34 devices
-r--r--r--   1 root     root          0 Sep 20 08:34 dma
-r--r--r--   1 root     root          0 Sep 20 08:34 fb
-r--r--r--   1 root     root          0 Sep 20 08:34 filesystems
dr-xr-xr-x   2 root     root          0 Sep 20 08:34 fs
dr-xr-xr-x   4 root     root          0 Sep 20 08:34 ide
-r--r--r--   1 root     root          0 Sep 20 08:34 interrupts
-r--r--r--   1 root     root          0 Sep 20 08:34 ioports
-r--------  `1 root     root   67112960 Sep 20 08:34 kcore
```

```
-r--------   1 root     root            0 Sep 20 08:16 kmsg
-r--r--r--   1 root     root            0 Sep 20 08:34 ksyms
-r--r--r--   1 root     root            0 Sep 20 08:34 loadavg
-r--r--r--   1 root     root            0 Sep 20 08:34 locks
-r--r--r--   1 root     root            0 Sep 20 08:34 mdstat
-r--r--r--   1 root     root            0 Sep 20 08:34 meminfo
-r--r--r--   1 root     root            0 Sep 20 08:34 misc
-r--r--r--   1 root     root            0 Sep 20 08:34 modules
-r--r--r--   1 root     root            0 Sep 20 08:34 mounts
dr-xr-xr-x   4 root     root            0 Sep 20 08:34 net
dr-xr-xr-x   3 root     root            0 Sep 20 08:34 parport
-r--r--r--   1 root     root            0 Sep 20 08:34 partitions
-r--r--r--   1 root     root            0 Sep 20 08:34 pci
-r--r--r--   1 root     root            0 Sep 20 08:34 rtc
dr-xr-xr-x   2 root     root            0 Sep 20 08:34 scsi
lrwxrwxrwx   1 root     root           64 Sep 20 08:34 self -> 15252
-r--r--r--   1 root     root            0 Sep 20 08:34 slabinfo
-r--r--r--   1 root     root            0 Sep 20 08:34 sound
-r--r--r--   1 root     root            0 Sep 20 08:34 stat
-r--r--r--   1 root     root            0 Sep 20 08:34 swaps
dr-xr-xr-x  10 root     root            0 Sep 20 08:34 sys
dr-xr-xr-x   4 root     root            0 Sep 20 08:34 tty
-r--r--r--   1 root     root            0 Sep 20 08:34 uptime
-r--r--r--   1 root     root            0 Sep 20 08:34 version
$
```

The root Directory

The root directory is the home directory for the root user. For security purposes, it is beneath the / directory rather than being a subdirectory of /home. For true security, it is further recommended that you move this directory to another location and rename it to a less obvious (and inviting) name.

One point of continuing confusion is the fact that both /root and / can be referred to as the "root" directory. Keep in mind that "/" is the root directory of the system, and /root is a subdirectory of / used as the home directory of the root user.

The sbin Directory

The /bin directory holds standard executables that most users utilize; the /sbin directory holds binary executables for system administration. Many of these utilities are used for booting the system and once resided in the /etc directory. The following list shows some of the files located in this directory:

- **dump**
- **fdisk**

- fsck
- halt
- ifconfig
- mkfs
- poweroff
- reboot
- shutdown

The tmp Directory

As the name implies, the tmp directory holds temporary files. Do not put in /tmp any file that you want to keep longer than the length of your current session because many systems clean (delete) all entries within this directory on either shutdown or startup.

Examples of files in /tmp are shadow copies of files opened for editing and any application's temporary files (stored between operations).

The usr Directory

Originally an acronym for *user-specific resources,* /usr is now an enormous directory with a large number of subdirectories. Figure 7.2 shows some of the common subdirectories in this structure.

Subdirectories beginning with X define the X Window environment. The bin subdirectory contains user binary (executable) files. The files placed here include:

- cut
- diff
- file
- grep
- killall
- nl
- passwd
- wc

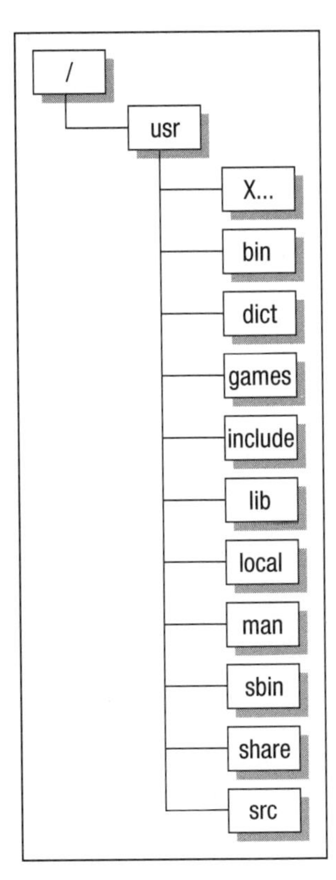

Figure 7.2 The standard subdirectory layout for usr.

As a general rule, necessary utilities for all users are stored in /bin, and utilities that are helpful to have (but not critical) are stored in /usr/bin. Utilities for the system administrative tasks are stored in /sbin. This is something to keep in mind for the exam.

The dict directory holds the word list used by the **spell** utility to check spelling in text files. The game directory does not hold third-party games and is usually empty except for **banner** or similar trivial utilities.

Not all the subdirectories beneath /usr are necessary, and they differ slightly based upon vendor and type of installation.

The include directory holds C program header files, and lib offers more libraries for C-based programs. The local directory is a temporary holding facility used during installation, and the subdirectories beneath it should be empty. The man directory holds the manual pages used for help and documentation purposes, if they are installed.

The sbin directory holds system-specific binaries. Most of the utilities in this subdirectory are related to managing the system—adding users and groups and working with networking. These are noncritical utilities because the system could function without them, and an administrator could manage without them as well: It is difficult, but certainly possible.

The share directory holds information specific to the machine for certain utilities. The src directory contains the operating-system source code.

The var directory

The name of the var directory derives from the word *variable*, and the data contained in this directory fluctuates in nature. Typically, a number of directories here hold dynamic files, such as spools, logs, and so on. Figure 7.3 shows a common set of subdirectories for the var directory.

The main directories to know among these variables are:

- *lock*—Locked files
- *log*—Log files, such as files created by login and logout (wtmp), files that record who is currently using the system (utmp), and files for the mail, spooler, and so on

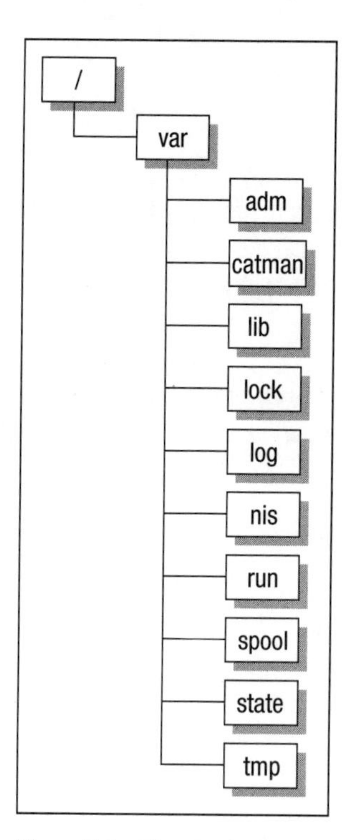

Figure 7.3 The standard subdirectory layout for var.

- *run*—Files needed for the run level
- *spool*—Spooled data waiting for processing (such as printing)
- *state*—System state variables

Other Directories

Other directories can exist beneath the / directory. The directories described so far are always present, but the following two directories can also be present:

- *install*—Holds information about the installation, such as scripts, errors, and so on.
- *lost+found*—Should be empty on a perfect system. When corruption occurs, however, the results appear in this directory.

Working with Hard Disks

To use a hard disk with Linux (and every operating system), the disk must have at least one partition. A partition is a portion of the disk (some or all) that has been properly formatted for storing data. Although the hard drive must have a minimum of one primary partition, it can have up to a total of four partitions with a DOS-style partition table (the default). Each partition must be formatted before use. A partition must be a primary partition for the operating system to be able to boot from it.

A primary partition (only one) can be further subdivided into extended partitions, known as *logical drives*. Using DOS-style partitions, you can create up to four logical drives from a primary partition, but none of them are bootable by the operating system.

You should remember that the maximum number of primary partitions you can have is four. The maximum number of partitions you can have when mixing and matching primary and extended is three primary partitions and four logical drives (for a grand total of seven).

The theoretical limit is 15 partitions on SCSI (Small Computer System Interface) disks and 63 partitions on IDE (Integrated Drive Electronics). The limitations mentioned previously are enforced with a DOS-style partition table.

All partitions must be referenced in the /dev directory, and the first partition on the first disk is either of the following:

- *hda1*—for IDE
- *sda1*—for SCSI

The name of the device has four fields:

- *The type of drive*—h for IDE or s for SCSI
- *The type of device*—d for disk
- *The number of the disk expressed in alphabetical format*—a for the first, b for the second, and so on
- *The number of the partition*—The numbers 1 through 4 are set aside for use on primary partitions, whether or not you have that many, and the logical drives start numbering with 5.

The disk should always have a minimum of two partitions: the filesystem itself (often referred to as *root*) and a swap partition. The swap partition contains the memory and some hard drive space. The swap partition size is always a minimum of the amount of RAM installed on the machine but can be larger (16MB is the minimum recommendation for hard drive space). For example, if you have 64MB installed on a machine and the swap partition needs 128MB, it can use a 64MB swap partition to read and write from as processing occurs. Using a swap partition larger than the amount of installed RAM is known as using virtual memory.

The maximum allowable size for a swap partition under current versions of Linux is 128MB, and you can tweak the size of the partition. If you run out of room within the partition (or you have not configured a swap partition), Linux automatically creates a swap file, but using a partition is preferred.

Linux can work with either swap files or swap partitions, but partitions provide more system efficiency.

One other note about hard drives: Linux prefers the number of cylinders on a drive to be 1,024 or less. With a larger number, you can encounter complications with software that runs at boot time (which is covered in Chapter 9) or booting and partitioning with other operating systems.

Creating Partitions and Filesystems

The primary tool to use in creating disk partitions is **fdisk**. The **fdisk** utility divides the disk into partitions and writes the partition table in sector 0 (known as the *superblock*). When run without parameters, **fdisk** displays a menu of choices with which you can interact. You can avoid the menu, however, and run **fdisk** with the following options:

- -l—Lists the partition tables.
- -v—Prints the version of **fdisk** only.

If you use neither of these options, **fdisk** first checks whether the number of cylinders on the default device (hda1) is greater than 1,024 and warns you if so. It then prompts for a command. You can start **fdisk** with a device other than the default by specifying it on the command line. For example, to start it with the third IDE drive, enter:

```
$ fdisk /dev/hdc
```

After the utility has started, entering **m** provides help in the form of a menu:

```
a    toggle a bootable flag
b    edit bsd disklabel
c    toggle the dos compatibility flag
d    delete a partition
l    list known partition types
m    print this menu
n    add a new partition
o    create a new empty DOS partition table
p    print the partition table
q    quit without saving changes
s    create a new empty Sun disklabel
t    change a partition's system id
u    change display/entry units
v    verify the partition table
w    write table to disk and exit
x    extra functionality (experts only)
```

The following examples illustrate what you can do with this utility, moving from simple actions to more complex ones. First, to see the partition table, you give the **p** command. The result resembles:

```
Disk /dev/had:  16 head, 63 sectors,  16383 cylinders
Units = cylinders of 1008 + 512 bytes

Device      Boot   Start   End     Blocks    Id   System
/dev/hda1   +      1       4063    2047720+  83   Linux
/dev/hda2          4064    4316    127512    82   Linux swap
/dev/hda3          4317    16383   6081768   83   Linux
```

The information here shows three partitions (1 through 3) on a single IDE disk (hda). The first partition is bootable, the second partition is the swap partition, and the third is the remainder of the drive.

To modify the system, assume the third partition is to be changed into two smaller partitions. First, enter the **d** command to delete the partition. A prompt asks which partition number (1 through 4). Enter 3, and it is gone.

To create a new partition, enter the **n** command. The prompt changes to:

```
e    extended
p    primary partition (1-4)
```

If you have already created other partitions, the prompts might not appear. For example, if you already have an extended partition, you cannot create another because it already exists. If you enter **p** for primary, you are next prompted for the number (1–4) to create; if you give a number already used, the command fails because you must first delete the partition before adding it again.

In this case, suppose you want to make two equally sized partitions from the space that was once the third partition; therefore, after entering **p** to the prompt earlier, the sequence becomes the following, with values you enter in italics:

```
Partition number (1-4): 3
First cylinder (4317-16383, default 4317): {Press Enter)
Using default value 4317
Last cylinder or +size or +sizeM or +sizeK _
(4317-16383, default 16383): 10350

Command (m for help): p

Disk /dev/had:  16 head, 63 sectors,  16383 cylinders
Units = cylinders of 1008 + 512 bytes

Device      Boot   Start   End    Blocks    Id   System
/dev/hda1   +      1       4063   2047720+  83   Linux
/dev/hda2          4064    4316   127512    82   Linux swap
/dev/hda3          4317    10350  3041136   83   Linux

Command (m for help): n
Command  action
   e     extended
   p     primary partition (1-4)
p
Partition number (1-4): 4
First cylinder (10531-16383, default 10351): {Press Enter)
Using default value 10351
Last cylinder or +size or +sizeM or +sizeK _
(10351-16383, default 16383): {Press Enter)
Using default value 16383
```

```
Command (m for help): p

Disk /dev/had:  16 head, 63 sectors,  16383 cylinders
Units = cylinders of 1008 + 512 bytes

Device       Boot   Start   End     Blocks     Id   System
/dev/hdal    +      1       4063    2047720+   83   Linux
/dev/hda2           4064    4316    127512     82   Linux swap
/dev/hda3           4317    10350   3041136    83   Linux
/dev/hda4           10351   16383   3040632    83   Linux
```

To change the third partition to a swap file, the sequence is:

```
Command (m for help): t
Partition number (1-4): 3
Hex code (type L to list codes): 82
Changed system type of partition 3 to 82 (Linux swap)
```

To then change the existing swap file (partition 2) to a Linux partition, run the preceding procedure, and type the hex code 83. Typing **L** at the hex code prompt shows all the possible filesystem types (as does pressing **l** at the main **fdisk** menu). Table 7.1 outlines a few of the types.

After making all the changes, you can quit **fdisk** and then format any partitions that need it. If you write the changes, an alert appears indicating that the partition table has been altered and the disks will be synchronized. You should reboot your system to ensure the table is properly updated.

You can make dozens of changes with **fdisk** and lose them all if you type **q** to quit the tool. If you want to save the changes you've made, you must write them with **w**.

You format the partitions with the **mkfs** (as in "make filesystem") utility. You must use options with this utility to indicate the type of filesystem to make (**-t**),

Table 7.1 Sample filesystem types.

Code	Filesystem Type
5	Extended
6	FAT16
7	HPFS
8	AIX
85	Linux Extended
86	NTFS
b	Windows 95 FAT32

the device, the size, and any other options. For example, to format the newly created fourth partition for DOS, the command is:

```
$ mkfs -t msdos /dev/hda4 3040632
```

Be extremely careful when using **fdisk** and **mkfs** because both have the ability to render a system inoperable if you use the incorrect parameters.

You can use the **mkfs** utility to format floppy disks as well as hard drives, but the utility **fdformat** is much simpler to use for floppy disks.

Maintaining Filesystem Integrity

Once the filesystem is created, you can gather information about it and perform troubleshooting using three tools: **df**, **du**, and **fsck**. The first two display information only and do not allow you to make any changes, but the latter can be a lifesaver in bringing a down system back up and operational once more.

The **df** utility shows the amount of disk free across filesystems. Table 7.2 (shown on page 152) describes a number of options or parameters you can use with the utility.

For example, the default output, and results with specified options, resemble:

```
$ df
Filesystem           1k-blocks      Used Available Use% Mounted on
/dev/hda1              1980969    573405   1305178  31% /
/dev/hda3              5871498      5212   5562198   0% /home
$
$ df -T
Filesystem     Type  1k-blocks      Used Available Use% Mounted on
/dev/hda1      ext2    1980969    573408   1305175  31% /
/dev/hda3      ext2    5871498      5212   5562198   0% /home
$
$ df -h
Filesystem             Size  Used Avail Use% Mounted on
/dev/hda1              1.9G  560M  1.2G  31% /
/dev/hda3              5.6G  5.1M  5.3G   0% /home
$
$ df -a
Filesystem           1k-blocks      Used Available Use% Mounted on
/dev/hda1              1980969    573406   1305177  31% /
/dev/hda3              5871498      5212   5562198   0% /home
devpts                       0         0         0   -  /dev/pts
/proc                        0         0         0   -  /proc
noname:(pid12019)            0         0         0   -  /auto
$
$ df -am
```

```
Filesystem          1M-blocks    Used Available Use% Mounted on
/dev/hda1                1934     560      1275  31% /
/dev/hda3                5734       5      5432   0% /home
devpts                      0       0         0   -  /dev/pts
/proc                       0       0         0   -  /proc
noname:(pid12019)           0       0         0   -  /auto
$
```

The "ext2" listed for filesystem type stands for second extended filesystem and is the default used by Linux. When thinking of Linux partitions and the abilities thereof (file names, links, etc.), it is always ext2 that is synonymous with that.

Whereas the **df** utility deals with partitions, the **du** utility shows disk usage by files and directories. From **df**, you can see that 560MB of hda1 is used, but you have no way of knowing what is using it. Using the **du** utility is the next step, showing how much space each item is using, beginning at whatever starting location you specify. For example, starting in the /root directory (the home directory of the root user), the utility shows the amount of space used by the subdirectories:

```
14      ./.seyon
2       ./Desktop/Autostart
2       ./Desktop/Trash
8       ./Desktop/Templates
20      ./Desktop
22      ./.kde/share/config
1       ./.kde/share/apps/kfm/tmp
1       ./.kde/share/apps/kfm/bookmarks
8       ./.kde/share/apps/kfm
6       ./.kde/share/apps/kdewizard/Work/Windows
7       ./.kde/share/apps/kdewizard/Work
1       ./.kde/share/apps/kdewizard/Themes
9       ./.kde/share/apps/kdewizard
1       ./.kde/share/apps/kpanel/applnk
1       ./.kde/share/apps/kpanel/pics
3       ./.kde/share/apps/kpanel
3       ./.kde/share/apps/kdisknav
5       ./.kde/share/apps/kwm/pics
6       ./.kde/share/apps/kwm
1       ./.kde/share/apps/kdisplay/pics
2       ./.kde/share/apps/kdisplay
2       ./.kde/share/apps/kdehelp
34      ./.kde/share/apps
1       ./.kde/share/icons/mini
2       ./.kde/share/icons
2       ./.kde/share/applnk
1       ./.kde/share/mimelnk
```

```
1       ./.kde/share/sounds
63      ./.kde/share
64      ./.kde
119     .
```

If you use the **-a** option, **du** lists files and not just directories. Table 7.3 lists other options that work with the **du** utility.

The grand utility in this section is **fsck**: the filesystem check utility. Not only does it check the filesystem, but if errors are encountered, it can correct them. The utility utilizes entries in the /etc/fstab file to tell which filesystems to check during startup if it is configured to run automatically. The **-A** option also tells the utility to use this file.

*Note: The /etc/fstab file is read by **fsck** and related utilities but never written to. As an administrator, you need to update the file—placing each filesystem on its own line—when you want to make modifications to the operation of system utilities.*

When you run **fsck**, it shells out to the appropriate interface based upon the filesystem in use. For example, with a Linux filesystem (ext2), a common series of events is:

Table 7.2 Options for the df utility.

Option	Description
-a	All (include those that have no blocks).
-h	Displays in "human readable" form.
-l	Local filesystems only.
-m	Displays the list in MB.
-t	Shows only those filesystems of a particular type.
-T	Shows the filesystem types.

Table 7.3 Options for the du utility

Option	Description
-b	Displays the list in bytes.
-c	Shows a grand total.
-h	Provides "human readable" output.
-k	Displays the list in KB.
-l	Shows the number of links.
-m	Displays the list in MB.
-s	Shows only totals.
-x	Shows only directories on this (not different) filesystems.

```
$ fsck -A
Parallelizing fsck version 1.14 (9-Jan-1999)
E2fsck 1.14, 9-Jan-1999 for EXT2 FS 0.5b, 95/08/09
/dev/hda1 is mounted.

WARNING!!! Running e2fsck on a mounted filesystem may cause
SEVERE filesystem damage.

Do you really want to continue (y/n)? y
Pass 1: Checking inodes, blocks, and sizes
Pass 2: Checking directory structure
Pass 3: Checking directory connectivity
Pass 4: Checking reference counts
Pass 5: Checking group summary information
/dev/hda3: 927/1521664 files (0.3% non-contiguous), 215482/6081768
blocks
$
```

Most of the other passes are self-explanatory, but the first requires further detail. An inode is a table entry that stores information about every file on the system. It is within the inode that information about the file is stored—in much the same way that a phone book holds information about people within a city.

Every item that appears in a directory listing has an inode associated with it. The inode holds the following types of information:

- A unique inode number
- The type of entry it is (file, directory, pipe, and so on)
- Permissions on the file in numerical format
- The physical size of the file
- The number of links to the entry (discussed later in this chapter)
- The owner of the file
- The group owning the file
- Times of creation, modification, and access
- A pointer to the actual location of the data on the disk

The inode numbers begin with 1 and increment from there: Files copied during installation have small numbers and recently created files have much larger numbers. When files and directories are deleted, their associated inode number is marked as usable once more.

When corruption occurs, files are dumped to the /lost+found directory, using their inode numbers as names. To see the inode numbers associated with files, you can use the **-i** option with **ls**:

```
$ ls -l
drwx------ 5     root root             1024 Sep 22 23:57 Desktop
-rw-r--r-- 1     root root               81 Sep 23 00:25 monday
-rw-r--r-- 1     root root              152 Sep 23 00:26 tuesday
-rw-r--r-- 1     root root               38 Sep 23 00:26 wednesday
$
$ ls -li
18471 drwx------ 5     root root             1024 Sep 22 23:57 Desktop
18535 -rw-r--r-- 1     root root               81 Sep 23 00:25 monday
18536 -rw-r--r-- 1     root root              152 Sep 23 00:26 tuesday
18537 -rw-r--r-- 1     root root               38 Sep 23 00:26 wednesday
$
```

When a file is moved, it maintains the same inode. When a file is copied, the original file maintains the same inode, but the new entry must have a new inode associated with it:

```
$ mv monday friday
$ ls -li
18471 drwx------ 5     root root             1024 Sep 22 23:57 Desktop
18535 -rw-r--r-- 1     root root               81 Sep 23 00:25 friday
18536 -rw-r--r-- 1     root root              152 Sep 23 00:26 tuesday
18537 -rw-r--r-- 1     root root               38 Sep 23 00:26 wednesday
$ cp friday monday
$ ls -li
18471 drwx------ 5     root root             1024 Sep 22 23:57 Desktop
18535 -rw-r--r-- 1     root root               81 Sep 23 00:25 friday
18538 -rw-r--r-- 1     root root               81 Sep 23 00:38 monday
18536 -rw-r--r-- 1     root root              152 Sep 23 00:26 tuesday
18537 -rw-r--r-- 1     root root               38 Sep 23 00:26 wednesday
$
```

Working with Links

The purpose of a link, purely and simply, is to allow one file to be referenced by more than one name. There are any number of reasons why you would want to, or need to, do this:

- *For historic purposes*—Assume you want to combine all the vendor information into a single file. In the past, marketing has always used a file called "vendor", but accounting kept its information in a file called "contacts", and admin called its file "references". When you create a single file, you can make it available by all three names so all parties can find it as they formerly did.

- *To make nonlocal files look local*—Assume that all users must use the same template when making system modification requests. This file can exist in the root user's home directory (/root), and you can create a link within each user's home directory (/home/user).

The utility you use to create links is **ln**. When you create a link, you merely create another pointer to an already existing entity; only one inode is used, not two. Because there is only one copy, you also save disk space.

When you link to a file to give others access, you must make certain they have appropriate permissions to access the file. Permissions are discussed in Chapter 8.

You can create two types of links: hard and symbolic.

Hard Links

The simplest of the two link types is the hard link. **ln** creates a hard link by default, and its use can be illustrated as follows:

```
$ ls -l
drwx------ 5    root root       1024 Sep 22 23:57    Desktop
-rw-r--r-- 1    root root         81 Sep 23 00:25    friday
-rw-r--r-- 1    root root         81 Sep 23 00:38    monday
-rw-r--r-- 1    root root        152 Sep 23 00:26    tuesday
-rw-r--r-- 1    root root         38 Sep 23 00:26    wednesday
$
$ ln monday thursday
$ ls -l
drwx------ 5    root root       1024 Sep 22 23:57    Desktop
-rw-r--r-- 1    root root         81 Sep 23 00:25    friday
-rw-r--r-- 2    root root         81 Sep 23 00:38    monday
-rw-r--r-- 2    root root         81 Sep 23 00:38    thursday
-rw-r--r-- 1    root root        152 Sep 23 00:26    tuesday
-rw-r--r-- 1    root root         38 Sep 23 00:26    wednesday
$
```

Notice that the attributes related to the time of the new entry (thursday) remained the same as those associated with monday and did not assume the current time—as would happen with a copy operation. This is because there is only one set of data, even though there are now two ways of referencing it. The second column from the left indicates the link count for files: the number of ways this same set of data can be referenced. The link count has incremented from 1 to 2.

Another way to verify that it is the same data is to view the inodes. Every entity must have its own inode, as discussed earlier. If, however, you have only one set of data and multiple ways of accessing it, all the access methods (names) share the same inode:

```
$ ls -i
18471 Desktop          18538 monday        18536 tuesday
18535 friday           18538 thursday      18537 wednesday
$
```

As you add links to the data, the link count increments; as you remove links, the link count decrements. The data that the links point to remains on the system as long as anything at all points to it. For example, the file thursday was linked to monday. If monday is deleted, thursday still remains, but the link count decrements to one: Linux does not care which file was created first. Only when the link count drops to zero does the data no longer exist on the system.

Every time you create a file from scratch, you create a link to the data (with a link count of one). When you remove the link (delete the file), the count becomes zero and the data goes away.

When you view the files graphically, as shown in Figure 7.4, you see no indication that they are links to each other.

To prove the link exists, however, any modification made to either file happens to both because they both reference the same data, as shown here:

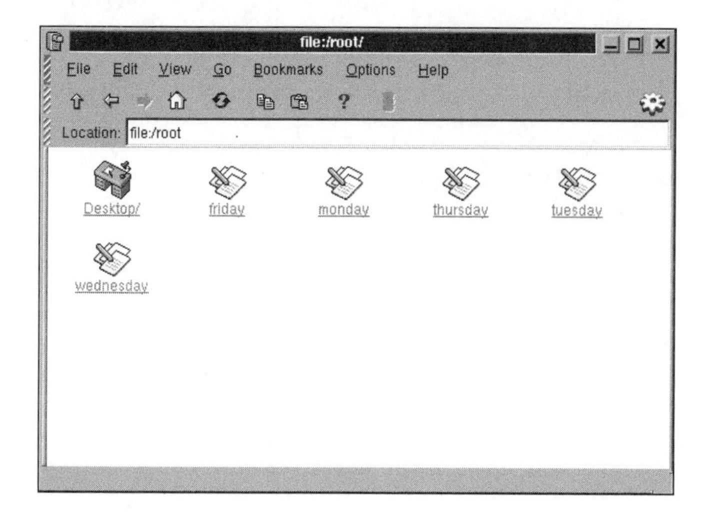

Figure 7.4 There is no indication, when viewed graphically, that two files are linked.

```
$ ls -l
drwx------ 5    root root       1024 Sep 22 23:57    Desktop
-rw-r--r-- 1    root root         81 Sep 23 00:25    friday
-rw-r--r-- 2    root root         81 Sep 23 00:38    monday
-rw-r--r-- 2    root root         81 Sep 23 00:38    thursday
-rw-r--r-- 1    root root        152 Sep 23 00:26    tuesday
-rw-r--r-- 1    root root         38 Sep 23 00:26    wednesday
$
$ cat >> monday
Ingredients include carbonated water, high fructose corn syrup
and/or sugar, citric acid, and natural flavoring.
{press Ctrl+d}
$
$ ls -l
drwx------ 5    root root       1024 Sep 22 23:57    Desktop
-rw-r--r-- 1    root root         81 Sep 23 00:25    friday
-rw-r--r-- 2    root root        194 Sep 24 15:09    monday
-rw-r--r-- 2    root root        194 Sep 24 15:09    thursday
-rw-r--r-- 1    root root        152 Sep 23 00:26    tuesday
-rw-r--r-- 1    root root         38 Sep 23 00:26    wednesday
$
```

The same effect of a change to one happening to both also applies to permissions, owners, groups, and so on. Hard links cannot exist across filesystems; they must always be local. Users can create links to files, but not to directories; the root user, however, can also create links to directories with the **-F** or **-d** options.

Symbolic Links

To make a symbolic link, you must use the **-s** option with **ln**. A symbolic link is what you might call a "shortcut" in the Windows operating systems: a small file that points to another file. The primary purpose for a symbolic link is to get around the shortcomings of hard links. As such, symbolic links allow users to link to directories and provide links to cross filesystems.

To understand how a symbolic link is created, consider the following example:

```
$ ls -l
drwx------ 5    root root       1024 Sep 22 23:57    Desktop
-rw-r--r-- 1    root root         81 Sep 23 00:25    friday
-rw-r--r-- 2    root root        194 Sep 24 15:09    monday
-rw-r--r-- 2    root root        194 Sep 24 15:09    thursday
-rw-r--r-- 1    root root        152 Sep 23 00:26    tuesday
-rw-r--r-- 1    root root         38 Sep 23 00:26    wednesday
$
$ ln -s friday saturday
$ ls -l
```

```
drwx------ 5    root root          1024 Sep 22 23:57    Desktop
-rw-r--r-- 1    root root            81 Sep 23 00:25    friday
-rw-r--r-- 2    root root           194 Sep 24 15:09    monday
lrwxrwxrwx 1    root root             6 Sep 24 15:49    saturday ->
   friday
-rw-r--r-- 2    root root           194 Sep 24 15:09    thursday
-rw-r--r-- 1    root root           152 Sep 23 00:26    tuesday
-rw-r--r-- 1    root root            38 Sep 23 00:26    wednesday
$
```

You should note several items about this transaction: The link count on friday did not change. The new file always has a first column equal to **lrwxrwxrwx** to indicate it is a link. The date and time on the new file are not equal to those for the old file but instead are the current date and time because a new file is created (with its own inode). To the right of the file name is a graphical indication of the file really being referenced. And the new file has a size associated with it, but the size is equal to the pointer only.

The last point is worth considering for a moment. The file friday has a size of 81, and saturday has a size of 6. This disparity in size is completely transparent to the user because any operation done on saturday is sent to friday instead. To illustrate:

pointer size is same

```
$ cat friday
this is the way that one and one
will equal two
and two and two
will equal four
$
$ cat saturday
this is the way that one and one
will equal two
and two and two
will equal four
$
$ wc friday
    4     18     81 friday
$ wc saturday
    4     18     81 saturday
$
```

In other words, saturday is just a symbolic (name) representation of friday. Whatever action you attempt is sent to the first file through the pointer held in the second. This behavior can lead to unexpected results: Because the file is a pointer, it can point to something that no longer exists or is currently unavailable. (Remember, symbolic links can span filesystems.) Consider the following sequence of events where the file being pointed to is removed:

```
$ rm friday
$ ls -l
drwx------ 5    root root      1024 Sep 22 23:57    Desktop
-rw-r--r-- 2    root root       194 Sep 24 15:09    monday
lrwxrwxrwx 1    root root         6 Sep 24 15:49    saturday ->
   friday
-rw-r--r-- 2    root root       194 Sep 24 15:09    thursday
-rw-r--r-- 1    root root       152 Sep 23 00:26    tuesday
-rw-r--r-- 1    root root        38 Sep 23 00:26    wednesday
$ wc saturday
wc: saturday: No such file or directory
$
```

This behavior can lead to frustration and aggravation for users because the error messages indicate that saturday does not exist, but every listing of the directory shows that it does. As an administrator, it is imperative for you to understand that the file does exist, but users see a pointer to a file that no longer does.

When you view a symbolic link graphically, as shown in Figure 7.5, the name is italicized and a small box holding an arrow appears at the bottom left of the icon.

A large number of the system files discussed at the beginning of this chapter are links to other items. For example, the /dev directory holds a plethora of symbolic links to devices that can be accessed via different names and in different locations.

Mounting and Unmounting

Linux is installed on a local filesystem. If that filesystem is large enough to hold everything you interact with, then that is all you need. In most cases, however, the

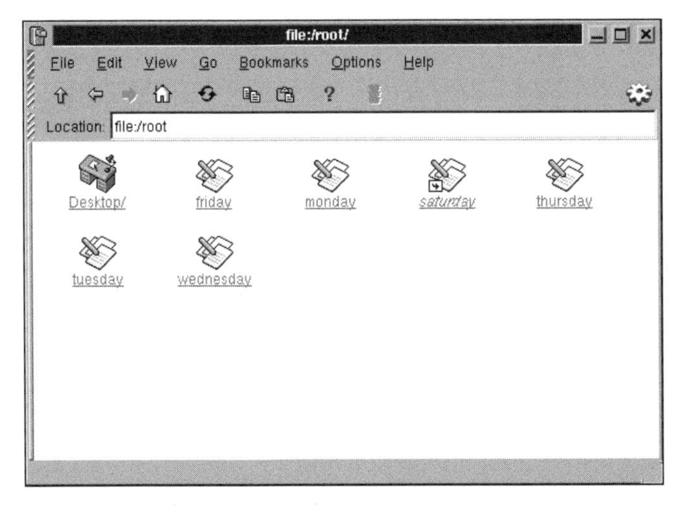

Figure 7.5 Symbolic links use slightly different icons than standard files.

local filesystem is not sufficient to hold everything you need. When that is the case, you can mount other filesystems to make them accessible within your environment.

You use the **mount** command without parameters to show what filesystems are currently available. A sample of the output is:

```
/dev/hda1 on / type ext2 (rw)
/dev/hda3 on /home type ext2 (rw)
devpts on /dev/pts type devpts (rw, gid=5,mode=620)
/proc on /proc type proc (rw)
noname: (pid11973) on /auto type nfs (rw)
```

This sample reads from the dynamic file /etc/mtab and indicates the device, the mount point, the type of filesystem, and the permissions (**rw** is read/write). In addition to read/write, filesystems can be mounted as read-only (**ro**), not allowing users (**nouser**), able to run binaries (**exec**) or not (**noexec**), not running certain files (**nosuid**), controllable by all users (**user**), and interpreting special devices on the filesystem (**dev**).

The entries listed here, and those that appear by default, appear in the /etc/fstab file—mentioned earlier in regard to the **fsck** utility. If you always want to mount additional filesystems, you should add their entries to this file. The command **mount -a** reads the fstab file and mounts and remounts all entries found within.

If you do not want filesystems always mounted, you can dynamically load other filesystems using the device name with the **mount** utility.

For example, to mount the CD, the command is:

```
$ mount /mnt/cdrom
```

The entry added to **mount** resembles:

```
/dev/hdc on /mnt/cdrom type iso9660 (ro,noexec,nosuid,nodev)
```

The /mnt directory holds readily accessible definitions for external devices such as the CD ROM and floppies. Options you can use with the **mount** command are:

- **-a**—Reads through the /etc/fstab file and mounts all entries.
- **-f**—Checks whether a filesystem can be mounted (but does not mount it). An error message returned means that it cannot be found, and no error message means that it was found in /etc/fstab or /etc/mtab.
- **-n**—Prevents the /etc/mtab file from being dynamically updated when a filesystem is added.
- **-r**—Mounts the filesystem as read-only.

- **-t**—Allows you to specify the type of the filesystem being mounted.
- **-w**—Mounts the filesystem as read/write (the default).

You can unmount a filesystem when it is no longer needed with the **umount** utility. To unload the CD, the command is:

```
$ umount /mnt/cdrom
```

Options that you can use with the **umount** utility are:

- **-a**—Unloads every entry in /etc/mtab.
- **-n**—Unloads but does not update /etc/mtab.
- **-r**—Remounts it as read-only if the unload fails.
- **-t**—Unloads all entries of a specific file type.

Working with Quotas

Quotas limit the amount of space available to a user or group. By default, Linux does not impose any quotas, so each user is limited in the amount of hard disk space she can consume only by the amount of space available on the system.

When used, quotas must be applied per partition, which offers flexibility in that the level applied to one partition can differ from that applied to another. Each quota operates independently of any other. For example, you can apply quotas on a partition limiting kristin to 7MB, evan to 5MB, and spencer to 3MB. This gives the three users a total of 15MB of storage space. If, however, they all belong to the sales group, which is limited to 10MB, then one or more of the users will not be able to store files after the 10MB limit is reached even though he has room left within the individual quota.

To turn on quotas, you must edit the /etc/fstab file. A current entry within the file would read:

```
/dev/hda3 /home ext2 defaults  1  2
```

The first field is the filesystem, and the second is the mount point. The third field is the filesystem type, and the fourth contains options for the filesystem. The fifth field identifies the order in which the filesystem would be used by a dump, and the sixth field is the order in which **fsck** would use it.

You make a modification to the fourth field to use quotas, changing the line to read:

```
/dev/hda3 /home ext2 defaults,usrquota  1  2
```

In some cases, it might be necessary for the kernel to be recompiled to support quotas, but not always. After the file is edited, go to the root of the partition where you want to apply the quota. As the root user, create a file called either quota.user or quota.group. The permissions on the file must be equal to read and write by the root user only (accomplished with the **chmod** command, which is discussed fully in Chapter 8). Thus, the sequence following the edit is:

```
$ touch quota.user
$ chmod 600 quota.user
```

You must then reboot. The utilities you can use are:

- **quotaon**—Enables the use of quotas. You can use the **-a** option to enable for every filesystem having **usrquota** in /etc/fstab; otherwise, you must specify the filesystem.
- **quotaoff**—Disables the use of the quotas.
- **edquota**—Edits and changes the quota limits. You use the **-u** option to specify a user or **-g** to specify a group. You can use the **-t** option for a "soft limit."
- **repquota**—Generates a report of disk usage and the specified quota (created with **edquota**). Options with this tool include **-a** to check all filesystems in /etc/fstab; **-g** to see the report for groups; **-u** to see the report for users (default); and **-v** to show numbers even if they are zero. Any user can run this utility to see her own numbers, but root sees the report for all users.
- **quota**—Shows the quotas in existence (similar to **repquota**). Any user can see his own, and root can see all.
- **quotacheck**—Scans the system and creates report files with the current usage (only available to root).
- **quotastats**—Shows the amount of used space for each individual user and group.

Note: Not all the utilities are available in all implementations of Linux.

By default, when a user or group reaches the quota limit, she is no longer allowed to save any further entries. Setting a soft limit means she can exceed the limit, but only for a short period of time (defined as a grace period, the default is 7 days).

Finding Files

Among all the files and all the different directories and subdirectories on a system, finding something specific can sometimes be a daunting task. A number of utilities in Linux can help ease this burden. This section outlines a few of the unique utilities and examines how they can be used to help find what you are looking for.

The utilities to be examined, in order, are:

- **locate**
- **updatedb**
- **which**
- **find** (and a companion, **xargs**)

The **locate** utility looks through a database file (instead of the actual directory tree) to find files that match a given name. The database is named locatedb and usually appears in a subdirectory in the /var directory. (Common locations include in /var/state or /var/lib.)

You update the locatedb database through the use of the **updatedb** command. By default, **updatedb** runs on a regular basis (usually once a day), but you can run it manually as well. The advantage to using **locate** (and thus locatedb) is that it is much faster to search a database for an entry than to search the entire filesystem. The downside is that you cannot find files created after the last time **updatedb** was run using the **locate** utility.

By default, **updatedb** moves through the filesystem and updates the locatedb database with entries anywhere it finds them. You can, however, create an optional file named updatedb.conf in the /etc directory. If the updatedb.conf file exists, then only directories listed in it are used to create the database.

An example of the use of the **locate** command is:

```
$ locate grep
/opt/kde/share/apps/kmail/pics/kmmsgreplied.xpm
/usr/bin/egrep
/usr/bin/fgrep
/usr/bin/grep
/usr/bin/zgrep
/usr/bin/zipgrep
/usr/doc/dosemu-0.98.5/bugreports.txt
/usr/doc/grep-2.2
/usr/doc/grep-2.2/ABOUT-NLS
/usr/doc/grep-2.2/AUTHORS
/usr/doc/grep-2.2/INSTALL
/usr/doc/grep-2.2/NEWS
/usr/doc/grep-2.2/README
/usr/doc/grep-2.2/THANKS
/usr/doc/grep-2.2/TODO
/usr/lib/python1.5/grep.pyc
```

```
/usr/lib/python1.5/grep.pyo
/usr/lib/xemacs-20.4/lisp/efs/dired-grep.elc
/usr/lib/xemacs-20.4/lisp/packages/igrep.elc
/usr/man/de/man1/egrep.1.gz
/usr/man/de/man1/grep.1.gz
/usr/man/man1/egrep.1.gz
/usr/man/man1/fgrep.1.gz
/usr/man/man1/grep.1.gz
/usr/man/man1/zgrep.1.gz
/usr/man/man1/zipgrep.1.gz
/usr/share/locale/de/LC_MESSAGES/grep.mo
/usr/share/locale/es/LC_MESSAGES/grep.mo
/usr/share/locale/fr/LC_MESSAGES/grep.mo
/usr/share/locale/ko/LC_MESSAGES/grep.mo
/usr/share/locale/nl/LC_MESSAGES/grep.mo
/usr/share/locale/no/LC_MESSAGES/grep.mo
/usr/share/locale/pl/LC_MESSAGES/grep.mo
/usr/share/locale/ru/LC_MESSAGES/grep.mo
/usr/share/locale/sl/LC_MESSAGES/grep.mo
/usr/share/locale/sv/LC_MESSAGES/grep.mo
/usr/share/vim/bugreport.vim
$
```

Similar to the **locate** command is the **which** command. Instead of looking through a database, however, **which** looks through the directories listed in your **PATH** statement. When it finds a match in a directory for a name you give, it stops immediately and reports what it found. How is this useful? Suppose your system has 14 versions of **grep**; **which** tells you the first one it finds via the path search, and thus the one that is executed when you use the command.

The following sample illustrates the very simple nature of **which**:

```
$ which grep
/usr/bin/grep
$
```

The find Utility

If you had to think of an analogy for the **find** utility, it would be the Swiss Army Knife in the real world or **grep** on steroids in the operating-system world. This tool is capable of looking at all entries in the filesystem and displaying results that meet given criteria. In many ways, it is the vast possibilities of the criteria you can specify that make this tool so powerful. The syntax is simply:

```
find [starting point] [criteria]
```

The default starting point is the present working directory, but you can specify any directory. Whatever the starting point, the search recursively moves from there to all subdirectories beneath it.

The criteria can be any of the options shown in Table 7.4.

To find all files named **grep** on a system, beginning with the root directory, you enter:

```
$ find / -name "grep"
/usr/bin/grep
$
```

Notice that you do not need to specify the **-print** option: It is the default action. Notice also that, unlike **locate**, **find** found an exact match, not just entries with the four letters somewhere in the name. If you want to find matches that are portions of words, you need to use the asterisk (*) wildcard (**find / -name "*grep*"**).

Once you find the match, you can perform an action on it, such as obtaining a long listing:

Table 7.4 Options for the find utility.

Option	Purpose
-atime *days*	Tests true if the file was accessed within the number of days specified.
-ctime *days*	Tests true if the file was changed within the number of days specified.
-exec *command*	Executes a command. You must specify that the command is for a group **{}** and continues on **\;**.
-group *name*	Tests true if the file belongs to the specified group.
-inum *number*	Tests true if the file has that inode number.
-links *number*	Tests true if the number of links is equal to the specified number.
-mount	Looks only on the local filesystem.
-mtime *days*	Tests true only if the file was modified within the number of days specified.
-name *file*	Tests true only if it matches the given name.
-perm *permission*	Tests true if it matches the given permissions.
-print	Prints the names of matching files.
-size *number*	Tests true if it matches the number of blocks or characters.
-type *type*	Tests true if it matches the specified type (**d**=directory, **f**=file, **b**=block file, and **c**=character file).
-user *name*	Tests true only if owned by the named user.

```
$ find / -name "grep" -exec ls -l {} \;
-rwxr-xr-x 1 root    root      70652  Aug 11 1999 /usr/bin/grep
$
```

Be very careful with the **-exec** option because you can specify anything following it—including **move**, **remove**, and so on. You can use the option **-ok** in place of **-exec** to force a prompt before every action is taken.

To find which files have been accessed, you use the **-atime** option. If the number following **-atime** is preceded by a plus sign (+), then **find** returns entries in which the access day was more than the number of days given. If the number following is preceded by a minus sign (-), then **find** returns entries in which the access day was less than the number of days given. For example, to find files in the current directory that have not been accessed for 10 days or more:

```
$ find . -atime +10
```

To find files that have been accessed within the last two days, type:

```
$ find . -atime -2
```

To find only directories beneath the current directory, type:

```
$ find . -type d
```

To find all files associated with the user edulaney, use:

```
$ find / -user edulaney
/home/edulaney
/home/edulaney/.bash_logout
/home/edulaney/.bashrc
/home/edulaney/.cshrc
/home/edulaney/.inputrc
/home/edulaney/.login
/home/edulaney/.logout
/home/edulaney/.profile
/home/edulaney/.tcshrc
/home/edulaney/.seyon
/home/edulaney/.seyon/phonelist
/home/edulaney/.seyon/protocols
/home/edulaney/.seyon/script.CIS
/home/edulaney/.seyon/script.PCBoard
/home/edulaney/.seyon/script.QWK
/home/edulaney/.seyon/script.unix
/home/edulaney/.seyon/startup
```

```
/home/edulaney/fileone
/home/edulaney/filethree
/home/edulaney/filetwo
/home/edulaney/.bash_history
$
```

Notice that the result includes directories and files that are visible and hidden.

xargs

As powerful as the **find** utility is, it is limited in the results it can return to values within the filesystem structure. The only real text within the structure is the name of the entity, not the data itself. (The pointer points to that.) To illustrate, suppose the user edulaney put out a memo several months back on acceptable use of the company refrigerator in the break room. Since then, user edulaney has quit the company and several new employees (who would benefit from knowing this policy) have joined. You want to find the file and reprint it.

About the closest you can get to accomplishing this task with **find** (and its results) is:

```
$ find / -user edulaney -type f -exec grep -i refrigerator {} \;
stored in the refrigerator overnight will be thrown out
$
```

You must use the **type f** option or else errors occur every time **grep** tries to search a directory. In this case, the line from the file is found, but there is no way of knowing what file contains it—rendering the result pretty much useless.

Enter the **xargs** utility: Analogous to a pipe, it feeds output from one command directly into another. Arguments coming into it are passed through with no changes and turned into input for the next command. Thus, the command can be modified to:

```
$ find / -user edulaney -type f | xargs grep -i refrigerator
/home/edulaney/fileone:stored in the refrigerator overnight
   will be thrown out
$
```

The desired file is indicated, so you can print it for the new employees.

Food for thought: If **xargs** works as a pipe, why wouldn't the following command suffice?

```
$ find / -user edulaney -type f | grep -i refrigerator
```

Answer: Because the **grep** operation takes place on the names of the files, not the content of the files. The **xargs** utility pipes the entire name (thus the contents) into the next command in succession (**grep**, in this case), not just the resulting file name.

Utility Summation

This chapter discussed several utilities. Table 7.5 lists them and their purposes.

Table 7.5 Utilities discussed in this chapter.

Utility	Purpose
mknod	Makes special (character and block) files.
fdisk	Divides the disk into partitions.
mkfs	Formats partitions.
df	Reports the amount of disk free space remaining.
du	Shows where disk utilization is occurring.
fsck	Checks the filesystem and corrects problems.
ln	Creates links: hard and symbolic.
mount	Loads a remote filesystem.
umount	Unloads a remote filesystem.
quotaon	Turns on user/group quotas.
quotaoff	Turns off user/group quotas.
edquota	Creates quotas for users or groups.
repquota, **quota**, **quotacheck**, and **quotastats**	Views quota usage.
locate	Finds a file from the locatedb database.
updatedb	Updates the locatedb database.
which	Finds a file from the **PATH** statement.
find	Locates a file based on given criteria.
xargs	Passes the output of one command into another.

Practice Questions

Question 1

Which file updates the database that the **locate** command uses to find matches for search names?

- ❍ a. locatedb
- ❍ b. fstab
- ❍ c. mtab
- ❍ d. updatedb

The correct answer to this question is d. The **updatedb** utility updates the database. Answer a is the name of the database the **locate** utility uses to find the files. Answer b is the file system table, and answer c is the mount table, neither of which relates to the locate utility.

Question 2

Which of the following files would be read by the command **mount -a**?

- ❍ a. /etc/mtab
- ❍ b. /etc/fstab
- ❍ c. /etc/update.conf
- ❍ d. /etc/mount

The correct answer to this question is b. The fstab file holds information about the filesystems known to it. Answer a—/etc/mtab—is where entries are written when the filesystems are loaded, so it is incorrect. The other two answers are invalid in relation to the question.

Question 3

You want to start using quotas on the third partition of your system's disk. To begin, you must edit the fstab file. To which field must you add the **usrquota** entry?

- ❍ a. First
- ❍ b. Second
- ❍ c. Third
- ❍ d. Fourth
- ❍ e. Fifth
- ❍ f. Sixth

The correct answer to this question is d. You must add the entry to the fourth field of the entry for the quotas to be invoked.

Question 4

What is the syntax used to create a symbolic link named "advise" to a file in the same directory named "please"? [Fill in the blank]

____

The correct answer to this question is:

```
ln -s please advise
```

Question 5

Which of the following locations could contain the kernel? [Check all correct answers]

- ❑ a. /
- ❑ b. /bin
- ❑ c. /boot
- ❑ d. /etc

The correct answers to this question are a and c. The default location for the kernel, which differs according to vendors and versions, is either root (/) or /boot. The /bin directory (answer b) holds executable files for all users, while the /etc directory (answer d) is used to hold configuration files; hence, these two choices are incorrect.

Question 6

Which of the following options can you use with the **find** utility to prompt a user before carrying out an operation?

- ❍ a. **-exec**
- ❍ b. **-query**
- ❍ c. **-ok**
- ❍ d. **-perm**

The correct answer to this question is c, which prompts you before carrying out an action. Answer a executes the same operation without first prompting the user; answer b is not an option for **find**; and answer d locates only files that meet the specified permissions.

Question 7

You are getting ready to begin system-administration tasks on your system. Before starting anything, you want to compile a list of utilities that are available only for this purpose (adding users, groups, and so on). Which directory contains the entries you are seeking?

- ❍ a. /usr/sbin
- ❍ b. /usr/bin
- ❍ c. /sbin
- ❍ d. /bin

The correct answer to this question is a. The /usr/sbin directory holds system-specific administrative binaries for use by the administrator. Answer b is used by all users, so it is incorrect. Answer c holds system utilities, but most are available for system purposes other than adding users and groups, such as formatting, checking the file systems, and so on; therefore, it is incorrect. Answer d is used by all users, so it is incorrect.

Question 8

On a SCSI hard drive, which of the following indicates the third partition on the second disk?

- ❍ a. hba3
- ❍ b. sba3
- ❍ c. sdb3
- ❍ d. hdc2

The correct answer to this question is c. The **s** indicates the type of disk, which is SCSI; the **d** indicates the type of device, which is disk; the **b** indicates the second disk; and the **3** indicates the third partition.

Question 9

Which utility can you use to format a partition?

❍ a. **format**

❍ b. **fdisk**

❍ c. **mkfs**

❍ d. **mount**

The correct answer to this question is c. You use the **mkfs** utility to format a partition. Answer a does not exist in Linux; answer b, **fdisk**, creates partitions; and answer d is used to load a remote filesystem

Question 10

The **fsck** utility has found a number of corrupted files, and you have chosen to correct the filesystem. To which directory are the corrupted files written?

❍ a. lost+found

❍ b. tmp

❍ c. etc

❍ d. /

The correct answer to this question is a. The /lost+found directory holds the corrupted files. Usually they are so corrupted that their names are no longer known, and thus the files are written here by inode number. The /tmp directory (answer b) holds temporary files that do not need to survive a reboot. The /etc directory (answer c) holds configuration files used by the system, while the root directory (answer d) is the starting point of all subdirectories.

Need to Know More?

/usr/src/linux/Documentation/devices.txt describes many of the entries in the /dev directory.

www.linuxdoc.org/HOWTO/Filesystems-HOWTO.html is not specifically limited to Linux (it includes NTFS and other filesystems), but it fully explains the Extended Filesystems (ext2 and so on) in the sixth section of the document.

www.linuxdoc.org/HOWTO/mini/Quota.html defines quotas and explains their requirements within Linux. The site addresses setup and configuration details, as well as corresponding utilities.

Users, Groups, and Permissions

Terms you'll need to understand:

- ✓ **passwd**
- ✓ **useradd**
- ✓ **pwconv**
- ✓ **pwunconv**
- ✓ **su**
- ✓ **usermod**
- ✓ **chpasswd**
- ✓ **userdel**
- ✓ **groupadd**
- ✓ **gpasswd**
- ✓ **grpconv**
- ✓ **grpunconv**
- ✓ **id**
- ✓ **newgrp**
- ✓ **groupmod**
- ✓ **groupdel**
- ✓ **umask**
- ✓ **chmod**
- ✓ **chown**
- ✓ **chgrp**
- ✓ SUID
- ✓ SGID
- ✓ Sticky bit

Techniques you'll need to master:

- ✓ Understanding how to add users and groups
- ✓ Comprehending file and directory permissions
- ✓ Recognizing the standard utilities available to add users and groups, as well as to change permissions on files and directories

In this chapter, you'll learn of utilities used to add users and groups to the system. You will also see the standard file and directory permissions available in Linux, as well as three special permissions.

Creating and Managing Users

During installation, Linux adds at least one user (root/superuser) to the system. It is the most powerful user on the system, literally able to do almost anything. After the installation, it is often necessary to add users and modify variables associated with existing ones. This section examines both tasks.

To understand what is involved, it is important to know the files the operating system uses to deal with users. The first file of importance is the /etc/passwd file. Fields are delimited by colons, and the following is a sample:

```
root:x:0:0:root:/root:/bin/bash
bin:x:1:1:bin:/bin:
daemon:x:2:2:daemon:/sbin:
adm:x:3:4:adm:/var/adm:
lp:x:4:7:lp:/var/spool/lpd:
sync:x:5:0:sync:/sbin:/bin/sync
shutdown:x:6:11:shutdown:/sbin:/sbin/shutdown
halt:x:7:0:halt:/sbin:/sbin/halt
mail:x:8:12:mail:/var/spool/mail:
news:x:9:13:news:/var/spool/news:
uucp:x:10:14:uucp:/var/spool/uucp:
operator:x:11:0:operator:/root:
games:x:12:100:games:/usr/games:
gopher:x:13:30:gopher:/usr/lib/gopher-data:
ftp:x:14:50:FTP User:/home/ftp:
man:x:15:15:Manuals Owner:/:
majordom:x:16:16:Majordomo:/:/bin/false
postgres:x:17:17:Postgres User:/home/postgres:/bin/bash
mysql:x:18:18:MySQL User:/var/lib/mysql:/bin/false
nobody:x:65534:65534:Nobody:/:/bin/false
col:x:500:100:Caldera Systems OpenLinux User:/home/col:/bin/bash
edulaney:x:501:100:emmett:/home/edulaney:/bin/bash
kdulaney:x:502:100:karen:/home/kdulaney:/bin/tcsh
sdulaney:x:503:100:spencer:/home/sdulaney:/bin/zsh
```

The seven fields are:

- *The login name of the user*—This must be unique per system but is free text that can be edited and modified with any editor at any time. Among the entries shown in the example, **bin** is the owner of executables, **daemon** is used for system services, and **adm** owns the log files. Other entries are users (such as edulaney) or individual services (such as FTP).

- *The password*—This can be an encrypted entry held within this field or an "x". With the latter case, the single character merely indicates that the values are stored elsewhere—in the /etc/shadow file.

Keep in mind that placing the passwords in the shadow file adds a level of security. Everyone can read the passwd file, but only the root user can read the shadow file.

- *The numerical user ID (UID)*—This incremental number, which is unique for every user, is how the operating system truly references the user. (Remember, the login name is changeable text.) The root user is always number 0, and maintenance or service accounts use small numbers (typically up to 99). Regular user accounts typically start at 500 (but this differs per Linux vendor) and increment from there. For security reasons, you can rename root to any other text value, but the number 0 is always the identifier.
- *The numerical group ID (GID)*—This identifies the default group associated with the user. The root group is always 0, and lower numbers represent system groups. Regular users are assigned groups beginning with a number listed in the /etc/login.defs file.
- *Free text used for descriptive purposes*—One of the main utilities that uses this field is **finger**, which simply returns information about a user to anyone querying.
- *The home directory of the user*—This is where users start when they log in and where files are held to define environmental variables.

Within the bash shell, the home directory can always be referenced by a tilde (~). For example, if a user wishes to copy a file named "example" from a directory he is currently in to his home directory, he can enter: **mv example ~**

- *The shell to use for the user*—If nothing appears here, the default shell is used.

The /etc/shadow file holds the password and information about the aging parameters. An example is:

```
root:awYeiEwzMpfo6:11144:0::7:7::
bin:*:10547:0::7:7::
daemon:*:10547:0::7:7::
adm:*:10547:0::7:7::
lp:*:10547:0::7:7::
sync:*:10547:0::7:7::
shutdown:*:10547:0::7:7::
```

```
halt:*:10547:0::7:7::
mail:*:10547:0::7:7::
news:*:10547:0::7:7::
uucp:*:10547:0::7:7::
operator:*:10547:0::7:7::
games:*:10547:0::7:7::
gopher:*:10547:0::7:7::
ftp:*:10547:0::7:7::
man:*:10547:0::7:7::
majordom:*:10547:0::7:7::
postgres:*:10547:0::7:7::
mysql:*:10547:0::7:7::
nobody:*:10547:0::7:7::
col:aw2tRWQHBhQK6:11144:0::7:7::
edulaney:aw0VvUAsWpigo:11144:0::7:7::
kdulaney:awzIG94wrzGqY:11144:0::7:7::
sdulaney:awf7Zbxwu.NmQ:11144:0::7:7::
```

The eight fields are:

- *The login name of the user*—The only fields that must match the /etc/passwd file.
- *An encrypted hash of the password*—If no password is defined, an asterisk (*) is used. Under no conditions can this field be blank for a functioning user.
- *The day the password was last changed*—This is expressed in the number of days that have passed since 1/1/1970.
- *Minimum password age*—This is expressed in how many days a user must wait between making password changes.
- *Maximum password age*—This is expressed in how many days a user is allowed to keep this password.

An empty field indicates there is no restriction.

- *The number of days before the password expires when a warning starts appearing about changing the password*—This provides a quasi-grace period by telling users to change their password before it expires.
- *The number of days after the password expires to wait before disabling the account*—This is the true grace period after users have avoided all messages to

change their password and now have only a few days to continue using the account before it becomes disabled.

➤ *The expiration date for the password*—In days since 1/1/1970.

Creating User Accounts

You can create new users manually or by using utilities. To do so manually, simply append an entry to the /etc/passwd file. (It is strongly recommended that you make a backup copy of the file before changing it.) You can leave the password field blank and then assign a password using the **passwd** utility. If you simply leave it blank, it is a valid account without a password:

```
$ cat >> /etc/passwd
evan::504:100:EvanD:/home/evan:/bin/bash
{Press Ctrl+D}
$
$ passwd evan
New user password: {Enter password}
Retype new user password: {Enter password again}
passwd: all authentication tokens updated successfully
$
$ tail -1 /etc/passwd
evan:petKv.fLWG/Ig:504:100/home/evan:/bin/bash
$
```

Any user can use the **passwd** utility to change her own password. Only the root user, however, can use it to change the password of another user.

Notice that this method places the encrypted password in the /etc/passwd file itself and does not utilize the /etc/shadow file. Provided the home directory exists, and the user is the owner of it (see the discussion of **chown** later in this chapter), the user becomes an authenticated user.

A utility provided with Linux (most vendors also have their own utilities as well) to simplify this process is **useradd**. You must use options with the utility; a key one is **-D** to display default settings:

```
$ useradd -D
GROUP=100
HOME=/home/%s
SHELL=/bin/bash
SKEL=/etc/skel
PASS_MIN_DAYS=0
```

```
PASS_MAX_DAYS=-1
PASS_WARN_DAYS=7
PASS_INACTIVE=-1
PASS_EXPIRE=-1
$
```

You use these defaults to create a new user with this utility. The defaults come from the text file /etc/login.defs. Therefore, the following sequence is possible:

```
$ useradd kerby
$ tail -1 /etc/passwd
kerby:x:508:100:Caldera OpenLinux User:/home/kerby:/bin/bash
$ tail -1 /etc/shadow
kerby:*not set*:11213:0:-1:7:-1:-1:
$
$ passwd kerby
New user password: {Enter password}
Retype new user password: {Enter password again}
passwd: all authentication tokens updated successfully
$ tail -1 /etc/shadow
kerby:M3cMnQDwHjRD6:11213:0:-1:7:-1:-1:
$
```

Note that this code uses the /etc/shadow file, and the values used to create the entries in the two files come directly from the defaults shown in Table 8.1.

The example did not use the **SKEL** variable. By default, **useradd** makes the entries in the passwd and shadow files but does not create the home directory for the user. If you use the **-m** option, **useradd** also creates the home directory for the user and copies files from the **SKEL** location (a skeleton, or template, of files that you want copied for every new user) into the new directory. In typical implementations, /etc/skel holds the following files:

- .bash_logout
- .bashrc

Table 8.1 Values used to create new accounts.

Default	Results in /etc/passwd and /etc/shadow.
GROUP	Becomes the fourth field of passwd.
HOME	Becomes the sixth field of passwd, with the **%s** variable becoming the name given on the command line (which becomes the first field of both passwd and shadow).
SHELL	Becomes the seventh field of passwd.
PASS variables	Entered into appropriate fields of shadow.

- .cshrc
- .inputrc
- .login
- .logout
- .profile
- .seyon
- .tcshrc

All the files are hidden files used for processing (setting up variables, the environment, and so on) with the various shells. Their purposes are further explored in Chapter 9.

You can use a number of options with **useradd** to override default settings:

- -c—Specifies the free text (the fifth field of passwd) associated with the user. Most Linux implementations default to an empty entry here or a deviation of the name.
- **-d**—Specifies a home directory different from /home/*{username}*.
- -e—Changes the expiration date (with the format *mm/dd/yyyy*).
- -f—Sets the variable defining how many days after expiration the account becomes disabled. The default of **-1** prevents it from being disabled even after expiration.
- -g—Specifies a different GID.
- -r—Switches to a root directory.
- -s—Chooses a different shell.
- -u—Specifies a UID: By default, the next available number is used. If you try to use a number already in use, the utility fails and identifies which user already has that number.

Switching between the passwd and the shadow Files

In the earlier example for creating a new user, the encrypted password appears in the /etc/passwd file and not the /etc/shadow file. If you want to make manual additions and still use /etc/shadow, the **pwconv** utility comes in handy. This utility reads the entire passwd file and converts new entries into shadow file entries.

The opposite of **pwconv** is **pwunconv**, which takes entries from the shadow file and places them in the appropriate format in the passwd file. As a final step, **pwunconv** removes the shadow file completely.

The su Utility

The entries in the passwd file represent valid accounts that can log in. Any user can sit at the system and give the correct username and password combination to log in as that user. Any user already logged in can also use the **su** utility to change identity to another user if he knows the other user's password. This creates a sort of subshell, where one user becomes another and can revert back to his own identity by typing **exit**.

Although there are dozens of harmful reasons why one user might want to become another, there are legitimate reasons as well. The command **su** without a username following it tries to make the user the superuser (root), which requires the password for that account. As an administrator, you can log in as a typical user without root permissions and begin your day. The lack of root permissions can be a blessing because it can keep you from deleting entries you unintentionally typed, for example. When a user presents a problem, you can use **su** to become root—with all its rights and privileges as if you had logged in as such—fix the problem, and then use **exit** to get back to your regular account.

Managing User Accounts

Once an account is created, you can manage and modify it manually or through the use of utilities. For example, if a user named Karen Dulaney marries and changes her name to Karen Brooks, you can edit the passwd and shadow files and change the first field of each from kdulaney to kbrooks. Because the same UID stays in place, all files associated with her continue to remain so. You can rename the home directory and make the change in passwd as well. (The home directory and username should always match, for administrative purposes.)

If Karen gets promoted to administration, it might be necessary to remove her from the users group and place her in the root group. You can do this by manually editing the /etc/passwd file and changing the GID field.

Just as **useradd** can help you simplify the addition of users to the system—and avoid manual entries—**usermod** is meant to simplify changing existing values. You must use options or flags with the utility; the possibilities follow:

- **-c**—Replaces the descriptive text with a new value.
- **-d**—Alters the home directory.
- **-e**—Changes the password expiration date.

- **-f**—Sets the inactive parameter.
- **-G**—Changes the secondary group membership. You can provide more than one group as long as the entries are separated by commas.
- **-g**—Changes the GID.
- **-l**—Changes the login name.
- **-m** (must be used with **-d**)—Makes the new home directory.
- **-p**—Changes the password.
- **-s**—Changes to a different shell.
- **-u**—Changes the UID.

Most of the values require that the user be logged off while the change is made. An example of a change is:

```
$ grep krist /etc/passwd
kristin:petKv.fLWG/Ig:506:100:kristin:/home/kristin:/bin/bash
$ usermod -l kristen kristin
$ grep krist /etc/passwd
kristen:petKv.fLWG/Ig:506:100:kristin:/home/kristin:/bin/bash
$ ls -l /home
drwxr-xr-x 4 evan users 1024 Jul 6 11:16 evan
drwxr-xr-x 4 kristin users 1024 Aug 8 10:29 kristin
drwxr-xr-x 4 spencer users 1024 Jul 6 11:16 spencer
$ usermod -d /home/kristen -m kristen
$ ls -l /home
drwxr-xr-x 4 evan users 1024 Jul 6 11:16 evan
drwxr-xr-x 4 kristen users 1024 Aug 8 10:29 kristen
drwxr-xr-x 4 spencer users 1024 Jul 6 11:16 spencer
$ grep krist /etc/passwd
kristen:petKv.fLWG/Ig:506:100:kristin:/home/kristen:/bin/bash
$
```

The **usermod** utility has the **-p** option to let you change passwords, but you should tackle that task with the **passwd** utility discussed earlier. The standalone utility is safer because it requires you to enter the value twice and thus helps you avoid entering a value that is off by one character (preventing you from logging in).

If you need to change a large number of passwords (think system break-in), you can perform a batch change with the **chpasswd** utility. To use it, create a text file with one entry per line. Each line consists of the username and new password, separated by a colon. For example:

```
$ cat > changes
kristen:spea23ker
evan:pho78ne
kdulaney:fla98sh
{Ctrl+D}
$
$ chpasswd < changes
$
```

The passwords are in clear text, and for that reason you want to remove the batch file from your system as soon as possible. An alternative is to use encrypted passwords and use the **-e** option with **chpasswd**.

Encourage users to choose good passwords. These consist of at least six characters; mix letters, characters, and numbers; and are not easily guessed.

Removing Users

When a user account is no longer needed, you can deal with the situation in a number of ways. The first question you must address is why the account is no longer needed. Once you know that, you can formulate a plan for dealing with it. Table 8.2 offers some scenarios and methods of proceeding.

Table 8.2 Disabling and removing accounts.

Perceived Reason for Not Needing Account	Proposed Solution
User has been temporarily transferred to Siberia.	For a temporary situation, you do not want to delete the account; so doing removes all references that might be needed later. To disable the account temporarily, edit the /etc/passwd file and place a pound sign (**#**) at the beginning of the line. This makes the entire line a comment and disables the account. Alternatively, you could place a period or similar character in the second field of /etc/passwd, which makes the password unusable and effectively disables the account.
User's password has been jeopardized by a hacker.	Change the password to another value. For greater security, change the login name and home directory.
User has left the organization.	Remove the account from /etc/passwd and /etc/shadow and delete the home directory.

You can also use the **userdel** utility to remove a user. This utility removes the user from system files (passwd and shadow), but you must still remove any files associated with the user.

Working with Groups

Just as it is important to know the parameters behind user variables in order to understand how to work with them, you must also understand group constructs. The primary file holding group information is /etc/group, a sample of which follows:

```
root::0:
wheel::10:
bin::1:bin,daemon
daemon::2:bin,daemon
sys::3:bin,adm
adm::4:adm,daemon
tty::5:
disk::6:
lp::7:daemon,lp
mem::8:
kmem::9:
operator::11:
mail::12:mail
news::13:news
uucp::14:uucp
man::15:
majordom::16:
database::17:
mysql::18:
games::20:
gopher::30:
dip::40:
utmp::45:
ftp::50:
nobody::65534:
users::100:
```

Each entry in the file has four fields. The first field is the text name (a maximum of eight characters) associated with the group (used for **ls -l** listings and the like). The third field is the numerical group ID (GID), which must be unique on the system. The second field—blank in all cases by default—holds a password that can be required for use. The fourth field can be used to list the members of the group.

Creating a New Group

To create a new group, you can manually edit the /etc/group file and append an entry to it. If you do so, you must be certain to use a unique text name and GID number. You can also use the **groupadd** utility to simplify the operation:

```
$ groupadd -g 101 sales
$ tail -1 /etc/group
sales::101:
$
```

The **-g** option specifies the GID number to use. If the number is not unique, the utility fails. As a general rule, GID numbers 0 through 99 are reserved for system groups:

```
$ groupadd -g 101 marketing
A group with GID 101 already exists.
$
```

Similarly, if you attempt to reuse a group name, the utility fails:

```
$ groupadd -g 102 sales
A group with name sales already exists.
$
```

The only option available with **groupadd** is **-g**. To define your group further, you can resort to manual editing or you can use the **gpasswd** utility. When issued with only the name of a group, **gpasswd** prompts for a password to associate with the group:

```
$ gpasswd sales
Changing the password for group sales
New Password: {Enter value}
Re-enter new password: {Enter value again}
$ tail -1 /etc/group
sales:QJHexo2Pbk7TU:101:
$
```

If you tire of the password, or find it unwieldy, you can use the **-r** option to remove it. Using the **-a** option, it is possible to add users to the group. The reverse option is **-d**, which removes users from the group:

```
$ gpasswd -r sales
$ tail -1 /etc/group
sales::101:
$ gpasswd -a edulaney sales
Adding user edulaney to sales
$
```

```
$ tail -1 /etc/group
sales:!:101:edulaney
$
```

The exclamation mark appears in the second field as a placeholder to identify that other users can join. You can remove it by again issuing the **-r** command. If you attempt to add a nonexistent user using the **-a** option, the utility fails. If you attempt to add users to a nonexistent group, the utility fails. You cannot add or delete more than one user at a time with **gpasswd**.

You can use the **-A** option in place of **-a** if the user you are adding will act as administrator for the group. To specify an administrator, you must use shadow passwords for the group file. Shadow passwords are stored in /etc/gshadow and add an additional level of security because this file is readable only by root (whereas /etc/group is readable by all).

The simplest way to convert group passwords to the gshadow file is to use the **grpconv** utility. This tool extracts data from the second field of the group file, replaces it with an "x", and creates the gshadow file. The gshadow file consists of four fields per entry, in the format:

```
Group name:password:administrator:users
```

The sequence of events for adding additional users and declaring an administrator is:

```
$ tail -1 /etc/group
sales:!:101:edulaney
$ gpasswd -a kristen sales
$ gpasswd -a kerby sales
$ gpasswd -a martha sales
$ gpasswd sales
Changing the password for the group sales
New Password: {Enter password}
Re-enter new password: {Enter password again}
$
$ tail -1 /etc/group
sales:0E5ux7C9.1pAS:101:edulaney,kristen,kerby,martha
$ grpconv
$ tail -1 /etc/group
sales:x:101:edulaney,kristen,kerby,martha
$ cat gshadow
root:::
wheel:::
bin:::bin,daemon
daemon:::bin,daemon
```

```
sys:::bin,adm
adm:::adm,daemon
tty:::
disk:::
lp:::daemon,lp
mem:::
kmem:::
operator:::
mail:::mail
news:::news
uucp:::uucp
man:::
majordom:::
database:::
mysql:::
games:::
gopher:::
dip:::
utmp:::
ftp:::
nobody:::
users:::
sales:0E5ux7C9.1pAs::edulaney,kristen,kerby,martha
$
$ gpasswd -A walker sales
$ tail -1 /etc/group
sales:x:101:edulaney,kristen,kerby,martha
$ tail -1 /etc/gshadow
sales:0E5ux7C9.1pAs::edulaney,kristen,kerby,martha
$
```

Notice that the administrative user for the group does not appear as a user in the /etc/group file and appears only in the third field of the /etc/gshadow file. To move the passwords back to the group file and delete gshadow, you can use the **grpunconv** utility.

Picking a Group

When a user is a member of more than one group, her default group is the one defined by the fourth field of the /etc/passwd file. The **id** utility shows information about the user, including all the groups of which the user is a member:

```
$ id
uid=501(edulaney) gid=100(users) groups=100(users),101(sales)
$
```

To change groups, use the **newgrp** utility with the name of the other group you want to make your default. Nongroup members trying to become a part of the group have to give a password, but group members do not:

```
$ id
uid=501(edulaney) gid=100(users) groups=100(users),101(sales)
$ newgrp sales
$ id
uid=501(edulaney) gid=101(sales) groups=100(users),101(sales)
$ newgrp marketing
Password: {Enter value}
$ id
uid=501(edulaney) gid=102(marketing) groups=100(users),
101(sales),102(marketing)
$
```

The **gpasswd -R** option prevents users from using **newgrp** and changing to a group that requires a password (a group for which they are not defined members):

```
$ gpasswd -R marketing
$ gpasswd -R sales
$ id
uid=501(edulaney) gid=100(users) groups=100(users),101(sales)
$ newgrp marketing
Password: {Enter value}
Sorry.
$ id
uid=501(edulaney) gid=100(users) groups=100(users),101(sales)
$ newgrp sales
uid=501(edulaney) gid=101(sales) groups=100(users),101(sales)
$
```

The **gpasswd -R** option does not apply to users who are members of the group, but only to those who must supply passwords to become members of the group.

Modifying Groups

After groups are created, you can modify their entries by manually editing the files using **gpasswd** or the **groupmod** utility. **groupmod** allows you to change values (name and GID) associated with the group in both the /etc/group and /etc/gshadow files. The two parameters you can use are:

- **-g**—Specifies a new GID.
- **-n**—Changes to a new text name.

Here's an example:

```
$ tail -1 /etc/group
sales:x:101:edulaney,kristen,kerby,martha
$ groupmod -g 105 sales
$ tail -1 /etc/group
sales:x:105:edulaney,kristen,kerby,martha
$ tail -1 /etc/shadow
sales:/aQ8k5kYaVcj6:walker:edulaney,kristen,kerby,martha
$
$ groupmod -n business sales
$ tail -1 /etc/group
business:x:105:edulaney,kristen,kerby,martha
$ tail -1 /etc/shadow
business:/aQ8k5kYaVcj6:walker:edulaney,kristen,kerby,martha
$
```

You can delete groups that are no longer needed by manually removing the lines from the files or by using the **groupdel** command. You cannot use the utility if any user indicates the group as his default group, and the utility removes the entry only from /etc/group. To remove entries from /etc/gshadow, you must run the **grpconv** utility again.

File and Directory Permissions

Permissions determine who can and cannot access files and directories, as well as what type of access they have. The first 10 characters of an **ls -l** listing of any entity resemble the following:

```
-rwxrwxrwx
```

The first character identifies the type of entity: - for a standard file, **d** for directory, **b** for a block device (such as a tape drive), **c** for a character device, **l** for a link, or **p** for a pipe. The remaining nine characters fit into three groups, as shown in Figure 8.1.

When a user attempts to access a file, the first check confirms whether she is the owner of the file. If she is, the first set of permissions applies to her. If she is not, a check then confirms whether she is a member of the group owning the file. If she is a member of the group, the middle set of permissions applies to her. If she is not the owner of the file, and not a member of the owning group, then the third set of permissions applies to her.

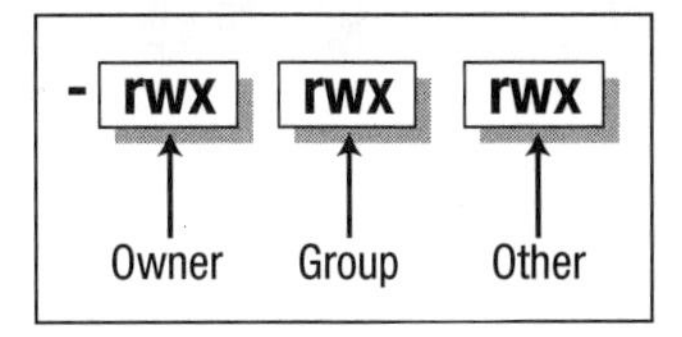

Figure 8.1 Permissions are shown divided into three sections.

Standard Permissions

The available permissions you can assign to an entity—owner, group, or other—are:

- **r**—Enables you to read a file. This is the only permission you need to copy a file as well. When applied to a directory, it grants the ability to read (see) the files within the directory.
- **w**—Enables you to write a file. Writing allows you to change the contents, modify, overwrite, and so on. When applied to a directory, it allows you to delete and move files within the directory (even if you don't specifically have write permission for an individual file).
- **x**—Executes the file if it contains scripts or can otherwise be run by the system. On a directory, it allows you to change to that directory. When applied in conjunction with read permissions on a directory, it allows you to search the directory.
- - (dash)—Indicates the absence of a permission. For example, **r-x** indicates that the user can read and execute but not write.

The 10 fields in the permissions are:

- The type of entity (file, directory, and so on)
- Whether the owner can read
- Whether the owner can write
- Whether the owner can execute
- Whether the group can read
- Whether the group can write
- Whether the group can execute
- Whether others (not the group or owner) can read
- Whether others can write
- Whether others can execute

Table 8.3 Symbolic permissions and their values.

Permission	Numeric Value
r	4
w	2
x	1
-	0

These permissions have numeric values as well, as shown in Table 8.3.

The numeric values make it possible to add permissions together and express them in an easy-to-understand way. For example, if a file grants a user the permissions **rwx**, the numeric value is 4(r)+2(w)+1(x)=7. The full set of permissions for the file can be computed as shown in Figure 8.2.

Table 8.4 extrapolates on the numerical conversion and outlines a few of the possible values for a file's permissions:

The default permissions for all newly created files are 666 (**rw-rw-rw-**) and directories are 777 (**rwxrwxrwx**). This number is altered, however, by the presence of a variable known as **umask**. The **umask** variable is equal to a number that is subtracted from the default permissions to arrive at the permissions that apply per user.

To see the value of **umask**, simply enter the command at a prompt:

```
$ umask
022
$
```

With a **umask** of 022, the permissions assigned to new files become 644 (**rw-r--r--**) and to directories 755 (**rwxr-xr-x**), as shown in Figure 8.3 (see page 194).

You can change the value of **umask** by specifying a different value on the command line (**umask 15**, for example), and this value is used for the session. The

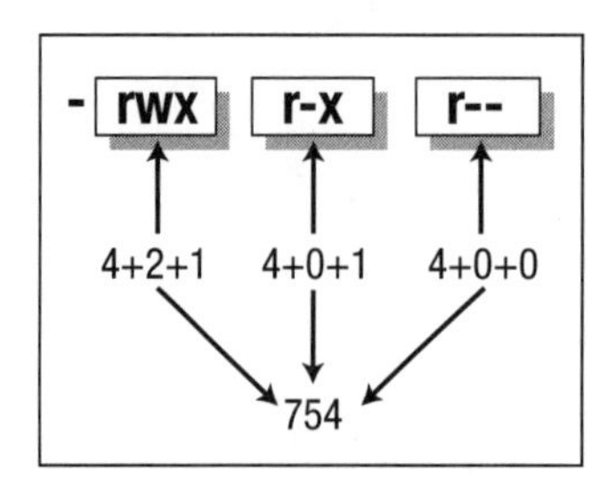

Figure 8.2 Numeric values are shown for the file's permissions.

Table 8.4 Examples of permission values.

Numerical Value	Permissions
1	--------x
2	-------w-
3	-------wx
4	------r--
5	------r-x
6	------rw-
7	------rwx
10	-----x---
11	-----x--x
22	----w--w-
33	----wx-wx
55	---r-xr-x
77	---rwxrwx
100	--x------
101	---x-----x
111	--x--x--x
222	-w--w--w-
311	-wx--x--x
322	-wx-w--w-
400	r--------
444	r--r--r--
511	r-x--x--x
544	r-xr--r--
644	rw-r--r--
666	rw-rw-rw-
755	rwxr-xr-x
777	rwxrwxrwx

variable is defined in the login information (discussed in Chapter 9) and reverts back to its normal value at the beginning of each session.

Changing Values

To change permissions on a file or directory, you can use the **chmod** utility. The arguments the utility accepts can be either numeric or symbolic. For example, to change the permissions of a file to allow all to read and write to it, enter the following:

Files:	Directories:
666 -rw-rw-rw-	777 drwxrwxrwx
-022 -----w--w-	-022 -----w--w-
644 -rw-r--r--	755 drwxr-xr-x

Figure 8.3 Computing default permissions are shown for newly created entities after subtracting the value of **umask**.

```
$ ls -l turbo
-rw-r--r--  1  root   root                          14  Sep 6 22:42  turbo
$ chmod 666 turbo
$ ls -l turbo
-rw-rw-rw-  1  root   root                          14  Sep 6 22:42  turbo
$
```

In symbolic format, **u** signifies user, **g** is group, and **o** is other. You can choose to add to existing permissions:

```
$ ls -l turbo
-rw-r--r--  1  root   root                          14  Sep 6 22:42  turbo
$ chmod go+w turbo
$ ls -l turbo
-rw-rw-rw-  1  root   root                          14  Sep 6 22:42  turbo
$
```

or specify exact permissions:

```
$ ls -l turbo
-rw-r--r--  1  root   root                          14  Sep 6 22:42  turbo
$ chmod ugo=rw turbo
$ ls -l turbo
-rw-rw-rw-  1  root   root                          14  Sep 6 22:42  turbo
$
```

You use the plus sign (+) to add to the existing permissions, but the minus sign (–) removes from existing permissions. The equal sign (=) ignores existing permissions and sets the value to whatever is specified. A **-c** option causes **chmod** to echo back the names of files that are changed, and **-f** cancels the display of any error messages.

In conjunction with **chmod**, the **chown** utility changes the owner of the entity. The syntax is:

```
chown {new user} {entity}
```

To change the owner of a file, the sequence is:

```
$ ls -l turbo
-rw-rw-rw-  1  root    root            14  Sep 6 22:42  turbo
$ chown edulaney turbo
$ ls -l turbo
-rw-rw-rw-  1  edulaney   root         14  Sep 6 22:42  turbo
$
```

Keep in mind the fact that changing the owner of a file does not change permissions or any other values, just as changing permissions does not change the owner, and so on.

If you are changing a directory, and you want to change recursively all the entities beneath, use the **-R** option.

A cousin of the other two utilities, **chgrp** changes the group associated with the entity. Once again, the **-R** option is available to change recursively all the files and subdirectories beneath a directory. The root user can make any group changes she wants; for a user to do so, however, he must be the owner of the file and belong to the group where he is making the change.

If you are the root user changing both the owner and group at the same time, you can use **chown** and separate the two values by a colon:

```
$ ls -l turbo
-rw-rw-rw-  1  edulaney   root         14  Sep 6 22:42  turbo
$ chown kristen:business turbo
$ ls -l turbo
-rw-rw-rw-  1  kristen    business     14  Sep 6 22:42  turbo
$
```

The command fails if either the owner or the group does not exist. You can also use **chown** to change only the group by using only the second part of the argument:

```
$ ls -l turbo
-rw-rw-rw-  1  kristen    business     14  Sep 6 22:42  turbo
$ chown :users turbo
$ ls -l turbo
-rw-rw-rw-  1  kristen    users        14  Sep 6 22:42  turbo
$
```

Special Permissions

You can use three special permissions in rare circumstances. Read, write, and execute always apply (or their absence is expressed), but sometimes you need to do more with a file or directory. The three special permissions are:

- Set user ID (SUID)
- Set group ID (SGID)
- Sticky bit

These are discussed in the following sections.

SUID

The Set user ID permission applies when you want a user to run an executable file that she normally cannot. For example, only the root user should be able to do function *xyz* (start backups, do restores, log in to other devices, and so on) because of the security ramifications, but you need the users to run a shell script to perform this action because you don't have time to do it personally.

You can create the shell script as root and set the SUID permission such that whoever runs the script becomes root only within the framework of that script. Before and after the script, she is merely a user, but the script runs as if being called by the root user.

The numerical permission of SUID, 4000, is added to the value of other permissions. When applied, it changes the **x** in the execute field for the owner's permission to an **s**:

```
$ ls -l turbo2
-rwxrwxrwx  1  root   root               542  Sep 9 20:02  turbo2
$ chmod 4777 turbo2
$ ls -l turbo2
-rwsrwxrwx  1  root   root               542  Sep 9 20:02  turbo2
$
```

Remember: The value of using this permission is that the process runs as the owner of the person who created it (root, in this case) and not as the person executing it. The same operation in symbolic format is:

```
chmod u+s turbo2
```

SGID

Similar in nature to SUID, the Set group ID permission applies when you need the person executing the file to be a member of the group owning the file (and not the owner). This changes the **x** in the group permission to an **s**, and the numerical value is 2000:

```
$ ls -l turbo2
-rwxrwxrwx  1  root   root            542  Sep 9 20:02  turbo2
$ chmod 2777 turbo2
$ ls -l turbo2
-rwxrwsrwx  1  root   root            542  Sep 9 20:02  turbo2
$
```

In symbolic syntax, the command is:

```
chmod g+s turbo2
```

Sticky Bit

This last permission does not work as the other special permissions do. With a numeric value of 1000, its operations differ when applied to a directory versus a file. When applied to a directory, it prevents users from deleting files from folders that grant them the write permission unless they are the owner of the file. By default, any user who has write permission to a directory can delete files within that directory even if he doesn't have write permission to that file.

When applied to a file, the file becomes "sticky." The first time the file is run or accessed, and loaded into memory, it stays loaded into memory or swap space so that it can run faster than it would if read from the drive.

If the file is not executable, the last permission bit (**x** for the other category) becomes **T**. If the file is an executable file, or the permission applies to a directory, the last bit becomes a **t**. When you apply the permission via **chmod** and symbolic letters, the **t** appears regardless of the type of entity being changed.

Utility Summation

This chapter discussed a plethora of utilities. Table 8.5 lists them and their purposes.

Associated Utilities

Several utilities serve minor purposes or provide information overlapping with other utilities listed in this chapter. Table 8.6 lists them for purposes of real-world knowledge and exam preparation.

Table 8.5 Utilities discussed in this chapter.

Utility	Purpose
passwd	Changes or sets the password for a user account.
useradd	Adds a new user to the system.
pwconv	Converts passwords into the shadow file.
pwunconv	Removes passwords from the shadow file and places in passwd.
su	Changes from one user account to another.
usermod	Modifies user variables.
chpasswd	Changes passwords with a batch file.
userdel	Removes user accounts.
groupadd	Adds a new group to the system.
gpasswd	Adds or modifies variables for an existing group.
grpconv	Converts passwords from the group file to gshadow.
grpunconv	Removes passwords from gshadow and places in group.
id	Shows user variables.
newgrp	Switches between default groups.
groupmod	Changes variables on an existing group.
groupdel	Removes a group from the system.
umask	Subtracts a numeric variable from the default permissions when creating new files and directories.
chmod	Changes an entity's permissions.
chgrp	Changes an entity's group association.
SUID	Sets the user ID when running a file.
SGID	Sets the group ID when running a file.
Sticky bit	Changes the operation of files and directories.

Table 8.6 Related utilities.

Utility	Purpose
adduser	Not available in all Linux implementations, this tool works similarly to **useradd**. It automatically looks for the first available UID and GID and creates the login, home directory, and mail directory for the user, as well as reminds you to set the password.
chfn	Changes "finger" information—text values about the user. The first field it changes is the descriptive field (fifth) of the /etc/passwd file.
chsh	Changes only the user's shell and no other variables. When used with the **-l** option, it lists valid shells on the system.
groups	Shows the groups a user belongs to.
grpck	Can be used to verify that /etc/group and gshadow are synced and correct.
pwck	Can be used to verify that /etc/passwd and shadow are correct.

Practice Questions

Question 1

Karen is adding seven new users to the system, and she wants to use the **useradd** utility. Where will the default come from for the minimum number of days new users can use the passwords?

- ❍ a. /etc/shadow
- ❍ b. /etc/group
- ❍ c. /etc/login.defs
- ❍ d. /etc/passwd

The correct answer to this question is c. The default values used by **useradd** utility come from login.defs. Answer a is incorrect because the shadow file holds encrypted passwords and not values used by **useradd**. Answer b is incorrect because the group file contains only group accounts, not user accounts. Answer d is incorrect because the password file gets values added to it by **useradd**, but does not affect the way the utility runs.

Question 2

Which of the following set of permissions is represented by the numeric value 44?

- ❍ a. **------rw-**
- ❍ b. **----rw----**
- ❍ c. **----r--r--**
- ❍ d. **-r--r-----**

The correct answer to this question is c. When the numerical value has fewer than four digits, you assume the leading digits are zeros, so 44 becomes 0044, and the permissions are ----r--r--. Answer a equals 6, answer b is 60, and answer d equals 440; therefore, they are all incorrect.

Question 3

You want to remove the encrypted passwords from the /etc/passwd file and create an /etc/shadow file that contains them. What command will you use to perform this? [Fill in the blank]

____

The correct answer to this question is:

```
pwconv
```

This creates the /etc/shadow file by taking entries from the /etc/passwd file.

Question 4

Which of the following represents a valid entry in the /etc/passwd file for a user account if the user's login name is brisco?

- ❍ a. **brisco:x:5:100:brisco:/home/brisco:/bin/bash**
- ❍ b. **brisco:x:5:100:brisco:/home/brisco:**
- ❍ c. **x:brisco:543:100:brisco:/home/brisco:/bin/bash**
- ❍ d. **brisco:x:543:100::/home/brisco:/bin/bash**

The correct answer to this question is d: The empty fifth field is the free-text description that is not needed. Answer a does not represent a "user" account with a UID of 5; such a low number is used by a system account and not a user account, so it is incorrect. Answer b is identical to answer a, except the last field (shell) has been left off, meaning that the default shell is used; the same low UID exists, so it is incorrect. Answer c reverses the first and second fields, so it too is incorrect.

Question 5

You want to manually create a new user account for a user by the name of "logan". This user will be a member of the "remote" group, and his password will be stored in the passwd file. Which of the following steps must you do to accomplish this? [Check all correct answers]

- ❑ a. Run the **pwconv** utility.
- ❑ b. Append an entry to the /etc/passwd file.
- ❑ c. Run the **passwd** utility.
- ❑ d. Append an entry to the /etc/shadow file.
- ❑ e. Create a home directory for logan.
- ❑ f. Change the home directory group to remote.
- ❑ g. Change the home directory owner to logan.

The correct answers to this question, in the order you will perform the tasks, are b, c, e, f, and g. You must be the root user to accomplish them. Answer a will move the password to the /etc/shadow file, so it is incorrect. Answer d is not necessary because the password will be stored in /etc/passwd; therefore, it is incorrect.

Question 6

Harold is an administrator for D. S. Technical. He usually logs on as a regular user (UID 157), but this morning he had to solve problems with backups and thus logged on as root (UID 0). While a process ran in the background, he used the command **su harold** to finish some other tasks. Mary knocks on his door and reports that because she didn't change her password before it expired, her account has been disabled. He types **su**. Given this scenario, what user will he become with this command?

- ❍ a. root
- ❍ b. harold
- ❍ c. mary
- ❍ d. He will be logged out.

The correct answer to this question is a. No matter how convoluted the scenario, any time you use the command **su** without a username, you become the root user. He is already Harold (choice b), but could become so again with the command **su harold**, or he could become mary (choice c) with the command **su mary**. He will not be logged out (choice d) unless he uses the **exit** command or something similar.

Question 7

What will be the permissions on the executable file "portable" when you use **chmod** with the numerical value 1777?

❍ a. **-rwsrwxrwx**

❍ b. **-rwxrwsrwx**

❍ c. **-rwxrwxrwt**

❍ d. **-rwxrwxtwT**

The correct answer to this question is c. Because the file is executable, the last bit becomes a **t**. Answer a represents a value of 4777, so it is incorrect. Answer b represents 2777, so it is incorrect. Answer d has a last bit of T, which indicates the file is not executable; therefore, it too is incorrect.

Question 8

Martin needs to perform some administrative tasks. Which option can he use with the **usermod** utility to change the login name for a user?

❍ a. **-c**

❍ b. **-l**

❍ c. **-p**

❍ d. **-s**

The correct answer to this question is b. The **-l** option will change the login name. Answer a, the **-c** option, will change the descriptive text; answer c, the **-p** option, will change the password; and answer d, the **-s** option, will change the shell.

Question 9

Which of the following commands will change the group of the file "purchase" to "orderlies"?

- ❍ a. **gpasswd -a purchase orderlies**
- ❍ b. **chgrp purchase orderlies**
- ❍ c. **groupmod purchase orderlies**
- ❍ d. **chown orderlies purchase**

The correct answer to this question is d, because the **chown** command is used to change the ownership of files. Answer a will add a user—purchase—to the group orderlies, so it is incorrect. Answer b reverses the two variables in its syntax; therefore, it is incorrect. Answer c will not work as given—**groupmod** is used to change only GID (-**g**) or text name (-**n**)—so it is incorrect.

Question 10

Which command can you use to change all passwords on the system as part of a batch process?

- ❍ a. **passwd**
- ❍ b. **chpasswd**
- ❍ c. **usermod -p**
- ❍ d. **useradd**

The correct answer to this question is b, because **chpasswd** is a batch file program that can change multiple passwords. Answers a and c will change passwords one at a time, and answer d will create users but not change them once they exist.

Need to Know More?

Siever, Ellen, and Stephen Spainhour, et al. *Linux in a Nutshell, 3rd Edition*. Sebastopol, CA: O'Reilly & Associates, 2000. ISBN: 0-59600-025-1. Chapter 3 contains an alphabetic listing of Linux utilities.

Welsh, Matt, and Matthias Kalle Dalheimer, et al. *Running Linux, 3rd Edition*. Sebastopol, CA: O'Reilly & Associates, 1999. ISBN: 1-56592-469-X. Chapter 4 covers basic commands and concepts.

www.tml.hut.fi/~viu/linux/sag/sag-06.2.html/index.html is the *Linux System Administrator's Guide*. Chapter 9 covers the management of user accounts, including how to create and delete a user.

http://wire.xenitec.on.ca:457/OSAdminG/ssC.suid_sgid.html provides a look at SUID and SGID bits and security.

http://wire.xenitec.on.ca:457/OSAdminG/ssC.bitclearing.html describes SUID, SGID, and sticky-bit clearing on writes.

9

Booting Linux

Terms you'll need to understand:

- ✓ Runlevel
- ✓ **init**
- ✓ **telinit**
- ✓ **shutdown**
- ✓ **halt**
- ✓ **reboot**
- ✓ **poweroff**
- ✓ LILO and **lilo**
- ✓ **dmesg**
- ✓ **last**

Techniques you'll need to master:

- ✓ Understanding the Linux boot process
- ✓ Comprehending which files are necessary for Linux to boot
- ✓ Recognizing the steps that take place when a user logs on

In this chapter, you'll learn about the boot process employed by Linux. I first address a number of key files and concepts and then put the items together to walk through the entire boot. You will also see the steps involved when a user logs on to the system, and thus you'll see the full cycle from boot to daily operation.

Understanding Runlevels

Before diving into booting the system, it is important to understand the concept of runlevels. Many operating systems have only two runlevels—functioning and off (halted). Linux, however, has seven different levels of functionality, as shown in Table 9.1.

At level 0, the system is in a *shutdown* state requiring a manual reboot. This can be called a *halt*, or *powerdown*, as well as a shutdown. When you change to this level, files are synchronized with the disk, and the system is left in a state where it is safe to power it off.

Level 1, also known as *administrative mode*, puts the system in single-user mode. This allows only one user (traditionally the root user) to access the system and prevents anyone else from getting in. Often, it restricts the login to only one terminal as well: that defined as the console. This is the level you use when rebuilding the kernel and performing similar tasks.

Level 2 is *multiple-user mode*—allowing more than one user to log in at a time. At this level, background processes (daemons) start up and additional filesystems (root is always mounted), if present, are mounted. Network File System (NFS) is not running.

Level 3, also known as *network mode*, is exactly the same as level 2, only with networking, or NFS, enabled.

Level 4 is left to each vendor to define.

Table 9.1 Linux system runlevels.

Runlevel	Purpose
0	The system is down.
1	Only one user permitted.
2	Multiple users permitted, but without NFS.
3	Multiple users and NFS.
4	Differs per implementation.
5	The X environment.
6	Shut down and reboot.

Level 5 is also known as a *hardware state*. The command prompt is available, and users are allowed to log in and out of the X environment.

Level 6 represents a *shutdown and automatic reboot:* the same result as changing to runlevel 0 and then rebooting the machine. It can be called a "warm boot" because power is never removed from the components; runlevel 0 represents a "cold boot" because power must be turned off and then restored.

An easy way to summarize the runlevels is that 2, 3, and 5 are operational states of the computer; it is up and running, and users are allowed to conduct business. All other runlevels involve some sort of maintenance or shutdown operation, preventing users from processing; the exception is level 4, which differs across implementations.

Typing the command **runlevel** at a prompt shows two values: the previous runlevel and the current runlevel:

```
$ runlevel
N 5
$
```

In this case, the current runlevel is 5, and the **N** means there is no previous level (None). These values are derived from the /var/run/utmp log file, which keeps track of all changes. If this file is corrupt, or the values cannot be found within it, the only value returned is **unknown**.

Changing Runlevels

You can use two commands to change the runlevel of a machine: **shutdown** and **init**. In reality, the **shutdown** command is nothing more than an interface to **init**, offering a few friendly features.

The **init** utility resides in the /sbin directory and must be followed by a number (0 through 6) or the letters **S** or **s**. The numbers identify which runlevel to change to, and the **S** and **s** signify single-user mode. (**S** allows only root, but **s** does not care which single user.) To change to runlevel 2, the command is:

```
init 2
```

The **telinit** utility works the same as **init**, and, for exam purposes, can be used in its place. In reality, it is but a link to **init**.

The **shutdown** utility offers a few more options. It informs all users currently logged in that the system is changing state and allows a time (delay) to be specified before the change takes place. Options that work with the utility are:

- -F—Forces **fsck** to run after the reboot (the default).
- -f—Prevents **fsck** from running after the reboot, thus creating a fast reboot.
- -h—Halts after shutdown (level 0).
- -k—Sends out a warning to all users but does not really change state.
- -r—Reboots after shutdown (level 6).
- -t—Specifies the number of seconds before the change begins.

If no parameters are specified, the default runlevel that **shutdown** attempts is level 0. An example of using the utility is:

```
$ shutdown -h -t3 now
```

This forces a change to runlevel 0 (**-h**) three seconds (**-t**) from the current time (**now**). Notice that you must always specify a time. If any text follows the time, it is interpreted as the warning message to send to users. You can also notify users by using the **write** command to send a message to individual users or by using **wall** to write to all users and tell them of the upcoming shutdown.

Finally, if you want to stop a shutdown after you have summoned it, but before it has begun, you can call **shutdown** once more with the -c (cancel) option.

By default, only the root user can run **shutdown**. You can create a file in the /etc directory named "shutdown.allow" to list other users you want to be able to run the command.

Three minor utilities exist as links to the **shutdown** utility:

- **halt**—Implements **shutdown -h**.
- **reboot**—Implements **shutdown -r**.
- **poweroff**—The same as **halt**.

Regardless of which command you use to shut down the system, you must use one of them to halt processes and close files properly. If you do not shut down the system properly, the filesystem has a strong chance of becoming corrupted.

The inittab File

The main file for determining what takes place at different runlevels is the /etc/inittab (initialization table) file. This text file is colon-delimited and divided into four fields. The first field is a short ID, and the second identifies the runlevel at which the action is to take place (blank means all). The third field is the action to take place, and the last field is the command to execute.

The following file is representative of what every inittab file looks like, although this one comes from Caldera OpenLinux. I added numbering to the beginning of each line to facilitate easier discussion following the listing.

```
1   #
2   # inittab This file describes how the INIT process should
3   # set up the system in a certain runlevel.
4   #
5   # Author: Miquel van Smoorenburg,
      #         <miquels@drinkel.nl.mugnet.org>
6   # Modified for RHS Linux by Marc Ewing
      # and Donnie Barnes
7   # Modified for COL by Raymund Will
8   #

9   # The runlevels used by COL are:
10  #   0 - halt (Do NOT set initdefault to this)
11
12  #   1 - Single user mode (including initialisation of
    #       network interfaces, if you do have networking)
13  #   2 - Multiuser, (without NFS-Server und some such)
14  #       (basically the same as 3, if you do not have
    #       networking)
15  #   3 - Full multiuser mode
16  #   4 - unused
17  #       (should be equal to 3, for now)
18  #   5 - X11
19  #   6 - reboot (Do NOT set initdefault to this)

20  #
21  # Default runlevel.
22  id:5:initdefault:

23  # System initialization.
24  s0::sysinit:/bin/bash -c 'C=/sbin/booterd; [ -x $C ] && $C'
25  si::sysinit:/bin/bash -c 'C=/etc/rc.d/rc.modules;
       [ -x $C ] && $C default'
```

```
26  s2::sysinit:/bin/bash -c 'C=/etc/rc.d/rc.serial;
       [ -x $C ] && $C'
27  bw::bootwait:/etc/rc.d/rc.boot

28  # What to do in single-user mode.
29  ~1:S:wait:/etc/rc.d/rc 1
30  ~~:S:wait:/sbin/sulogin

31  l0:0:wait:/etc/rc.d/rc 0
32  l1:1:wait:/etc/rc.d/rc 1
33  l2:2:wait:/etc/rc.d/rc 2
34  l3:3:wait:/etc/rc.d/rc 3
35  l4:4:wait:/etc/rc.d/rc 4
36  l5:5:wait:/etc/rc.d/rc 5
37  l6:6:wait:/etc/rc.d/rc 6
38  # Normally not reached, but fallthrough in case of emergency.
39  z6:6:respawn:/sbin/sulogin

40  # Trap CTRL-ALT-DELETE
41  ca:12345:ctrlaltdel:/sbin/shutdown -t3 -r now

42  # Action on special keypress (ALT-UpArrow).
43  kb::kbrequest:/bin/echo "Keyboard Request—edit
       /etc/inittab to let this work."

44  # When our UPS tells us power has failed, assume we have
45  # a few minutes of power left. Schedule a shutdown for 2
46  # minutes from now. This does, of course, assume you have
47  # power installed and your UPS connected and working
       correctly.
48  pf::powerfail:/sbin/shutdown -h +5 "Power Failure;
       System Shutting Down"

49  # If battery is fading fast — we hurry...
50  p1::powerfailnow:/sbin/shutdown -c 2> /dev/null
51  p2::powerfailnow:/sbin/shutdown -h now "Battery Low..."

52  # If power was restored before the shutdown kicked in,
       # cancel it.
53  po:12345:powerokwait:/sbin/shutdown -c "Power Restored;
       Shutdown Cancelled"


54  # Run gettys in standard runlevels
55  1:12345:respawn:/sbin/getty tty1 VC linux
56  2:2345:respawn:/sbin/getty tty2 VC linux
```

```
57  3:2345:respawn:/sbin/getty tty3 VC linux
58  4:2345:respawn:/sbin/getty tty4 VC linux
59  5:2345:respawn:/sbin/getty tty5 VC linux
60  6:2345:respawn:/sbin/getty tty6 VC linux

61  # Run kdm in runlevel 5
62  gu:5:respawn:/bin/sh -c 'C=/etc/rc.d/rc.gui;[ -x $C ]&&$C;
       [ -x $C ]||init 3'
```

Line 22 is very important because it identifies the default runlevel the system initially attempts after each boot. Lines 31 through 37 identify that at each runlevel, the shell script **rc** (beneath /etc/rc.d) is to run—using a different variable for each level. What this script does is look for other scripts within subdirectories of /etc/rc.d based on the runlevel—in /etc/rc.d/rc0.d, /etc/rc.d/rc1.d, and so on. Within those subdirectories are script files that start with either an **S** or a **K**. Scripts that start with **K** identify processes or daemons that must be killed when changing to this runlevel, and scripts starting with **S** identify processes or daemons that must be started when changing to this runlevel.

Line 41 prevents Ctrl+Alt+Del from being an active keyboard sequence and runs for runlevels 1 through 5. Line 62 fires up the graphical user interface (GUI) in runlevel 5. Lines 55 through 60 start the terminals to allow for login. Notice that tty1 (line 55) works with runlevels 1 through 5, but the other terminals are accessible only in runlevels 2 through 5. If the terminals get killed off, they are started back again thanks to the action of **respawn**. Other actions that can be specified are:

- **boot**—Runs at boot time.
- **bootwait**—Runs at boot time and prevents other processes until finished.
- **kbrequest**—Sends a request for keyboard action or inaction.
- **off**—Doesn't run the command.
- **once**—Runs the command only once.
- **ondemand**—Same as **respawn**.
- **powerfail**—Runs in the event of a power-failure signal.
- **powerokwait**—Waits until the power is back on before continuing.
- **sysinit**—Runs before any users can log on.
- **wait**—Allows completion before continuing.

The **init** daemon is responsible for carrying out changes in relation to runlevels. This daemon is summoned by the **init** utility. (Remember, the **init** utility is also called by **telinit** and **shutdown**.)

The **init** daemon is one of the first services to come alive upon a boot, and it reads and executes entries in the /etc/inittab file. After it finishes, the **init** daemon stays active and respawns any processes that are supposed to run but die off, as well as interacts with the log files (utmp and wtmp beneath /var or /etc).

If you modify the /etc/inittab file, the changes you make are not active until the system reboots or you run the command:

```
init q
```

Enter LILO

All of the details given so far in this chapter (runlevels, inittab, and so on) remain the same for Unix and Linux. Linux differs from Unix, however, in that it also has the Linux Loader (LILO). LILO allows Linux to coexist on your machine with other operating systems: Up to 16 images can be swapped back and forth to designate what operating system is loaded on the next boot.

By default, LILO boots the default operating system each time, but you can enter the name of another operating system at the boot: Prompt or force the prompt to appear by pressing Shift, Ctrl, or Alt during the boot sequence. Entering a question mark (or pressing Tab) shows the available operating systems as defined in the /etc/lilo.conf file: This text file can range from simple to complex based on the number of operating systems you have. An example follows of the file with only one operating system (Linux) (with numbering added to facilitate discussion):

```
1   #
2   # /etc/lilo.conf - generated by Lizard
3   #

4   # target

5   boot = /dev/hda1
6   install = /boot/boot.b

7   # options

8   prompt
9   delay = 50
10  timeout = 50
11  message = /boot/message

12  default = linux
```

```
13  image = /boot/vmlinuz-pc97-2.2.10-modular
14  label  = linux
15  root   = /dev/hda1
16  vga    = 274
17  read-only
18  append = "debug=2 noapic nosmp"
```

Line 5 identifies the partition to boot from, and line 6 specifies the boot sector file. Lines 8 through 12 identify the default, defined as **linux**, and **prompt** and **timeout** both have values of 50 deciseconds: You must press Shift or another key within this time period or LILO begins loading the default. Line 13 specifies the name of the kernel, line 14 identifies its label, and line 16 names the root partition. The remaining lines identify the type of file system and so on.

You can make changes to the file that are active when you run /sbin/lilo. Different options you can use with the **lilo** command are:

- **-b**—Specifies the boot device.
- **-C**—Uses a different configuration file.
- **-D**—Uses a kernel with a specified name.
- **-d**—Specifies how long the wait should be in deciseconds.
- **-I**—Prompts for the kernel path.
- **-i**—Specifies the file boot sector.
- **-m**—Specifies the name of the map file to use.
- **-q**—Lists the names of the kernels (which are held in the /boot/map file).
- **-R**—Sets as a default for the next reboot.
- **-S**—Allows you to overwrite the existing file.
- **-s**—Tells LILO where to store the old boot sector.
- **-t**—Tests the running of LILO without changing anything.
- **-u**—Uninstalls LILO.
- **-v**—Changes to verbose mode.

Related Boot Files and Utilities

You should be aware of a few other files and utilities before walking through a boot. The first of these is the **dmesg** utility, which allows you to display bootup messages generated from LILO (in /var/log/messages). By default, when you type in **dmesg**, the messages are displayed on your screen. If you encounter a problem, however, and you want to save the messages for troubleshooting purposes, you can use the command:

```
dmesg > {filename}
```

It generates a file similar to the following:

```
Linux version 2.2.10 (root@tuvok.calderasystems.com)
   (gcc version egcs-2.91.66 19990314 (egcs-1.1.2 release)) _
#1 SMP Tue Aug 10 19:01:45 MDT 1999
mapped APIC to ffffe000 (0024f000)
mapped IOAPIC to ffffd000 (00250000)
Detected 150004465 Hz processor.
Console: colour VGA+ 80x30
Calibrating delay loop... 299.01 BogoMIPS
Memory: 30692k/32768k available (920k kernel code,
   416k reserved, 652k data, 88k init)
VFS: Diskquotas version dquot_6.4.0 initialized
Checking 386/387 coupling... OK, FPU using exception
   16 error reporting
Checking 'hlt' instruction... OK.
Intel Pentium with F0 0F bug - workaround enabled.
POSIX conformance testing by UNIFIX
per-CPU timeslice cutoff: 1.56 usecs.
CPU0: Intel Pentium MMX stepping 04
SMP motherboard not detected. Using dummy APIC emulation.
PCI: PCI BIOS revision 2.10 entry at 0xf0200
PCI: Using configuration type 1
PCI: Probing PCI hardware
Linux NET4.0 for Linux 2.2
Based upon Swansea University Computer Society NET3.039
NET4: Unix domain sockets 1.0 for Linux NET4.0.
NET4: Linux TCP/IP 1.0 for NET4.0
IP Protocols: ICMP, UDP, TCP, IGMP
Initializing RT netlink socket
Starting kswapd v 1.5
vesafb: framebuffer at 0x000a0000, mapped to 0xc00a0000,
   size 128k
vesafb: mode is 640x480x4, linelength=80, pages=50719
vesafb: scrolling: redraw
Console: switching to colour frame buffer device 80x30
fb0: VESA VGA frame buffer device
Detected PS/2 Mouse Port.
Serial driver version 4.27 with no serial options enabled
ttyS00 at 0x03f8 (irq = 4) is a 16550A
```

```
pty: 256 Unix98 ptys configured
Real Time Clock Driver v1.09
RAM disk driver initialized:  16 RAM disks of 4096K size
PCI_IDE: unknown IDE controller on PCI bus 00 device 11,
   VID=10b9, DID=5219
PCI_IDE: not 100% native mode: will probe irqs later
PCI_IDE: simplex device:  DMA disabled
ide0: PCI_IDE Bus-Master DMA disabled (BIOS)
PCI_IDE: simplex device:  DMA disabled
ide1: PCI_IDE Bus-Master DMA disabled (BIOS)
hda: IBM-DTNA-22160, ATA DISK drive
hdc: UJDCD8730, ATAPI CDROM drive
ide0 at 0x1f0-0x1f7,0x3f6 on irq 14
ide1 at 0x170-0x177,0x376 on irq 15
hda: IBM-DTNA-22160, 2067MB w/96kB Cache, CHS=525/128/63
hdc: ATAPI 8X CD-ROM drive, 128kB Cache
Uniform CDROM driver Revision: 2.55
Floppy drive(s): fd0 is 1.44M
FDC 0 is a National Semiconductor PC87306
md driver 0.90.0 MAX_MD_DEVS=256, MAX_REAL=12
raid5: measuring checksumming speed
raid5: MMX detected, trying high-speed MMX checksum routines
pII_mmx   :   229.362 MB/sec
p5_mmx    :   275.844 MB/sec
8regs     :   112.776 MB/sec
32regs    :    76.200 MB/sec
using fastest function: p5_mmx (275.844 MB/sec)
md.c: sizeof(mdp_super_t) = 4096
Partition check:
hda: hda1 hda2
VFS: Mounted root (ext2 filesystem) readonly.
Freeing unused kernel memory: 88k freed
parport0: PC-style at 0x378 [SPP,PS2]
Linux PCMCIA Card Services 3.0.14
kernel build: 2.2.10 #1 SMP Thu Aug 5 20:42:02 MDT 1999
options:  [pci] [cardbus]
Intel PCIC probe:
TI 1131 PCI-to-CardBus at bus 0 slot 4, mem 0x68000000,
   2 sockets
host opts [0]: [isa irq] [no pci irq] [lat 32/176] [bus 32/34]
host opts [1]: [isa irq] [no pci irq] [lat 32/176] [bus 35/37]
ISA irqs (scanned) = 5,7,10,11,12 status change on irq 11
cs: IO port probe 0x1000-0x17ff: clean.
cs: IO port probe 0x0100-0x04ff: excluding 0x178-0x17f
   0x378-0x37f 0x408-0x40f 0x480-0x48f 0x4d0-0x4d7
cs: IO port probe 0x0a00-0x0aff: clean.
VFS: Disk change detected on device fd(2,0)
```

Notice the order of operations as the system comes up. Other files to be aware of are:

- /var/log/messages
- /etc/conf.modules
- /etc/modules.conf
- utmp
- wtmp

cron and other processes write to the first file, messages, which can be useful in troubleshooting problems. Some of the contents of this file are displayed by the **dmesg** command. The second and third files are one and the same but differ according to the vendor. (Some systems use conf.modules, and others use modules.conf.) The purpose of this file is to hold information used by the kernel to identify the machine. The file is a C++ source file and usually not accessed by administrators unless corruption has occurred.

I mentioned the utmp and wtmp files earlier in the chapter. They are log files that are counterparts of each other and exist in either /etc or elsewhere. If elsewhere, then utmp is beneath /var/run and wtmp is beneath /var/log. By default, when the system starts, entries are written to utmp; when the system is properly shutdown, entries are written to wtmp.

You can use the **last** command to look at the most recent entries in wtmp—showing users and system state changes:

```
$ last
root     pts/0                    Mon Oct  9 14:58   still logged in
root     :0                       Mon Oct  9 14:21   still logged in
reboot   system boot  2.2.10      Mon Oct  9 14:15           (03:01)
root     pts/1                    Mon Oct  9 11:35 - down    (02:15)
root     pts/0                    Mon Oct  9 11:35 - down    (02:15)
root     :0                       Mon Oct  9 11:34 - down    (02:16)
reboot   system boot  2.2.10      Mon Oct  9 11:33           (02:16)
root     pts/0                    Tue Oct  3 11:18 - crash (6+00:15)
root     :0                       Mon Oct  2 16:31 - 11:28 (6+18:56)
reboot   system boot  2.2.10      Mon Oct  2 16:23         (6+21:26)
root     :0                       Mon Sep 25 16:32 - 17:20  (00:48)
reboot   system boot  2.2.10      Mon Sep 25 16:29           (00:51)
root     :0                       Mon Sep 25 16:18 - 16:25  (00:06)
reboot   system boot  2.2.10      Mon Sep 25 16:06           (00:18)

wtmp begins Mon Sep 25 16:06:45 2000
```

Putting It All Together

Having looked at different elements of the boot, you can put it all together and run through the steps of a boot from start to finish:

1. When any machine starts, it first performs a POST (Power-on self test) to verify that all is internally present that should be. This occurs regardless of operating system.

2. The boot loader for the operating system begins. With Linux, that is LILO. By default, it waits 50 deciseconds (5 seconds) for you to press a key and identify another operating system you want to boot. If you don't press any key, the default of Linux is loaded.

3. The kernel is loaded from the hard drive, floppy drive, or other specified location into memory. By default, it is located within the /boot directory and exists in compressed state: As it loads into memory, it uncompresses.

4. The kernel is booted, and messages are written to /var/log/messages.

5. The system loads modules, default, and other from /etc/modules.conf or /etc/conf.modules.

6. The kernel passes control to the **init** daemon, which begins reading the /etc/inittab file. Because of this, the **init** daemon always has a process ID of 1 and is the parent of many other daemons.

7. Normally, a check of the filesystem (**fsck**) is carried out, and the local filesystem is mounted. Other operations can include mounting remote filesystems and cleaning up temporary files.

8. The system begins changing to the runlevel specified by the initdefault parameter. In so doing, it runs scripts beneath the /etc/rc.d directory and usually starts other processes or daemons, such as a print server, **cron**, **sendmail**, and so on.

9. The terminals become active for login (getty has initiated), and the boot process is finished.

Enter the User

After the system is up, the user can use it. The **init** daemon has started a getty process for each terminal, telling it to listen for a connection. If you run **ps -ef**, you see a getty process running on each terminal that can log in and that does not currently have a user using it. The program responsible for printing the login prompt is the command **getty** ("get a tty"). **getty** prompts for the user's login name.

I discussed this login name, which is assigned by the system administrator, in Chapter 6. Most often, the login name is the user's initials, first name, last name, or some variation. The username is considered a known entity for anyone wanting to send a message to or interact with the user, and it also appears in directory listings as the owner of files and directories.

Once the user enters a login name, getty spawns, or starts, the /bin/login utility. The **login** utility prompts the user to enter his or her password. The user enters the password (which does not display on the screen for security reasons). If the user enters the password incorrectly, the system responds with a generic message stating that the login is incorrect.

The **login** command accepts the password entered by the user and encrypts it using the same mechanism used by the **passwd** command to put the password in the /etc/passwd file. If the encrypted values match, the password is correct. Otherwise, the password entered by the user is incorrect. The **login** command cannot decrypt the password once it has been encrypted. When the password is entered properly, the next phase of the system files (utmp/wtmp) is updated.

The system runs the /etc/profile shell script to set up variables for all users, and then the user is moved to his home directory and his login shell (as specified in the /etc/passwd file) is invoked. If customization files appear within the home directory (such as .profile for bash or .login for C shell), they are executed next; the user's initial environment is configured, and the shell starts executing.

Utility Summation

This chapter discussed only a handful of utilities. Table 9.2 lists them and their purposes.

Table 9.2 Utilities discussed in this chapter.

Utility	Purpose
runlevel	Shows the current runlevel of the system.
init	Changes the runlevel.
telinit	Same as **init**.
shutdown	An interface to **init** with more options.
halt, **poweroff**, and **reboot**	An interface to **shutdown**.
lilo	Configures the Linux Loader.
dmesg	Displays the LILO messages.
last	Views the most recent entries in the wtmp file.

Practice Questions

Question 1

In what directory does the inittab file reside?

❍ a. /bin

❍ b. /dev

❍ c. /var

❍ d. /etc

The correct answer to this question is d. The initialization table must exist beneath the /etc directory to be used by the system. Answer a is incorrect because this directory stores binary files. Answer b is incorrect because this directory holds device definitions. And answer c is incorrect because this directory holds log files and other varying data.

Question 2

How many fields does each entry of the inittab file have?

❍ a. Two

❍ b. Three

❍ c. Four

❍ d. Five

❍ e. Six

❍ f. Seven

The correct answer to this question is c. Each entry must have four fields. The first field is a unique identifier for the entry. The second field is the runlevel at which the job will run. The third field identifies the action associated with the job, and the fourth field contains the process itself.

Question 3

Marco has just finished editing the inittab file and adding new entries to **respawn**. He does not want to shut down the system but wants the processes to begin immediately. What command must he enter for the new inittab file to be read and active? [Fill in the blank]

____

The correct answer to this question is:

```
init q
```

This will force the file to be reread and all lines within it activated for the current runlevel.

Question 4

Sandra wants to tune network parameters on the system and restrict access to local users while she is doing so. Which runlevel should she use that will allow for multiple users on the system and will not allow for NFS to be active?

- ❍ a. 1
- ❍ b. 2
- ❍ c. 3
- ❍ d. 5

The correct answer to this question is b. Runlevel 2 allows for multiple user mode without NFS. Answer a allows only one user at runlevel 1, so it is incorrect. NFS is active with runlevel 3, so answer c is incorrect. Answer d allows for the use of the X environment, so it is incorrect.

Question 5

Which runlevel is equivalent to performing a cold boot?

❍ a. 0

❍ b. 1

❍ c. 5

❍ d. 6

The correct answer to this question is a. When you change to runlevel 0, the system is completely halted and shut down. You must power-off and power-on to start the system again (boot cold). Answer b does not involve shutting down the system, so it is incorrect. Answer c does not involve shutting down the system, so it is also incorrect. Answer d (runlevel 6) is a shutdown and automatic restart and thus equivalent to a warm boot; therefore, it is incorrect.

Question 6

Martin has just pleaded with your boss to be granted the ability to shut down his system. What is the best way for you to accomplish this without affecting other operations?

❍ a. Make the /sbin/shutdown utility available to him.

❍ b. Make him a member of the root group.

❍ c. Add him to /sbin/shutdown.allow.

❍ d. Create /etc/shutdown.allow.

The correct answer to this question is d. The shutdown.allow file does not exist by default, so you must create it in /etc and add Martin. With answer a, the **shutdown** utility is available to everyone but can only be run by root by default. Answer b makes him a member of root, which opens the door to many other problems. And answer c has the needed file beneath the wrong directory.

Question 7

You want all users of the system to have the variable **OFFICE** set to **ANDERSON** when they log in. Where should you place this variable?

❍ a. .profile

❍ b. getty

❍ c. /etc/profile

❍ d. /bin/login

❍ e. ./etc/inittab

❍ f. /etc/modules.conf

The correct answer to this question is c. The /etc/profile script holds variables that apply to all users. In answer a, you place individual variables in individual home directories, which does not accomplish the task for all users, so it is incorrect. Answer b allows a screen to listen for a login, so it is incorrect. Answer d is where the action is passed during a logon and is a binary file, so it is incorrect. Answer e is a text file used by the **init** daemon to initialize the system—not for holding variables—so it is incorrect. Answer f identifies system modules to be loaded during boot of the system and does not hold values for users, so it is incorrect.

Question 8

Which option can you use with the **shutdown** command to force the system to come up more quickly than it normally does?

❍ a. **-f**

❍ b. **-F**

❍ c. **-q**

❍ d. **-x**

The correct answer to this question is a. The **-f** option will prevent **fsck** from running and will save time during the reboot. Answer b forces **fsck** to run, which slows down the, down and answers c and d are options that do not exist for the **shutdown** command.

Question 9

Which action in the inittab file identifies the runlevel that the system will attempt on the next system boot?

❍ a. **boot**

❍ b. **wait**

❍ c. **initdefault**

❍ d. **sysinit**

The correct answer to this question is c. The **initdefault** action identifies the runlevel and the entry resembles:

```
id:5:initdefault:
```

Answer a identifies actions to occur at boot, so it is incorrect. Answer b specifies that booting should wait until these actions complete, so it is incorrect. Answer d identifies system processes to run at a particular runlevel before any users can log on, so it is incorrect.

Question 10

Which command will display the messages created by the last iteration of LILO?

❍ a. **dmesg**

❍ b. **last**

❍ c. **init**

❍ d. wtmp

The correct answer to this question is a—reading from /var/log/messages. Answer b displays entries for wtmp; answer c changes runlevels; and answer d is a file and not a command.

Need to Know More?

Hare, Chris, and George Eckel, et al. *Inside UNIX.* Indianapolis, IN: New Riders Publishing, 1994. ISBN: 1-56205-401-5. Chapter 24 addresses runlevels and the login process.

Leblanc, Dee-Ann. *General Linux I.* Scottsdale, AZ: The Coriolis Group, 2000. ISBN: 1-57610-567-9. Chapter 4 discusses booting, initialization, shutdown procedures, and runlevels.

http://judi.greens.org/lilo/ is the Unofficial Linux Loader user's mutual support page.

www.scc.com/mirrors/LDP/HOWTO/mini/LILO.html is the LILO mini-how-to, which describes how to boot, work with huge disks, and troubleshoot with a rescue floppy.

www.wwnet.com/~stevelim/booting.html discusses booting multiple operating systems with LILO.

Documentation

Terms you'll need to understand:

- ✓ **man**
- ✓ **whatis**
- ✓ **--help**
- ✓ **info**
- ✓ **whereis**
- ✓ **apropos**

Techniques you'll need to master:

- ✓ Understanding how to access local help
- ✓ Comprehending methods for writing documentation and providing support
- ✓ Recognizing the starting locations for finding resources on the Internet

In this chapter, you'll learn about the help utilities used to document utilities and features in Linux. You will also learn how to write documentation for your own system and how to provide support to users. Finally, I address resources outside the system and available over the Internet.

Using Local Documentation

A number of methods are available in all Linux implementations for finding help on the operation of utilities. Additionally, many vendors add their own documentation and utilities for simplifying the process. In this section, I describe the common utilities, namely:

- **man**
- **--help**
- **info**

The man Utility

The **man** (as in manual) utility dates back to the early days of Unix. Using whatever page utility is defined in the user's environmental variables for PAGER, it displays document files found in the /usr/man subdirectories. The PAGER variable is usually equal to **less** or **more**.

On some systems, **PAGER** can be **MANPAGER**. Other variables are available, but not needed, including **MANPATH** (the location of the manual files), **MANSECT** (defining the sections of the pages), and **MANWIDTH**.

The directories beneath /usr/man, and their purposes, include those shown in Table 10.1.

Table 10.1 Subdirectories for man files.

Subdirectory	Descriptions Contained Within
man1	Shell utilities and user commands
man2	System calls
man3	libc calls
man4	/dev descriptions
man5	/etc and other configurable files (such as protocols)
man6	Games
man7	Linux system files, conventions, and so forth
man8	root user/system administration utilities

When you enter the command to display a manual page (**man**), the subdirectories in Table 10.1 are searched until the first match is found. For example, if you enter the command:

```
man nice
```

the directories are searched until the first match of a manual page describing the **nice** utility is found. Linux displays the manual page using the utility specified by the **PAGER** variable. An example of the output follows (with line numbering added to aid the discussion):

```
1    NICE(1)                                                    NICE(1)
2
3
4    NAME
5         nice - run a program with modified scheduling priority
6
7    SYNOPSIS
8      nice  [-n  adjustment] [-adjustment] [—adjustment=adjust_
9       ment] [—help] [—version] [command [arg...]]
10
11   DESCRIPTION
12     This documentation is no longer being maintained and may
13     be inaccurate or incomplete. The Texinfo documentation is
14     now the authoritative source.
15
16     This manual page documents the GNU version of nice. Note
17     that most shells have a built-in command by the same name
18     and with similar functionality.
19
20     If no arguments are given, nice prints the current
21     scheduling priority, which it inherited. Otherwise, nice
22     runs the given command with its scheduling priority
23     adjusted. If no adjustment is given, the priority of the
24     command is incremented by 10. The superuser can specify a
25     negative adjustment. The priority can be adjusted by nice
26     over the range of -20 (the highest priority) to 19 (the
27     lowest).
28
29   OPTIONS
30     -n adjustment, -adjustment, —adjustment=adjustment
31          Add adjustment instead of 10 to the command's pri_
32          ority.
33
34     —help Print a usage message on standard output and exit
35          successfully.
```

```
36
37      —version
38          Print version information on standard output then
39          exit successfully.
40
41
..
66 FSF                          GNU Shell Utilities                    1
```

The **nice** utility does not have a great deal to it, which makes it a good choice for dissecting as an example of the output available from **man**. Using the **more** or **less** utilities to display the page (whichever is defined by the **PAGER** variable), you can move through the documentation in a number of ways after the first screen appears, as shown in Table 10.2.

Examining the actual display: Line 1 gives the name of the utility, and the parentheses identify what subdirectory the documentation is coming from. In this case, the **1** indicates it is a shell utility or user command for which the documentation was found and displayed. If documentation is found for other entities named "nice", they are not displayed because the default action is to display only the first entity found.

To check for more than one set of documentation on the system by the same name, you can use the **whatis** command:

```
$ whatis nice
nice (1)     - run a program with modified scheduling priority
nice (2)     - change process priority
(END)    (press q}
$
```

In this case, another set of documentation for **nice** does appear under man2. The list displayed comes from a whatis database created with the **makewhatis** utility

Table 10.2 Keys to use with man.

Key Combination	Movement
Enter	Scroll down the next line.
Space	Scroll down the next page.
b	Scroll up to the previous page.
q	Quit.
/	Search for the first page containing specified text.

in /usr/sbin. To see the second set of documentation instead of the first, the command is:

```
man 2 nice
```

which specifies that you want the documentation for **nice** from the man2 directory. (You use **3** for man3, **4** for man4, and so on.)

Lines 4, 7, 11, and 29 of the manual file begin sections for Names, Synopsis, Description, and Options, respectively. Based upon the complexity of the utility and other features, you can also see sections for See Also, Diagnostics, Files, Bugs, and History. Occasionally, you might also see an Author section, but it is rare.

Line 5 is a short synopsis of what the utility does and matches the line returned by the **whatis** utility. Lines 8 and 9 describe the options you can use, and lines 30 through 41 provide more detail on the workings of each.

To conserve space, the manual files are stored in compressed format; each time you run one, however, the entry is written to /var/catman to allow the **man** utility to display the page more quickly the next time you request that entry (because it doesn't have to reformat). Beneath /var/catman is a subdirectory for each man subdirectory, which is where you can find manual files that have been requested.

Various options you can use with **man** (which can be ascertained with the command **man man**) include:

- -a—Displays all pages matching the text given and does not quit after the first. (Matches are found by checking the subdirectories, not with the whatis database.)
- -C—Uses different configuration parameters for the display.
- -K—Searches files for a term in all the manual pages and shows the title page of each if a match is found. This is the most global search you can do.
- -k—Shows all the manual pages with the same name (as found in the whatis database) and does not stop after displaying the first. This differs from -K in that the former searches the entire page, and **-k** searches only the header.
- -M—Specifies the path to check (versus all subdirectories of /usr/man).
- -P—Specifies a different pager to be used.

Using --help

As was shown in the manual entry for **nice**, with many utilities and commands, you can follow the name of the utility with --**help**. This provides a terse online help for the utility, showing syntax only. For example:

```
$ nice --help
Usage: nice [OPTION]... [COMMAND [ARG]...]
Run COMMAND with an adjusted scheduling priority.
With no COMMAND, print the current scheduling priority. ADJUST
   is 10 by default. Range goes from -20 (highest priority) to
   19 (lowest).

  -ADJUST                     increment priority by ADJUST first
  -n, —adjustment=ADJUST      same as -ADJUST
      —help                   display this help and exit
      —version                output version information and exit

Report bugs to sh-utils-bugs@gnu.ai.mit.edu
$
```

This is an abbreviated version of only some of the manual entry (syntax only). Whether the help appears in this manner depends upon the programmer creating the utility. Most of the newer (and GNU) utilities and commands do include the **--help** option, but it is far from standard, it is rare with older utilities, and it is never available with applications.

Getting info

You can use the **info** utility to display documentation on the GNU utilities. The syntax is either:

```
Info
```

or

```
info {utility name}
```

Calling **info** with no utility name shows a main menu screen similar to the following:

```
File: dir,  Node: Top

Info main menu
==============

  A few useful info commands are:
    h   Enter a short tutorial on info.
    d   Return to this menu.
    ?   List all info commands.
    q   Quit info.
```

```
Not all of the topics shown below may be available on your
   system.

* Menu:


Miscellaneous:
==============

* As: (as).                     The GNU assembler.
* Bash:(bash).                  The GNU Bash Features Guide.
* Bfd: (bfd).                   The Binary File Descriptor library.
—Info: (dir)Top, 205 lines –Top————————
```

As the display states, you are really looking at the top (head) of a file named dir. This file contains a list of all the utilities for which the **info** command works, organized by sections (miscellaneous, GNU file utilities, programming languages, and so on). Following each asterisk is the name of the item, and within each set of parentheses is the text you type to see the entry for it. For example, to see the info for bash, at the command line you type:

```
$ info bash
```

Within the menu, you can also press "m" to invoke a menu prompt and then type the shortcut string (**bash** in this case). The first screen lists the commands for navigating within the tool (h, d, and so on) and their functions. You use the down arrow to scroll through the list one line at a time; pressing the Enter key selects that entry and shows you its information. The files are in hypertext format, so more often than not making one selection leads you to another menu.

To illustrate, start the utility without any parameters:

```
$ info
```

Using the down arrow to scroll through the list to:

```
* gzip:(gzip).                  The GNU compression utility.
```

and pressing Enter invokes the menu of options specific to it:

```
File: gzip.info,  Node: Top,  Up: (dir)

This file documents the 'gzip' command to compress files.

* Menu
```

```
* Copying::             How you can copy and share 'gzip'.
* Overview::            Preliminary information.
* Sample::              Sample output from 'gzip'.
* Invoking gzip::       How to run 'gzip'.
* Advanced usage::      Concatenated files.
* Environment::         The 'GZIP' environment variable.
* Tapes::               Using 'gzip' on taps.
* Problems::            Reporting bugs.
* Concept Index::       Index of concepts.
```

From here, you make your selection and choose to read the information relevant to what you are attempting to accomplish. Pressing "q" quits, and pressing "d" takes you back to the main menu.

Notice the two empty colons following each choice on the **gzip** submenu. This means that you cannot type **info** followed by any shortcut text to arrive at that location. Very rarely is shortcut text available for use on anything but the main menu.

Other keys that work within **info** are the spacebar for scrolling down and the Delete key for scrolling up. Just as files for the manual documentation reside in /usr/man, the files for the **info** utility reside in /usr/info.

Other Local Documentation

You can find information in other locations, and other utilities serve limited purposes within this scope. Two utilities to recognize are:

- **whereis**
- **apropos**

The **whereis** utility lists all the information it can find about locations associated with a file, including man documentation (if any). For example:

```
$ whereis nice
nice: /usr/bin/nice /usr/man/man1/nice.1.gz
.../usr/man/man2/nice.2.gz
$
```

The search is limited to specific directories only, so catman is not included to show whether the manual has been formatted, and so forth. The first listing, in this case, concerns the binary itself, and the other two are the man entries. If no man entry exists, nothing is shown there, but source files or related files are shown. For example:

```
$ whereis info
info: /usr/src/../info  /usr/bin/info /usr/local/info
   /usr/man/../info
$
```

The **apropos** utility uses the whatis database to find values and returns the short summary information about the listing shown earlier with **whatis**. The difference is that **apropos** scans the database and reports all matches—not just exact matches—to the utility name:

```
$ apropos nice
nice (1)    - run a program with modified scheduling priority
nice (2)    - change process priority
renice (8)    - alter priority of running processes
skill, snice (1)    - report process status
(END)    (press q}
$
```

Other locations where you can find documentation locally include the subdirectories beneath /usr/doc. This directory is filled with subdirectories, and the three to know are:

- *FAQ*—Files and further subdirectories of frequently asked questions. FAQs here describe Linux, security, and other related topics.
- *HOWTO*—This directory holds subdirectories with descriptions of how to perform tasks. This is generally a link to /pub/Linux/docs/HOWTO.
- *{application name}*—The documentation for applications you run can write themselves to this directory for easy location. For example, the 1.7 version of the ABC program should write its documentation to /usr/doc/ABC-1.7.

Within the last subdirectory, you can commonly find further documentation for many of the standard utilities as well as new applications. For example, entries commonly appear for shells, compression utilities, and so on.

Other local documentation depends on the vendor, and you need not know it for the exam; however, it is helpful to acknowledge it in the real world. The graphical interface almost always provides a means of obtaining help. Figure 10.1 shows the documentation available from the menu within Caldera's OpenLinux.

Finding Remote Resources

In addition to the resources available locally, numerous resources are available across the Internet. These resources fit two categories: Web sites and newsgroups. The former provide static information that can change daily or infrequently but

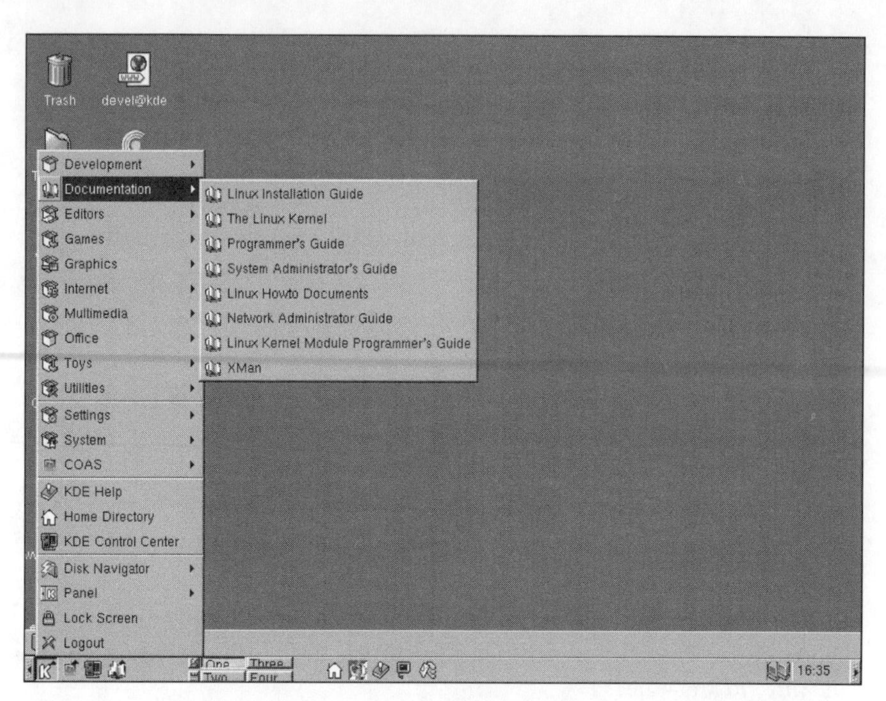

Figure 10.1 Most versions of Linux offer a means of reading documentation through the graphical interface.

that allow you to obtain information without providing any specific interaction. Newsgroups, on the other hand, consist of ongoing threads of communication between individuals who decide to participate. You can post a question specific to your situation in a newsgroup and (you hope) read answers from one or more knowledgeable individuals attempting to help. You would never use a newsgroup to post a common question for which you could easily find the answer elsewhere.

Table 10.3 lists sites that provide Linux or utility-oriented resources. Because the Internet is a constantly changing entity, it is possible that not all the sites listed here will still exist in the future, and it is possible that newer or better sites will come into being: Never underestimate the power of a good search engine for informing you about all changes.

Even though the site might represent a software vendor, or a version of Linux other than the one you are running, you should never dismiss a site. The simple reason is that many of the Linux sites post FAQs and help files for the operating system in general in addition to promoting their products.

The following newsgroups can be invaluable aids in solving specific problems you can experience. The wonderful thing about newsgroups is that—for the ma-

Table 10.3 Linux information sites.

Category	Site	Description
Documentation	**www.kde.org**	The organization behind the K Development Environment (KDE) interface
Documentation	**www.linuxdoc.org**	Linux Documentation Project (LDP)—invaluable for finding HOWTO information
Documentation	**www.linuxlookup.com**	LinuxLookup—how-tos and reviews
Documentation	**www.linuxnewbie.com**	Generic information for new users
Exam	**www.lpi.org**	Linux Professional Institute
Exam	**www.lpi.org/faq.html**	Frequently asked questions about the LPI exams
Exam	**www.lpi.org/p-glossary.html**	All the terms needed for the LPI exam
News	**webwatcher.org**	Linux Webwatcher
News	**www.embedded.com**	Linux News
News	**www.linux.com**	Linux.com
News	**www.linux.org**	Linux Online
News	**www.linuxgazette.com**	Linux Gazette
News	**www.linuxjournal.com**	Linux Journal
News	**www.linuxplanet.com**	LinuxPlanet
News	**www.linuxtoday.com**	LinuxToday
News	**www.lwn.net**	Linux Weekly News
News	**www.maximumLinux.com**	Maximum Linux Magazine
News	**www.slashdot.org**	Slashdot
News	**www.ugu.com**	Unix Guru's Universe
Software	**www.Linuxtapecert.org**	Enhanced Software Technologies
Software	**www.freshmeat.com**	Freshmeat
Software	**www.linuxapps.com**	LinuxApps
Software	**www.linuxmall.com**	Linux Mall
Standards	**www.fsf.org**	Free Software Foundation
Standards	**www.li.org**	Linux International
Standards	**www.usenix.org**	Usenix
Vendor	**www.calderasystems.com**	Caldera OpenLinux
Vendor	**linux.corel.com**	Corel
Vendor	**www.debian.org**	Debian

(continued)

Table 10.3 Linux information sites *(continued)*.

Category	Site	Description
Vendor	**www.linuxcare.com**	LinuxCare
Vendor	**www.linux-mandrake.com**	Mandrake
Vendor	**www.redhat.com**	RedHat
Vendor	**www.slackware.com**	Slackware
Vendor	**www.suse.com**	SuSE
Vendor	**www.turbolinux.com**	TurboLinux

jority of them—their names are self-explanatory, which can prevent you from posting a question in the wrong location:

- comp.os.linux.advocacy
- comp.os.linux.announce.html
- comp.os.linux.answers
- comp.os.linux.development.apps
- comp.os.linux.development.system
- comp.os.linux.hardware
- comp.os.linux.misc
- comp.os.linux.networking
- comp.os.linux.setup
- comp.os.linux.x

Both AltaVista and Deja.com archive the newsgroups, and you can search them for solutions that have been posted in the past before submitting new questions.

You can also subscribe to Linux mailing lists to see mail threads on particular topics. To subscribe, send a message to **majordomo@vger.rutgers.edu** with the topic "subscribe" and the name of the mailing list. Again, the names are self-explanatory:

- linux-admin
- linux-alpha
- linux-apps
- linux-c-programming
- linux-config

- linux-doc
- linux-kernel
- linux-laptop
- linux-newbie
- linux-sound
- linux-standards

Writing Documentation

As a system administrator, one of the most important things you can do to ensure that your systems run smoothly is to provide documentation for the actions you undertake. Using common sense, you can often ascertain such things as:

- *The method of documentation*—Printed or electronic? If it is electronic, can it exist within another document, or must it be a standalone document? If it is printed, is it a subset of a large document or a standalone entity?
- *The scope of the documentation*—Should it address only a change that was made, or should it be all-inclusive? Any time you make a major change to the operation of a site, you need to document exactly what was done. Needless to say, you should also make only one major change at a time to fully realize the ramifications of that change before making others.
- *The target audience*—Will you use this note to jog your memory 6 months from now, or is it something to distribute to all users? If you are writing for yourself, you can get by with a few lines of terse notes. For distribution to users, documentation should be specific and offer as much background information as possible.

Electronic documentation can exist as comment lines within script files, such as:

```
# here we compare the two reports
# and look for only the changes between
# them
```

It can also be HTML files. For the exam, you need not know how to create the documentation, but you should recognize that doing so is advisable and that you should have a plan for distributing documentation to the appropriate personnel. You should also know that some of the simplest documentation can create itself—such as log files. Elements that are imperative to include in good documentation are file locations, any configuration changes, and the resources involved (applications, scripts, source code, and so on).

Providing Support

Just as creating proper documentation involves a great deal of common sense, so too does providing support to users. You must possess not only technical skills, but also interpersonal skills, as well as the ability to think and react quickly.

You should always make users feel as if you are listening to their concerns and trying to understand their problems. You should treat them with politeness and guidance—whether it is over the telephone, through an electronic medium (such as email), or in person. Treat them with the same respect and empathy you would want extended to you. Although their problems may be nothing more than minor annoyances you can fix in less than a minute, to them the problems represent critical issues (or even crises).

When solving a problem, punctuality and accountability are also important. When you tell a user you will be there at 3:00 P.M., make every attempt to arrive at that time. When you solve the problem, the user should be confident that the problem is solved and that you will take responsibility if it recurs.

Understand that crises tend to occur in clusters. When more than one crisis occurs at a time, it is imperative to prioritize and tend the most severe problems first. If two users call at the same time—one cannot print the images he downloaded from a Web site and the other can't get payroll checks to run—know that the latter is the first issue to tackle.

For the exam, apply common sense to any questions pertaining to customer support, and you will have no difficulty answering them correctly.

Utility Summation

I discussed only a handful of utilities in this chapter. Table 10.4 lists them and their purposes.

Table 10.4 Utilities discussed in this chapter.

Utility	Purpose
man	Displays the manual pages.
whatis	Shows what manual pages are available.
--help	Displays command-line help from within some files.
info	Displays help from the /usr/info files.
whereis	Shows the location of the utility and all related files—including any man entries.
apropos	Shows what manual pages are available but scans the entire entry and does not require exact matches.

Practice Questions

Question 1

Karen wants to know what directory contains the calendar utility (**cal**) to make certain the correct one runs when she enters the command. Which of the following commands will show her what directory of the **cal** utility she is using?

- ❍ a. **whereis cal**
- ❍ b. **whatis cal**
- ❍ c. **apropos cal**
- ❍ d. **which cal**

The correct answer to this question is d. The differences among these four utilities can be difficult to remember. The **which** utility, discussed in Chapter 7, will search your **PATH** statement to find the utility that runs when you enter the command. In this case, it returns a value similar to /usr/bin/cal. Answer a will show (by searching a preset number of directories) the executables with the same name and the man pages, so it is incorrect. Answer b will offer the short synopsis from the whatis database, so it is incorrect. Answer c will display every header that contains "cal" from the whatis database; therefore, it, too, is incorrect.

Question 2

Which of the following searches is the most inclusive?

- ❍ a. **man -K du**
- ❍ b. **apropos du**
- ❍ c. **info du**
- ❍ d. **whatis du**

The correct answer to this question is a. The **-K** option will search all manual pages—not just headers—for every occurrence of **du**. Answer b will search only the whatis database; answer c will just display information on the **du** utility; and answer d will search only the whatis database.

Question 3

William has just installed version 6.4.2 of the commercial BASF editor. Giving the full path, where should documentation for the application now reside? [Fill in the blank]

____

The correct answer to this question is:

```
/usr/doc/BASF-6.4.2
```

Applications should create subdirectories beneath the /usr/doc directory. The syntax for these subdirectories is {name}-{version}.

Question 4

Which environmental variable should you change to use **more** in place of **less** when viewing manual pages?

- ❍ a. **MORE**
- ❍ b. **PAGER**
- ❍ c. **MAN**
- ❍ d. **MANMORE**

The correct answer to this question is b. The value of the **PAGER** variable determines what utility will be used to show the contents of the manual pages. The other variable choices listed do not exist.

Question 5

You are viewing the main menu of the **info** utility and want to see more information about the **sed** stream (which has the shortcut string of **sed**). What should you type to reach this?

❍ a. **sed**

❍ b. F1+ **sed**

❍ c. **msed**

❍ d. **gsed**

The correct answer to this question is c. You must type "m" to invoke the menu prompt and then enter the string for the shortcut. Answer a is incorrect because it will not bring up the menu to allow you to move to **sed** quickly. Answer b is incorrect because the function key serves no purpose in **info**. And answer d is incorrect because g will not bring up the menu allowing you to move quickly to the **sed** description.

Question 6

Beneath which /usr/man subdirectory are device descriptions located?

❍ a. man1

❍ b. man2

❍ c. man3

❍ d. man4

❍ e. man5

❍ f. man6

❍ g. man7

❍ h. man8

The correct answer to this question is d. The entries in man4 are for /dev descriptions. The other answer choices are incorrect for the following reasons: Choice a is incorrect because man1 is used for shell utilities and user commands. In choice b, man2 is used for system calls. Answer choice c is incorrect because man3 is used for libc calls. man5, listed in answer e, is used for /etc and other configurable files (such as protocols). Answer f is incorrect because man6 is used for games. man7, the choice in answer g, is used for Linux system files, conventions, and so forth. And answer h is incorrect because man8 is used for root user/system administration utilities.

Question 7

You are scrolling through the man description for the **uniq** utility and unintentionally move two screens at one time. To view the screen you skipped, what key should you press to accomplish this in the fewest steps?

- ❍ a. p
- ❍ b. b
- ❍ c. u
- ❍ d. :

The correct answer to this question is b. Pressing the "b" (for back) key will take you to the previous page. The other choices are incorrect. Answer a will take you to the top of the page, answer c will take you back half a window, and answer d will take you to the command window and accomplishes nothing toward moving backward through the document.

Question 8

kill has two manual pages—one beneath the man1 subdirectory and the other beneath the man2 subdirectory. How can you view only the documentation beneath man2?

- ❍ a. **man 2 kill**
- ❍ b. **man kill 2**
- ❍ c. **man kill(2)**
- ❍ d. **man (2)kill**

The correct answer to this question is a. You first specify the subdirectory and then the utility or command name. Answer b would bring up the kill entry from man1, which is not the desired result. Answer c is the incorrect syntax and would look for an entry named "kill(2)", which does not exist. And answer d would look for an entry named "(2)kill", which also does not exist.

Question 9

You have viewed the man pages for the **uniq** command. The next time you issue **man uniq**, the pages display faster. This happens because they are stored in a formatted file in what directory?

❍ a. usr/man

❍ b. var/man

❍ c. var/catman

❍ d. usr/catman

The correct answer to this question is c. After the pages are viewed once, /var/catman stores a formatted copy to make the display appear more quickly on subsequent issues of the command. Answer a holds the compressed—original—entries, and thus is incorrect. Answers b and d are directories that do not exist.

Question 10

Which command will show only the syntax options for the **nice** command?

❍ a. **man nice**

❍ b. **nice --help**

❍ c. **info nice**

❍ d. **whatis nice**

The correct answer to this question is b. Using the **--help** option shows syntax and nothing more. Answer a will show all the documentation it can about the utility—including, but not limited to, the syntax; therefore, it is incorrect. Answer c will also show all the documentation it can, so it is incorrect. Answer d will show what man pages exist for **nice**, so it, too, is incorrect.

Need to Know More?

Bogue, Robert, and Emmett Dulaney. *A+ Certification Interactive Workbook*. Upper Saddle River, NJ: Prentice Hall, 2000. ISBN: 0-13084-847-6. Chapter 7 addresses the topic of customer satisfaction and the keys to effective customer satisfaction.

Weiss, Martin, and Emmett Dulaney. *i-Net+ Exam Cram*. Scottsdale, AZ: The Coriolis Group, 2000. ISBN: 1-57610-673-X. Chapter 10 covers HTML basic commands and concepts, and Chapter 14 looks at business concepts.

Administering the System

Terms you'll need to understand:

- ✓ Logging
- ✓ /etc/syslog.conf
- ✓ **lastlog**
- ✓ **logger**
- ✓ **logrotate**
- ✓ **at**
- ✓ **atq**
- ✓ **atrm**
- ✓ **cron**
- ✓ **crontab**
- ✓ Backup
- ✓ **tar**
- ✓ **cpio**
- ✓ **gzip**
- ✓ **compress**
- ✓ **pack**

Techniques you'll need to master:

- ✓ Understanding how to configure and monitor log files for administrative and security reasons
- ✓ Comprehending methods of automating jobs to run in the future
- ✓ Recognizing the importance of backups and how to implement them

In this chapter, you'll learn about the system-logging features you can turn on in Linux. I address two methods (**at** and **cron**) of scheduling unattended jobs to run in the future. You will also see the means by which you can perform backups and restores and come to understand their importance.

Configuring System Logs

Log files can easily be an administrator's best friend or your worst enemy. They can monitor the system and report on administrative and security issues 24 hours a day, seven days a week: creating fingerprints that allow you to see what is happening and who is doing it. If improperly implemented, they monitor so much information that you spend days looking through thousands of lines of unneeded entries trying to find a single item; they eat up precious disk space; and they serve little purpose.

An illustration of a negative aspect: I once worked in support for an electronic-monitoring corporation that sold computer systems to law-enforcement departments. When making the purchase, most departments had to scrape together the money to buy the system and would cut corners where they could, usually saving money by buying small hard drives or minimal RAM. Given the sensitive nature of house arrest, log files recorded everything that happened—every time a modem was accessed (thousands of times a day), every time a change was made to a person's information, and so on. The machines constantly ran out of hard-drive space, and on a weekly basis customer support had to dial in remotely and delete the log files—defeating the whole purpose of having them.

An illustration of a positive aspect: I once consulted for a company that had problems no one else had ever encountered. As soon as we fixed one problem, another occurred. The problems did not seem to make sense; instead of showing file corruption, the databases would completely disappear from the system—seemingly out of the blue without rhyme or reason. Users who could log on one day would come in the next and discover that their profiles contained variables that caused one error after another. Frustration was reaching an all-time high. A quick look at the logs showed a disgruntled employee had figured out a number of passwords, logged in as other users, did some damage, and then exited and acted as confused as everyone else.

The key to using log files effectively is to know what each of them does. Once you know that, you can realistically set your expectations and look for necessary data without being overwhelmed.

The Log Daemon

Although individual applications can have their own logging features, one log service runs just for the operating system. The service responsible for adding entries to the log files is **syslogd**—the system log daemon—which is spawned by the **init** daemon. When started, **syslogd** reads the /etc/syslog.conf file to see what to monitor. Very descriptive in nature, each line consists of the item you want to monitor followed by a period (.), the priority, white space, and the location of the log file.

You can use a comma (,) to separate multiple entries. You can also use a semicolon (;) to denote exceptions to the rule. This makes the syntax:

```
item.priority;exceptions log_file
```

Remember that the **syslog** daemon reads the syslog.conf file by default. You can, however, modify the startup files so that **syslogd** starts with the **-f** option, allowing you to use another configuration file in place of /etc/syslog.conf.

The following is an example of the default file created on OpenLinux (with line numbers added to aid the discussion that follows):

```
1    # Log all kernel messages to the console.
2    # Logging much else clutters up the screen.
3    # kern.*                       /dev/console

4    # Log everything (except mail and news) of level info
     or higher.
5    # Hmm—also don't log private authentication messages here!
6    *.info;news,mail,authpriv,auth.none          -/var/log/
     messages

7    # Log debugging too
8    #*.debug;news,mail,authpriv,auth.none        -/var/log/debug

9    # The authpriv file has restricted access.
10   authpriv.*;auth.*                            /var/log/secure
11   # true, 'auth' in the two previous rules is deprecated,
12   # but nonetheless still in use...

13   # Log all the mail messages in one place.
14   mail.*                                       /var/log/mail

15   # As long as innd insists on blocking /var/log/news
16   # (instead of using /var/log/news.d) we fall back to ...
17   news.*                                       /var/log/
     news.all

18   # Save uucp and news errors of level err and higher
19   # in a special file.
```

```
20  uucp,news.err                                    /var/log/spooler

21  # Everybody gets emergency messages, plus log them on
22  # another machine.
23  *.emerg                                             *
24  #*.emerg                                        @loghost
```

Remember that all lines starting with the pound sign (#) are comments. The first line executed is line 6, which sends all information-level (and above) messages to /var/log/messages. Messages not sent here (thanks to the semicolon) are those regarding news, mail, and authentication; they are recorded elsewhere.

Line 10 sends all private authorization messages (but not those for regular login) to /var/log/secure. Line 14 sends all mail messages to /var/log/main, and line 17 sends all news messages to /var/log/news.all. Line 20 sends uucp and news error messages to /var/log/spooler, and line 23 sends all emergency messages to everyone.

Some of the valid entries for the items field include:

- *—Everything
- **uucp**
- **news**
- **mail**
- **kern**—For kernel messages

A kernel log daemon on many systems—**klogd**—can be running for the sole purpose of logging kernel messages.

- **authpriv**—For private authentication
- **auth**—For general authentication such as login
- **lpr**—For the printer service
- **cron**—For the **cron** daemon
- **user**—For user processes

The 10 valid values for the priority field, in the order of priority from highest to lowest, are:

- **emerg**—For emergency

- **alert**
- **crit**—For critical
- **err**—For error
- **warning**
- **notice**
- **info**
- **debug**
- *—Everything
- **none**

Keep in mind that when you specify a priority, that priority represents a minimum. Messages are generated at that, and any higher, priority. If you want to log only for that priority, you can use the equal sign (=). For example, you can use ***.=err /var/log/errors**.

If you want to exclude one specific type of priority but get all others, you can use the exclamation mark (!). For example, to log all news messages except those that are critical, you could use:

```
news.*;news.!=crit
```

The location field can be anything. Some valid entries include:

- *—Everywhere
- **/dev/console**—To notify the current console user
- /var/log/{***name of log file***}

Because the /etc/syslog.conf file is read by **syslogd** at startup, you must restart the daemon for the changes to be active if you make changes to the file. The daemon will automatically restart upon death, and thus you can force it to read changes by first killing it off using either:

```
kill -HUP
```

or

```
kill -1
```

on the PID (process ID) number of the syslogd process (both values are the same, but one is a numeric representation while the other is symbolic). You can find the PID number of syslogd by running **ps –ef** or by looking at the value in the file /var/run/syslogd.pid. You can also use the command:

```
pidof syslogd
```

to arrive at the PID number of the process.

Files to Know

You should recognize a number of log files that exist by default. Table 11.1 summarizes the main files beneath /var/log.

You should know a few executables that are related to logging. The first is **logger**. This utility must be followed by the name of the file to write to and a message; it then inserts that message into the log file. For example, the system default is the message:

```
$ pwd
/var/log
$ tail messages
Oct 16 14:40:00 noname CRON[3823]: (root) CMD (/sbin/rmmod -a)
Oct 16 14:42:01 noname CRON[3825]: (root) CMD
   ([ -x /usr/sbin/cronloop ] && /usr/sbin/cronloop Hourly)
Oct 16 14:45:00 noname CRON[3829]: (root) CMD (/sbin/rmmod -a)
Oct 16 14:50:00 noname CRON[3832]: (root) CMD (/sbin/rmmod -a)
Oct 16 14:55:00 noname CRON[3838]: (root) CMD (/sbin/rmmod -a)
Oct 16 15:00:00 noname CRON[3858]: (root) CMD (/sbin/rmmod -a)
Oct 16 15:05:01 noname CRON[3896]: (root) CMD (/sbin/rmmod -a)
Oct 16 15:10:00 noname CRON[3921]: (root) CMD (/sbin/rmmod -a)
Oct 16 15:15:00 noname CRON[3925]: (root) CMD (/sbin/rmmod -a)
Oct 16 15:20:00 noname CRON[3934]: (root) CMD (/sbin/rmmod -a)
$ logger hey
$ tail messages
Oct 16 14:42:01 noname CRON[3825]: (root) CMD
   ([ -x /usr/sbin/cronloop ] && /usr/sbin/cronloop Hourly)
Oct 16 14:45:00 noname CRON[3829]: (root) CMD (/sbin/rmmod -a)
Oct 16 14:50:00 noname CRON[3832]: (root) CMD (/sbin/rmmod -a)
Oct 16 14:55:00 noname CRON[3838]: (root) CMD (/sbin/rmmod -a)
Oct 16 15:00:00 noname CRON[3858]: (root) CMD (/sbin/rmmod -a)
Oct 16 15:05:01 noname CRON[3896]: (root) CMD (/sbin/rmmod -a)
Oct 16 15:10:00 noname CRON[3921]: (root) CMD (/sbin/rmmod -a)
Oct 16 15:15:00 noname CRON[3925]: (root) CMD (/sbin/rmmod -a)
Oct 16 15:20:00 noname CRON[3934]: (root) CMD (/sbin/rmmod -a)
Oct 16 15:22:28 noname root: hey
$
```

Notice that each entry starts with the date and time and is followed by the name of the system, the caller, a colon (:), and the message.

Table 11.1 Common log files.

File	Purpose
cron	Logs events generated by the **cron** daemon.
lastlog	Shows the last time each user logged in (read by the **lastlog** command).
mail or maillog	Mails messages.
messages	The big one: where most events are logged by default.
news or news.all	Shows news messages.
secure	Provides security.
spooler	Spools messages.
uucp	Shows uucp events.
wtmp	Keeps track of logins and logouts; used by the **last** command; the counterpart to /var/run/utmp.

The next executable you should know is **logrotate**. This utility reads configuration files and compresses or deletes log files as specified. You use the **gzip** utility for the compression, and actions can take place daily, weekly, monthly (all courtesy of **cron**), or when set sizes are obtained.

At any time, an administrator can archive, delete, and compress log files manually. The sole purpose of **logrotate** is simply to automate the process. Commands you can use with this utility are:

- compress
- copytruncate
- create
- daily
- delaycompress
- errors
- extension
- ifempty
- include
- mail
- mailfirst
- maillast

- **missingok**
- **monthly**
- **nocompress**
- **nocopytruncate**
- **nocreate**
- **nodelaycompress**
- **nomail**
- **nomissingok**
- **noolddir**
- **notifempty**
- **olddir**
- **postrotate**
- **prerotate**
- **rotate**
- **size**
- **weekly**

The text file /var/state/logrotate shows the status of the utility in terms of the files it interacts with. An example of this file is:

```
logrotate state — version 1
/var/log/secure 2000-10-15
/var/log/mail 2000-10-15
/var/log/news.all 2000-10-3
/var/log/spooler 2000-10-3
/var/log/messages 2000-10-15
/var/log/xferlog 2000-10-3
/var/log/wtmp 2000-10-3
/var/log/lastlog 2000-10-3
```

Automating Tasks

Quite often, jobs that can run in your absence need to run either at odd hours or with a fair amount of frequency. If you want a job to run once, and it is convenient to run it when you are not around, you can schedule it using the **at** command. If you want a job to run with any degree of frequency (once a month every month, once a week, and so on), you can schedule it with **cron**.

Using at

The **at** command allows you to schedule a job to run at a specified time. The syntax is simply:

```
at {time}
```

You can specify the time in many ways. Some examples are:

- **17:31**—Runs the command at 5:31 in the afternoon.
- **now**—Runs now.
- **now + 5 days**—Runs five days from now at the exact same time.
- **17:31 Mar 14**—Runs at 5:31 in the afternoon on March 14th.
- **midnight**—Runs at midnight tonight. Other special words are **today, tomorrow**, and **noon**.

By default, only the root user can use the **at** command. You can change this, however, by using either the /etc/at.allow file or the /etc/at.deny file. By default, the at.deny file exists on most systems and holds system accounts that a user should not be using. If only the at.allow file exists, then only users who are listed there are allowed to use the **at** command. On the other hand, if the at.deny file exists, then all users are allowed to use the **at** command except those listed within this file.

When you give the **at** command and the time, the prompt changes to the PS2 prompt (>, by default), and you can enter as many commands as you want to run at that time. When you are finished, press Ctrl+D to return to the PS1 prompt.

You can list jobs that are spooled for future execution with the command:

```
at -l
```

or the command:

```
atq
```

Individual users see only their own entries, but the root user can see all. In reality, the listings are text files stored beneath /var/spool/atjobs. These text files hold a copy of environment information that applied when the user created the job, as well as the commands within the job itself. Prior to execution, the command can be stopped with either of the following commands and the job number:

```
at -d
```

or

```
atrm
```

The following is an example of scheduling a job to run at a later time. Notes about the action appear as comments:

```
$ pwd
/home/edulaney
$ cat myexample    # this file must be executable
logger # this is to show a successful execution
$
$ su root
Password:    # must become root user to see current messages
#
# tail -3 /var/log/messages
Oct 16 17:45:00 noname CRON[4259]: (root) CMD (/sbin/rmmod -a)
Oct 16 17:50:00 noname CRON[4262]: (root) CMD (/sbin/rmmod -a)
Oct 16 17:55:00 noname CRON[4275]: (root) CMD (/sbin/rmmod -a)
# exit
$
$ date +%H:%M    # to get the current hour and minute
17:57
$ at 18:05
> /home/edulaney/myexample
> {press Ctrl+D}
job 7 at 2000-10-16 18:05
$
$ atq
7   2000-10-16 18:05 a
$
```

This last listing shows it is the seventh job that has been assigned recently (as a user, you see only your own) and the date and time it will run. The **a** indicates an **at** job. There can be other jobs spooled. During the duration a job is spooled, a file represents it with an odd name (in cryptic format) beneath /var/spool/atjobs. In this case, an example of the file name is a0000700f71ec1, and its contents (which you must be root to see) are:

```
#!/bin/sh
# atrun uid=502 gid=100
# mail     root 0
umask 22
HOSTNAME=noname; export HOSTNAME
LOGNAME=edulaney; export LOGNAME
_ETC_PROFILE=1; export _ETC_PROFILE
```

```
HELPPATH=/usr/openwin/help; export HELPPATH
MAIL=/var/spool/mail/edulaney; export MAIL
PAGER=less; export PAGER
CLASSPATH=/usr/java/lib/classes.zip; export CLASSPATH
HOSTTYPE=i386; export HOSTTYPE
PATH=/usr/local/sbin:/sbin:/usr/sbin:/bin:/usr/bin:
   /usr/local/bin:/usr/X11R6/bin:/opt/teTeX/bin:/opt/kde/bin:
   /usr/java/bin; export PATH
KDEDIR=/opt/kde; export KDEDIR
HOME=/home/edulaney; export HOME
USER=edulaney; export USER
LESSCHARSET=latin1; export LESSCHARSET
JAVA_HOME=/usr/java; export JAVA_HOME
HOST=noname.nodomain.nowhere; export HOST
OSTYPE=Linux; export OSTYPE
OPENWINHOME=/usr/openwin; export OPENWINHOME
SHLVL=2; export SHLVL
cd /home/edulaney || {
   echo 'Execution directory inaccessible' >&2
   exit 1
}
/home/edulaney/myexample
```

Notice that all relevant information about the user is here: user ID, environmental variables, and so on. This prevents a user from running a command through **at** that he or she does not have access and permissions to run otherwise. The last line is the command to run: You should always provide the full path because there is no relative path for the service that runs the command.

When the time has elapsed and the command has run, the line will be added to the system log as shown in the following:

```
$ date +%H:%M
18:06
$ atq
$
$ su root
Password:
#
# tail -3 /var/log/messages
Oct 16 18:05:00 noname CRON[4318]: (root) CMD (/sbin/rmmod -a)
Oct 16 18:05:00 noname CRON[4325]: (root) CMD (/sbin/rmmod -a)
Oct 16 18:05:00 noname logger: this is to show a successful
   execution
# exit
$
```

A few other options exist with **at**: **-m** mails the user when the job is done, and **-f** feeds the lines into **at** from a file. An alias for the command is called **batch**. The **batch** utility works similarly, but it runs the processes only when system use is low.

One thing to keep in mind about **at** jobs is worth repeating: They are good for running one time. It is time consuming to schedule the same jobs every day because there is no trace of them to resurrect once they are finished executing. If you need to run jobs more than once, avoid **at** jobs, and investigate the use of **cron**.

Working with cron

You use **cron** to run commands at an interval, which can be any type of interval. **cron** reads a file of times and commands named **crontab** (as in "cron table") to find what must be run when. By default, every user can have her own crontab file. The default changes, however, if an /etc/cron.allow or /etc/cron.deny file exists. In the presence of the cron.allow file, only those users who appear within the file can create crontab files. In the presence of a cron.deny file, all users can use crontab files except those whose names appear within the cron.deny. The two files are optional and mutually exclusive: You would never have both on the same system. To check for a current crontab file, a user uses the command:

```
crontab -l
```

To remove it, he uses:

```
crontab -r
```

To edit it, he uses:

```
crontab -e
```

For the root user to see another user's files, such as for larry, she uses:

```
crontab -u larry
```

There is one entry per line in the file, and each line consists of six fields. The six fields are separated by white space. The first time you look at such a file, it will look like a garbled mess. To understand what you are seeing, remember that the six fields are:

- Minutes (0–59)
- Hours (0–23)
- Day of month (1–31)

- Month (1–12)
- Day of week (0=Sunday, 6=Saturday)
- Command to run

To illustrate:

```
$  pwd
/home/edulaney
$ cat example
logger # This is running every five minutes after the hour
$
$ crontab -l
no crontab for edulaney
$ crontab -e    # this opens a blank file within the editor
5 * * * * /home/edulaney/example
# exit the editor
$
```

This sets the shell script (which logs an entry to /var/log/messages) to run every five minutes after the hour, regardless of the hour (*), the day of the month (*), the month(*), or day of the week (*). Within each of the fields, the asterisk means all, but:

- A number means only when there is a match, such as the **5** in the example.
- A hyphen can indicate an inclusive range of numbers, as in **1–10**.
- A comma can separate numbers, as in **1,10**.

Some examples of specifications appear in Table 11.2.

The **cron** daemon, started by **init**, wakes up once a minute to look for jobs that are set to execute. The jobs are held in the spooler (/var/spool/cron) and come from the user crontabs or /etc/crontab. The **at** jobs are executed by the **at** daemon (**atd**) on most systems. (On others, **atrun** is started routinely by the **cron** daemon to look for **at** jobs.)

Backups

Every system has the ability to crash (sad to say). When it does, you can reinstall the operating system from the media it came upon and start over. What cannot be reinstalled from that media is all the data you've created since the system was started. Enter the lifesaving backups.

The true definition of backups is copies of your data stored on removable media. (You can copy files from one drive to another, but they do you no good if the

Table 11.2 Examples of cron syntax.

Syntax	Result
1 12 * * *	12:01 every day of the year
15 18 1 * *	6:15 in the evening on the first day of each month
1,16,31,46 * * * *	Every 15 minutes
30 0,12 * * *	12:30 in the morning and afternoon
20 10 31 10 *	Only on October 31st at 10:20
1 6 * * 1-5	At 6:01 every weekday morning

system gets hit by fire.) In recent times, the definition has broadened to include technologies such as clusters.

You need a complete understanding of the basic definition of "backups" for the exam.

Although the removable media can be anything from floppy disks to CD-RWs, most of the time tapes are the preferred medium. Most tapes allow you to store several gigabytes of data and provide a cheaper, more reusable media than other options.

One of the first things to realize is that one tape, used over and over, does not support a good backup strategy. You need to use multiple tapes, to be able to recover in the event of the failure of one, and rotate them. You need to store copies in safe locations, including off site (in case the entire building is blown away in a tornado). You should keep logs of what is on each tape so you can quickly identify what is there.

It is important to understand the difference between backups and archives. Archives are files that you copy from your system to store elsewhere and that you would not put back on the system if it crashes. Backups are files that you need and would put back on if the system crashed.

Several strategies dictate how you back up the data to tapes:

- *Daily*—Copies all the files changed each day to a tape.
- *Full*—Copies all files.
- *Incremental*—Copies all files added or changed since the last full or incremental backup.

- *Differential*—Copies all files added or changed since the last full backup.

Most real backup plans use some combination of these types. For example, full backups are best but require the most time to run. For that reason, you might run a full backup every Sunday and an incremental every other evening of the week. The amount of time it takes to run the incrementals is much shorter and roughly the same each night. If the system crashes on Friday, however, it will take quite a while to restore the full tape from Sunday, then the incremental from Monday, the incremental from Tuesday, the one from Wednesday, and the one from Thursday (a total of five tapes.)

Another possibility is to perform a full backup on Sunday and a differential each night. The amount of time to do the differentials gets longer each night, but if the system crashes on Friday, you only need two tapes: Sunday's full and Thursday's differential.

LPI also recognizes two other types of backups: copy and partial. A copy backup is simply a copy of a file to the media (think of copying one file to a floppy). A partial backup is just a copy of all the files within a single directory.

Just as important as a good backup strategy and adherence to it is the knowledge that you can restore the data if you have to. This assurance can come only from verifying that on a regular basis. Every so often, you should run a restore operation from a completed backup and verify that you can read back the data in its original form.

Utilities to Know

Linux includes a number of utilities that you can use to do your backups, such as **tar** and **cpio**. The **tar** utility (tape archiver) combines multiple files into a single file that can be copied to the media. The syntax for it is:

```
tar {options} {target_file} {source_files}
```

Both the target file and source files can be paths (such as /dev/tape). The options include:

- **c**—Creates a new file.
- **d**—Compares contents and displays the differences between the target and source.
- **f**—Specifies a file in which to place the archive.
- **p**—Keeps the permissions.
- **r**—Appends to an existing file.

- **t**—Shows the names of the files in the tar file.
- **u**—Adds only files that are new.
- **v**—Runs in verbose mode.
- **x**—Extracts files.
- **z**—Sends the output through **gzip** or **gunzip** depending on direction.

The following common command creates a new tar file on the tape and does so in verbose mode:

```
tar cvf /dev/tape {files}
```

The following command extracts and restores the files from the october.tar backup file:

```
tar xf october.tar
```

You use the **cpio** utility to copy in and out. It can do three basic actions, so you must specify one:

- **-i**—Extracts from an archive.
- **-o**—Makes a new archive.
- **-p**—Prints or passes through the files.

Options you can specify are:

- **d**—Creates directories if they are needed.
- **f**—Specifies a file.
- **t**—Shows the contents.
- **u**—Overwrites existing files.
- **v**—Runs in verbose mode.

The following example reads in files from a tape and displays them as it is operating (verbose mode):

```
cpio -iv < /dev/tape
```

The next example finds all files on the system starting with **ead** and copies them beneath the /home/ead directory, creating all the needed subdirectories in the process:

```
find / -name ead* | cpio -pdv /home/ead
```

Related Utilities

Backup utilities allow you to copy files from the system to the backup media or vice versa. Some utilities are designed to reduce or compress data so that it takes up less space. The most common of these are **gzip** (to compress) and **gunzip** (to uncompress). You can see the contents of the **gzip** file (without uncompressing) by using the **zcat** utility in place of **cat**.

Two other utilities that exist on some systems are:

- **pack** (and its counterpart, **unpack**)
- **compress** (and its counterpart, **uncompress**)

Utility Summation

This chapter discussed only a handful of utilities. Table 11.3 lists them and their purposes.

Table 11.3 Utilities discussed in this chapter.

Utility	Purpose
lastlog	Shows the last time each user logged on.
logger	Writes an event in the log file.
logrotate	Automates administration to log files.
pidof	Identifies the PID number of a process.
at	Runs commands at a different time.
atq	Sees what **at** jobs are spooled to run.
atrm	Removes **at** jobs before they run.
crontab	Creates and edits a crontab file.
tar	Copies files to or from a tape.
cpio	Copies files to and from one location to another.
gzip/gunzip	Compresses/uncompresses files.
pack/unpack	Compresses/uncompresses files.
compress/uncompress	Compresses/uncompresses files.

Practice Questions

Question 1

Which of the following **crontab** entries will run the **passwd.save** program at 12:45 in the morning, every morning?

❍ a. **45 0 * * * passwd.save**

❍ b. **0 45 * * * passwd.save**

❍ c. **12 45 * * * passwd.save**

❍ d. *** * 12 45 * passwd.save**

❍ e. **45 0 * * * /home/edulaney/passwd.save**

❍ f. *** * * 12 45 /home/edulaney/passwd.save**

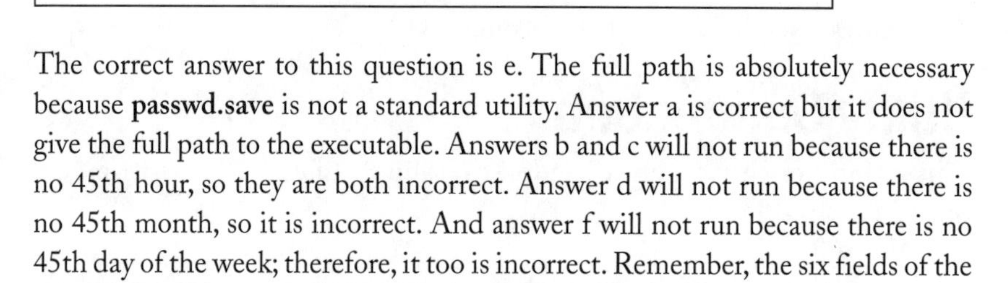

The correct answer to this question is e. The full path is absolutely necessary because **passwd.save** is not a standard utility. Answer a is correct but it does not give the full path to the executable. Answers b and c will not run because there is no 45th hour, so they are both incorrect. Answer d will not run because there is no 45th month, so it is incorrect. And answer f will not run because there is no 45th day of the week; therefore, it too is incorrect. Remember, the six fields of the file are minute, hour, day of month, month, day of week, and program.

Question 2

What utility can you use to write messages to the system file?

❍ a. **logger**

❍ b. **syslogd**

❍ c. **at**

❍ d. **cron**

❍ e. syslog.conf

❍ f. **system**

The correct answer to this question is a; the **logger** utility will write messages to the log files. Answer b will automatically write entries to the log files, so it is incorrect. Answer c will run commands at a later time, so it is incorrect. Answer d will run them with some frequency, so it is incorrect. Answer e is used to configure the system log daemon, so it is incorrect. And answer f is not a command related to this discussion, so it too is incorrect.

Question 3

Marco has created a report compiler that takes 6 hours to run. He wants it to start later when the system is slow to avoid adversely affecting other users. What command should he give to have the command start at 11:15 tonight? [Fill in the blank]

____

The correct answer to this question is:

```
at 23:15
```

This will bring him to the PS2 prompt, where he can enter the name of the utility.

Question 4

By default, what is the "system" log file where the majority of messages are written by the system log daemon?

- ❍ a. /var/etc/spooler
- ❍ b. /var/spool/message
- ❍ c. /var/log/messages
- ❍ d. /var/log/message

The correct answer to this question is c; the default system log is /var/log/messages. The other answer choices are incorrect because these files do not exist.

Question 5

In the absence of either an at.allow or at.deny file, which users are allowed to create jobs to run at a different time?

- ❍ a. Only root
- ❍ b. Only non-root users
- ❍ c. Root and other users
- ❍ d. No one

The correct answer to this question is a. Without an at.allow or at.deny file, only the root user can schedule future jobs with the **at** command and daemon. In order for non-root users only (answer b) to be able to use the service, their names must exist in an at.allow file that does not contain the root user. For all users to use the service, (answer c), their names should exist in the at.allow file. For no one to be able to use the service (answer d), all names should appear in an at.deny file.

Question 6 

Julio has decided that the system is excessively bogged down each night by too many users running **at** jobs. He has decided to create an at.allow file and place only those users who truly need to run future jobs in that file. In what directory must he store the at.allow file?

❍ a. /bin

❍ b. /boot

❍ c. /dev

❍ d. /etc

❍ e. /home

❍ f. /root

❍ g. /sbin

❍ h. /tmp

❍ i. /usr

❍ j. /var

The correct answer to this question is d. Both the at.allow and at.deny files need to be beneath the /etc directory to be active. This same directory is used for cron.allow and cron.deny files if they are needed as well. The /bin directory (answer a) holds binary files. The /boot directory (answer b) holds the boot files. The /dev directory (answer c) holds the device definitions. The /home directory (answer e) holds the user's home directories (all except root). The root user's home directory is /root (answer f). The /sbin directory (answer g) holds system executables. The /tmp directory (answer h) is used for files that are of a temporary nature. The /usr directory (answer i) holds user resources, and the /var directory (answer j) is used for log files and variable data.

Question 7

Which command will copy files from the system to an archive file that could be placed on a tape and stored elsewhere?

❍ a. **tar xv** x = extract

❍ b. **cpio -iv**

❍ c. **tar cv**

❍ d. **cpio -du**

❍ e. **cpio -pv**

❍ f. **cpio -dfv**

The correct answer to this question is c; this will copy files from the system to an archive file. Answer a will create an archive file, so it is incorrect. Answer b, by using the x parameter, will extract, so it is incorrect. Answer d can copy to and from but will not create a single archive file; therefore, it is incorrect. Answer e will not create a single archive file, so it is incorrect. Answer f also will not create a single archive file, so it too is incorrect.

Question 8

The administrator at Acme Togs manually performs a full backup every Friday after everyone else has gone home for the week. The system is automated to perform an incremental backup Saturday through Thursday night at 9:00 P.M. After a long holiday weekend, the administrator comes to work on Tuesday morning and finds that the system crashed at 7:00 Monday night. How many backup tapes will he need to use to restore the system?

❍ a. 1

❍ b. 2

❍ c. 3

❍ d. 4

The correct answer to this question is c. He must first restore the full backup from Friday night and then restore the incremental backups from Saturday and Sunday.

Question 9

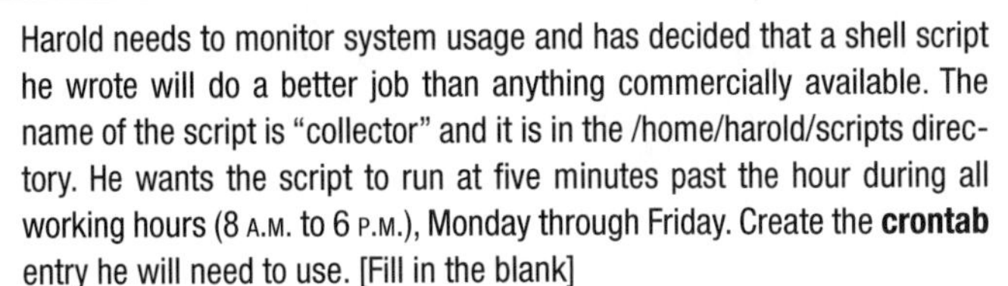

Harold needs to monitor system usage and has decided that a shell script he wrote will do a better job than anything commercially available. The name of the script is "collector" and it is in the /home/harold/scripts directory. He wants the script to run at five minutes past the hour during all working hours (8 A.M. to 6 P.M.), Monday through Friday. Create the **crontab** entry he will need to use. [Fill in the blank]

____

The correct answer to this question is:

```
5 8-17 * * 1-5 /home/harold/scripts/collector
```

This will cause the script to run at 8:05, 9:05, and so on until 17:05 (5:05 P.M.). He does not want the program to run after employees go home at 6:00 or before they come in at 8:00. This program will run regardless of the day of the month or the month (* *) but will run only Monday through Friday (**1–5**).

Question 10

By default, who can read entries in the messages file?

❍ a. Only root

❍ b. Only non-root users

❍ c. Root and other users

❍ d. No one

The correct answer to this question is a. By default, only the root user can read the entries in the messages file and other log files beneath /var/log.

Need to Know More?

Hare, Chris, and George Eckel, et al. *Inside UNIX.* Indianapolis, IN: New Riders Publishing, 1994. ISBN: 1-56205-401-5. Chapter 26 addresses the topics of **tar** and **cpio**.

http://uwsg.ucs.indiana.edu/usail/automation/cron.html is "Automating Tasks with **cron** Services." It provides an overview of the **cron** daemon and discusses file formats and the **crontab** command.

www.ee.pdx.edu/~rootd/catdoc/guide/TheGuide_230 provides a quick definition of the **tar** utility and links to "Backing Up Files on Tape."

www.elementkjournals.com/sun/9810/sun98al.htm is "Housekeeping with **cron**" by Don Kuenz, which discusses how to automate common administrative tasks.

www.ensta.fr/internet/unix/archive_compress/GNU-tar.html describes the GNU version of **tar**.

Where to Next

Step 1: Study and Pass

After reading the first 11 chapters of this book, you've been introduced to all the commands and concepts you need to know to take and pass LPI's Exam 101. At this point, you are ready to sign up for the exam and begin your last-minute cramming. As you cram, however, it will be useful to realize that not all the concepts are equally weighted on the exam. This is not to say that you should not know or study all the concepts, but you need to be more comfortable with your knowledge in some areas than in others.

The exam has 26 identifiable objective areas, with seven possible weights. Table 12.1 lists those objective categories and the weight each represents on the exam, from those with the highest objective weighting to the lowest.

The following sections offer each of the objective categories—in the same order as displayed in the table—and the commands and concepts that fall within each.

Process Text Streams Using Text-Processing Filters

For this objective, you must know how to send text files and output streams through the text-utility filters to get a desired result. The commands to know are:

- cut
- expand
- fmt
- head

Table 12.1 Weighting on Exam 101.

Weight	Objective
7	Process text streams using text-processing filters.
7	Manage users and group accounts and related system files.
5	Create, monitor, and kill processes.
5	Maintain the integrity of filesystems.
5	Use and manage local system documentation.
4	Work effectively on the Unix command line.
4	Tune the user environment and system environment variables.
4	Automate system administration tasks by scheduling jobs to run in the future.
3	Use Unix streams, pipes, and redirects.
3	Perform searches of text files making use of regular expressions.
3	Create partitions and filesystems.
3	Control filesystem mounting and unmounting.
3	Use file permissions to control access to files.
3	Boot the system.
3	Change runlevels and shut down or reboot the system.
3	Configure and use system log files to meet administrative and security needs.
3	Maintain an effective backup strategy.
2	Perform basic file management.
2	Modify process execution priorities.
2	Manage file ownership.
2	Create and change hard and symbolic links.
2	Find system files and place files in the correct location.
2	Find Linux documentation on the Internet.
1	Set and view disk quota.
1	Write system documentation.
1	Provide user support.

- join
- nl
- paste
- pr
- sed

- sort
- split
- tac
- tail
- tr
- wc

Manage Users and Group Accounts and Related System Files

For this objective, you must know how to add, remove, and suspend user accounts. You must know how to add and remove groups. The files to know are all beneath /etc: group, gshadow, passwd, and shadow. The utilities are:

- gpasswd
- groupadd
- passwd
- useradd
- userdel

Create, Monitor, and Kill Processes

Self-explanatory by nature, this objective includes moving jobs between the background and foreground as well as stopping, starting, and monitoring them. Commands are:

- bg
- fg
- jobs
- kill
- ps
- top

Maintain the Integrity of Filesystems

Here you need to know how to look for free space and what a filesystem and inode are. Commands to know are:

- df
- du
- fsck

Use and Manage Local System Documentation

In one word: **man**. Know that there are entries beneath /usr/doc and know how to view more than one manual page if multiples exist by the same name.

Work Effectively on the Unix Command Line

Yes, the exam concerns Linux, but all the main commands are from Unix. This objective does not contain any specific utilities but expects you to know how to work on the command line and recognize that you are working within a shell. You need to know about environmental variables, command history, command substitution, and the path.

Tune the User Environment and System Environment Variables

For this objective, it is important to know about the creation of new users. You should know that they need a home directory and that files from /etc/skel are copied to there by default. Users can modify their environments by modifying their /etc/profile files.

Automate System Administration Tasks by Scheduling Jobs to Run in the Future

This involves the **at** and **cron** facilities. Know about the configuration files (.allow and .deny) and the syntax for each command.

Use Unix Streams, Pipes, and Redirects

For this objective, you need to understand that output defaults to standard output but can be redirected, as can standard input and standard error. You can combine multiple commands by separating them with a semicolon (;) or send the output of one command into another by joining them with a pipe (|). The commands to know are:

- tee
- xargs

Perform Searches of Text Files Making Use of Regular Expressions

If it is a regular expression, you had best know it. This includes methods of looking for exact matches, multiple matches, and nonmatches (retrieving everything except . . .). Know how to use regular expressions with:

- grep
- sed

Create Partitions and Filesystems

Know how to create disk partitions and work with filesystems. The two tools to know are:

- fdisk
- mkfs

Control Filesystem Mounting and Unmounting

For this objective, know how to mount and unmount filesystems. Know how to configure the /etc/fstab file as well.

Use File Permissions to Control Access to Files

Understand how to use symbolic and numeric permissions when setting values. Know the default values assigned to directories and files and the special modes (SUID, SGID, and sticky bit). The tools to know are:

- chmod
- umask

Boot the System

For this objective, you need to know about LILO, the Linux Loader. You also need to know the files /etc/conf.modules, etc/lilo.conf, /etc/modules.conf, and /var/log/messages. The only utility to know is **dmesg**.

Change Runlevels and Shut Down or Reboot the System

You must understand the different runlevels and why one is used instead of another in a specific situation. You should recognize that you must notify users before changing levels and know how to use the commands:

- init
- shutdown

Configure and Use System Log Files to Meet Administrative and Security Needs

Know about the system logs and /var/log/messages. Know, as well, the system log daemon and the fact that it is configured via /etc/syslog.conf. You can manually truncate and compress the log files, or you can use the **logrotate** utility to automate the process.

Maintain an Effective Backup Strategy

For this objective, you need to know the different types of backups and understand their importance. You need to know the following utilities as well:

- cpio
- tar

Perform Basic File Management

This objective involves copying and moving files and directories as well as deleting them. Know that you can give actual names or use wildcards. When it comes to directories, you cannot delete a directory until you remove the entries in it, and deletion can occur recursively. Commands to know are:

- cp
- mv
- rm

Modify Process Execution Priorities

You must know how to change the priority of jobs and how priorities are used. The commands to know are:

- nice
- renice

Manage File Ownership

This objective requires the basic knowledge that every file belongs to an owner and a group. You can change the owner with the **chown** command, and you can change the group with the **chgrp** command.

Create and Change Hard and Symbolic Links

You must know the difference between hard links and symbolic links and the way to create both (**ln** versus **ln -s**).

Find System Files and Place Files in the Correct Location

Memorize the system directories. Know that the /bin directory holds executables, /etc holds configuration files, and so on. Know about the **updatedb** command and its configuration via the /etc/updatedb.conf file. Also know the following utilities:

- find
- locate
- which

Find Linux Documentation on the Internet

Know that the Internet can be a great place to find solutions to problems you are experiencing. Know that if you cannot find the information on your system locally, you have a good chance of finding it in newsgroup archives or through newsgroups or mailing lists. Be aware of the Linux Documentation Project and the fact that you can often find useful information on vendor sites as well.

Set and View Disk Quota

The weighting drops as low as possible beginning with this objective. Nevertheless, you should understand that quotas can prevent individual users from taking all the disk space and causing problems for others. You should know the commands:

- edquota
- quota
- quotaon
- repquota

Write System Documentation

Common sense must prevail here. When you make a significant change to your system, you should document it as thoroughly as possible. Know how to add comments to shell scripts, and realize what information is important to detail: file locations, configuration, steps in a procedure, and so on.

Provide User Support

Recognize that support can come through different mediums: face to face, through the mail, or over the telephone. Understand the importance of providing good support to solve problems and allow users to be productive.

Step 2: Prepare for Exam 102

After you have passed the 101 exam, you need to begin studying for LPI Exam 102. Passing both exams is a requirement for becoming certified at the entry level by the Linux Professional Institute (LPIC Level 1 certification).

Note: General Linux II Exam Cram *(Scottsdale, AZ: The Coriolis Group, 2001; ISBN: 1-57610-962-3) is a complement to this one, helping you to prepare for that exam.*

A few of the topics on the 102 exam are continuations of topics introduced on this exam, but most are new with the 102 exam. The exam has 32 identifiable objective areas, with 10 possible weights. Table 12.2 lists those objective categories and the weight each represents on the exam, from those with the highest objective weighting to the lowest. Following the table is a short list of the commands and concepts that match each objective.

TCP/IP Troubleshooting and Configuration

Weighing in higher than any other objective, this category tests knowledge of the basic files used to configure the system (/etc/hosts, /etc/hostname, /etc/host.conf, /etc/networks, and /etc/resolv.conf) and the following utilities and daemons:

- **dhcpd**
- **host**
- **ifconfig**
- **netstat**
- **ping**
- **route**
- **traceroute**

Use Red Hat Package Manager (rpm)

Package management is a big portion of this exam, and **rpm** is weighted the most heavily. You must know how to use it to install and uninstall packages, figure out the version, list the files within the package, and use it in conjunction with **grep**.

Table 12.2 Weighting on Exam 102.

Weight	Objective
10	TCP/IP troubleshooting and configuration.
6	Use Red Hat Package Manager (**rpm**).
5	Use Debian package management.
5	Make and install programs from source.
5	Customize or write simple scripts.
5	Configure and manage **inetd** and related services.
5	Operate and perform basic configuration of **sendmail**.
4	Set up SCSI and NIC devices.
4	Reconfigure, build, and install a custom kernel and modules.
4	Customize and use the shell environment.
4	Install and configure **Xfree86**.
4	Install and customize a window manager environment.
4	Fundamentals of TCP/IP.
4	Configure and use PPP.
4	Properly manage the **NFS**, **smb**, and **nmb** daemons.
4	Perform security admin tasks.
4	Set up host security.
3	Configure fundamental system hardware.
3	Configure modem and sound cards.
3	Install a boot manager.
3	Manage shared libraries.
3	Manage kernel modules at run time.
3	Install and configure local and remote printers.
3	Operate and perform basic configuration of Apache.
3	Set up and configure basic DNS services.
2	Design hard-disk layout.
2	Perform basic file-editing operations using **vi**.
2	Manage printers and print queues.
2	Set up user-level security.
1	Print files.
1	Set up XDM.
1	Identify and terminate runaway X applications.

Use Debian Package Management

The second most popular package-management utility, Debian, is important on the test as well. You must know how to perform the same functions with it as you would with **rpm** and edit the files and directories it works with.

Make and Install Programs from Source

This objective requires knowledge of **tar** files, compressed archives, and simple customization. The latter implies modifying paths, working with directories, and making and installing executables.

Customize or Write Simple Scripts

Create executable batch files that use some logic. The logic can be as simple as loop routines or as complicated as if-then tests. You must also have knowledge of SUID rights and exit values.

Configure and Manage inetd and Related Services

Know how to start services with **inetd**, as well as how to manually start and stop services. Also, the configuration (and, to some extent, use) of Telnet and FTP is required knowledge.

Operate and Perform Basic Configuration of sendmail

You must know how to modify the configuration files, create mail aliases, and manage the mail queue. You must also know how to use the commands:

- **mailq**
- **newalias**
- **sendmail**

Set Up SCSI and NIC Devices

Very self-explanatory, this objective dwells at the hardware level. The test requires knowledge of the SCSI BIOS, as well as an understanding of SCSI IDs and termination. For network interface cards, you need to know how to change the I/O and IRQ settings.

Reconfigure, Build, and Install a Custom Kernel and Modules

You must have basic knowledge of how to reconfigure the kernel and make a new one. You need to know how to reconfigure LILO and use the commands:

- depmod
- lilo
- make
- menuconfig
- oldconfig
- xconfig

and the files:

- /etc/conf.modules
- /etc/lilo.conf
- /etc/modules.conf
- /lib/modules/*kernel_version*/modules.dep
- /usr/src/linux/.config
- /usr/src/linux/Makefile

Customize and Use the Shell Environment

For this objective, you must know how to modify the shell environment the user is working in with a major emphasis on bash. You must have knowledge of the environment variables, as well as such files as .profile, .bash_login, and so on.

Install and Configure Xfree86

Know how to work within X and configure fonts and values. You must also know how to verify that the equipment you have (monitor, card) will work properly.

Install and Customize a Window Manager Environment

This objective tests how to customize window manager menus and work with .xinitrc, .Xdefaults, and .rc files.

Fundamentals of TCP/IP

Back to TCP/IP for more testing: Here you must know the basics of IP addressing and the default ports used by services. The utilities to know are:

- dig
- ftp

- **host**
- **ping**
- **telnet**
- **traceroute**
- **whois**

Configure and Use PPP

The Point-to-Point Protocol is used for remote and dial-up connections, and you must know how to configure, monitor, and manage it. All the steps used in establishing a connection are fair play for exam questions.

Properly Manage the NFS, smb, and nmb Daemons

You must know the methods by which remote filesystems are mounted via NFS, as well as how to use Samba. By virtue of the testing upon Samba and **smb** (the means by which Windows NT machines communicate), you must know a fair amount about Windows networking for this objective.

Perform Security Admin Tasks

This objective focuses on the implementation of security wrappers and the configuration of system password variables. You need to know how to find all SUID and SGID files and configure **ssh**.

Set Up Host Security

A continuation of the preceding objective, this one focuses on security from the network standpoint. You are tested about the configuration of **syslogd**, as well as how to work with CERT and BUGTRAQ.

Configure Fundamental System Hardware

"Fundamental hardware" consists of system BIOS, IRQs, I/O ports, and similar resources. You are expected to know the basics of ports and hard disks (including the history of Linux problems with drives above 1,024 cylinders).

Configure Modem and Sound Cards

This objective is self-explanatory for the most part; you must know how to configure modems for PPP, SLIP, and CSLIP. You must also know about DMA addresses and the different ways to configure dial-in versus dial-out services.

Install a Boot Manager

You must know not just any boot manager, but specifically LILO. The test requires knowledge of the configuration of /etc/lilo.conf.

Manage Shared Libraries

The knowledge of the existence and necessity of shared libraries forms the core knowledge for this objective. You must know the utilities:

- ldconfig
- ldd

Manage Kernel Modules at Run Time

For this objective, you need to understand the modules and which ones are appropriate to use in a given situation. The commands to know are:

- **insmod**
- **lsmod**
- **modinfo**
- **modprobe**
- **rmmod**

Install and Configure Local and Remote Printers

Working with the daemon (**lpd**) and configuring files to print are the topics of this objective. You need to know the files used in the process (/etc/apsfilterrc, /etc/magicfilter/, /etc/printcap, and /usr/lib/apsfilter/filter/). You must also know how to work with Samba printing and PostScript, as well as non-PostScript printing.

Operate and Perform Basic Configuration of Apache

You must know how to work with Apache configuration files, as well as how to start and stop the service. Working with **httpd** to provide Web services (but not customizing the actual **httpd** configuration files) forms the core of the objective.

Set Up and Configure Basic DNS Services

The Domain Name Service is used to translate hostnames (FQDN names) to IP addresses. As such, this objective is a further extension of the other TCP/IP objectives listed earlier. Necessary knowledge includes knowing how to work with the configuration files, how to use the **nslookup** command properly, and how to recognize the differences (and respond to them accordingly) in BIND implementations.

Design Hard-Disk Layout

A carryover of topics for Exam 101, this objective dictates that you know how to partition and work with swap space and mount points.

Perform Basic File-Editing Operations Using vi

Overlook the "basic" portion; this objective focuses on how to use the **vi** editor. You need to know how to create and edit files, with an emphasis on inserting, moving, replacing, and copying text.

Manage Printers and Print Queues

This objective tests knowledge of print-related utilities. For this objective, you need to know the following:

- **lpc**
- **lpq**
- **lpr**
- **lprm**

Set Up User-Level Security

Such issues in this objective include logins (the whole process thereof) and ways to monitor memory usage and process utilization.

Print Files and Set Up XDM

These two objectives are self-explanatory.

Identify and Terminate Runaway X Applications

The focus here is on applications that continue to run after the session ends. To pass this objective, simply know how to identify them and respond to them.

Step 3: Other Possibilities

After passing both exams listed here and becoming LPIC Level 1 certified, you can pursue many different paths if you want to continue down the certification path. LPIC Level 1 certifies you as knowing the basic functions of the Linux operating system and of system administration. This certification provides an excellent foundation upon which to build other certifications of a higher level.

Among the possibilities that exist after finishing LPIC Level 1, you might want to consider:

- *Becoming certified by LPI at Level 2*—Consisting of another two exams (201 and 202), this certification is geared toward the intermediate (rather than the beginning) administrator. It tests on implementation and troubleshooting of Internet gateways, servers, and Samba (in much greater detail than Exam 102). Exam 201 requires you to be able to track and solve problems, write **sh** and **sed** shell scripts, and fully understand internetworking. Exam 202 tests the knowledge of processes and booting and working with the kernel, libraries, bugs, and upgrades. More information appears at **www.lpi.org**.

Note: As of this writing, both exams are in development, but they are expected to be available soon.

- *Obtaining a vendor-specific certification*—LPI exams are intended to be vendor neutral and do not overly favor one vendor's implementation of Linux over another. If you are working exclusively with one vendor's Linux, and a mastery of the intricacies of its implementation will make you more valuable (both in terms of knowledge and market value), then you should investigate whether that vendor has a certification for its operating system. The best example is the Red Hat Certified Engineer (RHCE) certification. More information on it appears at **www.redhat.com/services/training**.

- *Obtaining another general Linux certification*—Both Sair and CompTIA (the organization behind the A+ and Network+ exams) offer their own vendor-neutral certifications. Sair has three levels (similar to LPI), with each consisting of four exams. More information on Sair and their exams/certification appears at **www.linuxcertification.com**. CompTIA offers a single-exam, single-level certification known as Linux+. More information on this exam appears at **www.comptia.org**.

Note: As of this writing, the Linux+ exam is not available, but it is expected to be available toward the end of 2001.

- *Becoming a certified trainer*—Several companies offer certification as Linux instructors. One of the best examples is Caldera's OpenLearning Instructor certification. Once you earn this certification, you receive free copies of OpenLinux betas and other resources you need to stay on top of the operating system. You also can teach in OpenLearning training centers (which are required to use certified instructors) and access resources not available to the general public. You must be LPI certified to be an OpenLearning Instructor. More information appears at **www.calderasystems.com/openlearning/instructor**.

Once you complete LPIC Level I certification, you can stop or continue on to other certifications. The Coriolis Group offers a number of other books about the other certifications, and you can find the most current list at **www.examcram.com**.

Whatever your choice, I wish you the best with the 101 exam and all your certification endeavors.

Sample Test

In this chapter, I provide pointers to help you develop a successful test-taking strategy, including how to choose proper answers, how to decode ambiguity, how to work within the LPI testing framework, how to decide what you need to memorize, and how to prepare for the test. At the end of the chapter, I include 70 questions on subject matter pertinent to the LPI 101 Certification Exam. Good luck!

Questions, Questions, Questions

You should have no doubt in your mind that you are facing a test full of specific and pointed questions. The LPI Exam 101 that you take will include 52 questions, and you will be allotted 90 minutes to complete the exam.

Questions for the LPI test belong to one of three types:

- Multiple choice with a single answer
- Multiple choice with multiple answers
- Fill in the blank

Always take the time to read a question at least twice before selecting an answer and always look for an Exhibit button as you examine each question. Exhibits include graphics information related to a question. An *exhibit* is usually a screen capture of program output or GUI (graphical user interface) information that you must examine to analyze the question's contents and formulate an answer. The Exhibit button brings up graphics and charts used to help explain a question, provide additional data, or illustrate page layout or program behavior.

Not every question has only one answer; many questions require multiple answers. Therefore, you should read each question carefully, determine how many answers are necessary or possible, and look for additional hints or instructions when selecting answers. Such instructions occur in brackets immediately following the question itself.

Picking Proper Answers

Obviously, the only way to pass any exam is to select enough of the right answers to obtain a passing score. LPI's exams are not standardized, however, as the SAT and GRE exams are; they are far more diabolical and convoluted. In some cases, questions are strangely worded, and deciphering them can be a real challenge. In such cases, you might need to rely on answer-elimination skills. Almost always, at least one answer for a question can be eliminated immediately because it matches one of these conditions:

- The answer does not apply to the situation.
- The answer describes a nonexistent issue, an invalid option, or an imaginary state.
- The answer can be eliminated because of information in the question itself.

After you eliminate all answers that are obviously wrong, you can apply your retained knowledge to eliminate further answers. Look for items that sound correct but refer to actions, commands, or features that are not present or are not available in the situation the question describes.

If you're still faced with a blind guess among two or more potentially correct answers, reread the question. Try to picture how each of the remaining answers would alter the situation. Be especially sensitive to terminology; sometimes the choice of words (*remove* instead of *disable*) can make the difference between a right answer and a wrong one.

Only after you've exhausted your ability to eliminate answers but remain unclear about which of the remaining possibilities is correct should you guess at an answer. An unanswered question offers you no points, but guessing gives you at least some chance of getting a question right; just don't be too hasty when making a blind guess.

You can wait until the last round of reviewing marked questions (just as you're about to run out of time or out of unanswered questions) before you start making guesses. Guessing should be a last resort, however.

Decoding Ambiguity

LPI's exams have a reputation for including questions that can be difficult to interpret, confusing, or ambiguous. The only way to beat LPI at its own game is to be prepared. You'll discover that many exam questions test your knowledge of things that are not directly related to the issue raised by a question. This means that the answers you must choose from, even incorrect ones, are just as much a part of the skill assessment as the question itself.

Questions often give away their answers, but you have to be Sherlock Holmes to see the clues. Often, subtle hints appear in the question text in such a way that they seem almost irrelevant to the situation. You must realize that each question is a test unto itself and that you need to inspect and successfully navigate each question to pass the exam. Look for small clues, such as one question toward the end of the exam that states the answer to a question that appeared earlier in the exam. Little things can point to the right answer if properly understood; if missed, they can leave you facing a blind guess.

Another common difficulty with certification exams is vocabulary. Be sure to brush up on the key terms presented in the Glossary at the end of this book the day before you take the test.

Working within the Framework

The test questions appear in random order, and many elements or issues that receive mention in one question might also crop up in other questions. It's not uncommon to find that an incorrect answer to one question is the answer to another question, and vice versa. Take the time to read every answer to each question, even if you recognize the answer to a question immediately. That extra reading might spark a memory or remind you about a feature or function that helps you on another question elsewhere in the exam.

Don't forget that you can revisit any question as many times as you like. If you're uncertain of the answer to a question, check the box that's provided so you can return to it later. You should also mark questions that you think might offer information that you can use to answer other questions. On fixed-length tests, I have usually marked somewhere between 25 and 50 percent of the questions on the exams I have taken. The testing software is designed to let you mark every question if you choose; use this framework to your advantage. Everything you'll want to see again should be marked; the testing software can then help you return to marked questions quickly and easily.

For fixed-length tests, I strongly recommend that you first read through the entire test quickly before getting caught up in answering individual questions. This will help jog your memory as you review the potential answers and can help identify questions that you want to mark for easy access to their contents. It will also let you identify and mark the tricky questions for easy return as well. The key is to make a quick pass over the territory to begin with—so that you know what you're up against—and then to survey that territory more thoroughly on a second pass, when you can begin to answer all questions systematically and consistently.

If you see something in a question or one of the answers that jogs your memory on a topic, or that you feel you should record if the topic appears in another question, write it down on your piece of paper.

Don't be afraid to take notes on what you see in various questions. Sometimes, what you record from one question—especially if it's not as familiar as it should be or reminds you of the name or use of some network device, utility, or network interface details—can help you on other questions later on.

Deciding What to Memorize

The amount of memorization you must undertake for an exam depends on how well you remember what you've read and how well you know the material by heart. If you're a visual thinker and can see a command line and how all the components of the operating system interact with each other in your head, you won't need to memorize as much as someone who's less visually oriented. However, the exam will stretch your abilities to memorize operating system features and utilities, including options and troubleshooting.

At a minimum, you should memorize the following kinds of information:

- The different files needed to boot
- The core command-line utilities for working with files
- The fundamentals of the filesystem hierarchy
- The different runlevels and how to obtain them
- How to work with documentation and provide support
- Troubleshooting the system

Don't forget that the Cram Sheet at the front of the book is designed to capture the material that's most important to memorize; use this to guide your studies as well.

Preparing for the Test

The best way to prepare for the test—after you've studied—is to take at least one practice exam. I've included one here in this chapter for that reason. The test questions are located in the pages that follow, and, unlike the preceding chapters in this book, the answers don't follow the questions immediately; you'll have to flip to Chapter 14 to review the answers separately.

Give yourself 90 minutes to take this exam, and keep yourself on the honor system—don't look back at the text in the book or jump ahead to the Answer Key. When your time is up or you've finished the questions, you can check your work. Pay special attention to the explanations for the incorrect answers; these can also help reinforce your knowledge of the material. Knowing how to recognize correct answers is good, but understanding why incorrect answers are wrong can be equally valuable.

Taking the Test

Relax. Once you're sitting in front of the testing computer, there's nothing more you can do to increase your knowledge or preparation. Take a deep breath, stretch, and start reading that first question.

You don't need to rush, either. You have plenty of time to complete each question and to return to those questions that you skip or mark for return. If you read a question twice and remain clueless, you can mark it if you're taking a fixed-length test. Don't spend more than 5 minutes on any single question—if it takes you that long to get nowhere, it's time to guess and move on.

You can read through the entire test and, before returning to marked questions for a second visit, you can figure out how much time you've got per question. As you answer each question, remove its mark. Continue to review the remaining marked questions until you either run out of time or complete the test.

Set a maximum time limit for questions and watch your time on long or complex questions. If you hit your limit, it's time to guess and move on. Don't deprive yourself of the opportunity to see more questions by taking too long to puzzle over questions, unless you think you can figure out the answer. Otherwise, you're limiting your opportunity to pass.

That's it for pointers. Here are some questions for you to practice on.

Sample Test

Question 1

Martin calls you on the telephone. He has a file named "marketinfo" that has 56,000 lines in it, and he wants to see only the last 10,000. Which of the following commands should you tell him to run?

❍ a. **tail +46000 marketinfo**

❍ b. **tail +10000 marketinfo**

❍ c. **tail -46000 marketinfo**

❍ d. **head +46000 marketinfo**

❍ e. **head -10000 marketinfo**

❍ f. **tail +46001 marketinfo**

Question 2

At the command line, Tim has given the command **TODAY=Friday**. Which of the following will show that the variable **TODAY** is equal to a value of Friday?

❍ a. **set**

❍ b. **env**

❍ c. **show**

❍ d. **display**

Question 3

Which of the following commands will send the errors from the abc application to a file, but not the standard output?

❍ a. **abc > abc.error**

❍ b. **abc 2 > abc.error 2>&1**

❍ c. **abc 2> abc.error**

❍ d. **abc >> abc.error**

Question 4

What environmental variable in the bash shell points to the command history file? [Fill in the blank]

____

Question 5

You wish to combine two files together such that the fields from each file are combined into a single output file. The first field of each of the two starting files is identical—equal to the employee number. Which utility should you use to create the output file?

- ❍ a. **join**
- ❍ b. **paste**
- ❍ c. **cat**
- ❍ d. **od**
- ❍ e. **sort**

Question 6

Tim has a large file that exceeds the size of a floppy's storage capacity. He wants to put the file on two floppies so he can take it with him when he joins the competition. What command can he use to make the file fit two floppies?

- ❍ a. **nl**
- ❍ b. **cut**
- ❍ c. **fmt**
- ❍ d. **split**

Question 7

You wish to find all the five-letter files in the current directory that end with the letter "c". What command should you use?

❍ a. **ls *c**

❍ b. **ls *c***

❍ c. **ls ????c**

❍ d. **ls ????c***

Question 8

Karen wants to sort the "defg" file and display its results on her screen. She also wants a copy of the sorted results to be saved in a file named "defg.sorted". What command should she use?

❍ a. **sort defg > defg.sorted 2>&1**

❍ b. **sort defg | tee defg.sorted**

❍ c. **sort defg ; tee defg.sorted**

❍ d. **defg > tee defg.sorted**

Question 9

Evan must run a cleanup utility every night until the programmers can fix the code that is causing problems on his system. This utility is very verbose and displays a message for every line of a file it goes through. Where can Evan send the output to avoid it being displayed on his screen or filling up a file?

❍ a. /dev/null

❍ b. /root

❍ c. /dev/root

❍ d. /dev

❍ e. /null

Question 10

Kristin started a process 3 hours ago that ties up many system - resources. She has written down in her documentation that she is supposed to start it at a lower priority, but she forgot to do so. What utility can she use at this point to reduce the priority of the process?

❍ a. **nice**

❍ b. **ps**

❍ c. **top**

❍ d. **jobs**

❍ e. **renice**

Question 11

Spencer has a notation from the central office that he is to run the **zzzz** utility today on his system and that it will probably run for 4 hours. The note says that he will need to start the job in the background. What syntax should he use to do this?

❍ a. **bg zzzz**

❍ b. **zzzz bg**

❍ c. **zzzz &**

❍ d. **& zzzz**

Question 12

Spencer forgot to start the job in the background, and it is currently running in the foreground. What should Spencer first type on his keyboard to move the job to the background?

❍ a. **bg**

❍ b. **jobs**

❍ c. **fg**

❍ d. **^Z**

Question 13

What search criteria would best be used to find the lines within the BRIO.TXT file about disks?

❍ a. **grep disks BRIO.TXT**

❍ b. **find disks BRIO.TXT**

❍ c. **sed disks BRIO.TXT**

❍ d. **search disks BRIO.txt**

Question 14

Allan wants to create a DOS partition on device sda3. What command should he use to do this? [Fill in the blank]

____

Question 15

Which of the following characters must exist for a path to be considered a relative path (rather than an absolute path)?

❍ a. \

❍ b. .

❍ c. ?

❍ d. #

Question 16

Madonna needs to change the permissions on the file "hope" (which are currently equal to 700) such that the group has read and write permissions, and other has only read. Which command will allow her to perform this change?

❍ a. **chmod g+rw:o+r hope**

❍ b. **chmod go+r,o-w hope**

❍ c. **chmod g+rw,o+r hope**

❍ d. **chmod g+rw;o+r hope**

Question 17

Tony has used the command **cat > fileone** to start creating a file. He is now in the middle of a line and would like to quit and save the text he has entered. What must he do?

❍ a. Press ^D once

❍ b. Press ^Z once

❍ c. Press ^D twice

❍ d. Press ^Z twice

❍ e. Press ^Z followed by ^D

Question 18

You suspect that Maude is taking up an enormous amount of disk space with images she is saving from Web sites. You know for a fact that because of the way permissions are set, the only place she can be saving these files is beneath her home directory. What tool can you use to see how much disk space she is using beneath her home directory?

❍ a. **quota**

❍ b. **quotaon**

❍ c. **df**

❍ d. **du**

Question 19

You are the administrator for ACME Plumbing. Due to recent growth, you have had to expand from the simple system you once had to something considerably more complicated. When your system comes up, you want to configure it to mount a number of remote filesystems automatically. What file must you edit to include the remote filesystems for automatic mounting?

❍ a. /etc/inittab

❍ b. /etc/fstab

❍ c. /etc/group

❍ d. /dev/mnt

Question 20

What would be the minimal permission(s) needed on a directory to be able to save a file within that directory?

❍ a. read

❍ b. write

❍ c. execute

❍ d. read and write

Question 21

What are the default permissions assigned to a newly created file if the **umask** is set to 44?

❍ a. **-rw--w--w-**

❍ b. **--w--w--w-**

❍ c. **-rw-r--r--**

❍ d. **-r--r--r--**

Question 22

What are the default permissions assigned to a newly created directory if the **umask** is set to 44?

❍ a. **d-wx-wx-wx**

❍ b. **d-wx------**

❍ c. **drwx-wx-wx**

❍ d. **drwxr--r--**

❍ e. **drw-r--r--**

❍ f. **dr--r--r--**

Question 23

As the administrator for D S Technical, you have created a script file users can run that will query their system and write an inventory of what they have into a text file. Due to its sensitive nature, the script must be run by root. The script must be run from each machine in order to work, and you have no inclination to spend 2 days walking from machine to machine running it. You decide to send email to the users telling them that they must run the script before the end of the day, and you give them the location to the file. What permissions should you assign to the file if it is currently owned by the root owner and root group? [Choose all correct answers]

- ❑ a. 777
- ❑ b. 1777
- ❑ c. 2777
- ❑ d. 4777

Question 24

You have created a script file named "getall" in your home directory (/home /workerbee), which you are currently working in. You assign permissions of 744 to the file and want to run it. By default, which of the following commands will execute the script? [Choose all correct answers]

- ❑ a. **getall**
- ❑ b. **/usr/workerbee/getall**
- ❑ c. **./getall**
- ❑ d. **../getall**

Question 25

Which of the following log files is considered to be the "system" log?

- ❍ a. /var/log/system
- ❍ b. /var/log/messages
- ❍ c. /etc/lilo.conf
- ❍ d. /etc/modules.conf

Question 26

Each time you give the command **man nice**, the entry from beneath the man1 subdirectory appears. You know there is an entry for **nice** beneath the man2 subdirectory as well. What command must you give to see only the entry beneath the man2 subdirectory? [Fill in the blank]

____

Question 27

Which command can you give to find out which manual subdirectories (and only manual subdirectories) have entries for **nice**?

- ❍ a. **whereis nice**
- ❍ b. **whatis nice**
- ❍ c. **which nice**
- ❍ d. **man nice**

Question 28

Which of the following variables determines which utility is used to display manual pages when the **man** command is used?

- ❍ a. **MORE**
- ❍ b. **MANPAGER**
- ❍ c. **MAN**
- ❍ d. **PAGER**

Question 29

Madison has added the commercial DSTECH editor (version 3.5.7) to her system. No printed documentation accompanied the CD, and now she wants to read the online documentation. Where should the documentation now reside?

- ❍ a. /usr/man/man8/DSTECH
- ❍ b. /usr/doc/DSTECH-3.5.7
- ❍ c. /usr/man/man8/DSTECH-3.5.7
- ❍ d. /usr/doc/3.5.7/DSTECH
- ❍ e. /usr/doc/DSTECH/3.5.7
- ❍ f. /usr/man/man8/DSTECH/3.5.7gz

Question 30

Which field of the /usr/passwd file contains free text that allows you to enter a description about the user?

- ❍ a. 5
- ❍ b. 4
- ❍ c. 3
- ❍ d. 2
- ❍ e. 1
- ❍ f. None

Question 31

In which files can passwords for users exist? [Choose all correct answers]

- ❑ a. passwd
- ❑ b. gpasswd
- ❑ c. shadow
- ❑ d. gshadow

Question 32

When creating users, Martin would like to have a number of template files automatically copied into their home directories. Where should these template files be placed?

❍ a. /etc/skel

❍ b. /home/skel

❍ c. /root/skel

❍ d. /skel

Question 33

You have created a new directory (/system/bin) that holds utilities you have written for internal use. After careful debugging and testing, all users on your system should be able to access these files. In order to do so, the directory needs to be added to the **PATH** statement. How would you best add this directory to the path of your existing 16 users?

❍ a. Add it to /etc/profile.

❍ b. Add it to /etc/skel.

❍ c. Add it to the .profile in each user's home directory.

❍ d. Make it the sixth field of each user's /etc/passwd entry.

Question 34

Karen is going on maternity leave for 6 weeks. Whether she will return after the 6 weeks is unknown at this time, but you have been told to act as if she will. How can you best disable her account while she is gone?

❍ a. Delete her .profile file in the home directory.

❍ b. Change her password to an entity that only you know.

❍ c. Add a pound sign as the first character of her entry in /etc/passwd.

❍ d. Use the **userdel** command to disable her account temporarily.

Question 35

You need to automatically enable archiving of log files on your system and have 12 files you want the archiving to occur to. What configuration file should be used to specify the 12 files? [Fill in the blank]

____

Question 36

Which type of backup can be used to get all the files that have been changed or created since the last full backup was done, even if a number of smaller backups have been done in the interim?

- ❍ a. Incremental
- ❍ b. Differential
- ❍ c. Common
- ❍ d. Component

Question 37

You wish to have an application run every night at 9:15 P.M. What should the specification in the crontab file resemble?

- ❍ a. * 15 22 * *
- ❍ b. * 22 15 * *
- ❍ c. 22 15 * * *
- ❍ d. 15 22 * * *
- ❍ e. * * 15 22 *
- ❍ f. * * 22 15 *
- ❍ g. * * * 22 15
- ❍ h. * * * 15 22

Question 38

You wish to allow all users except the three temporary employees to use the **at** functions. The three temporary employees are Bob, Jan, and Shannon. Where should the restriction for them be placed?

❍ a. at.allow

❍ b. cron.allow

❍ c. cron.deny

❍ d. at.deny

Question 39

You are showing a new user how to combine two files into a single file by appending the output of one to the end of another. You tell him that he should never use the following syntax:

```
cat fileone filetwo > fileone
```

What is your reason?

❍ a. The **cat** command will read only one file at a time.

❍ b. Two greater-than signs (>>) must always be used when combining files.

❍ c. Using "**cat >**" and going to the same file you are reading from first empties the contents.

❍ d. You *can* combine files in this way.

Question 40

To find the current time on a system, what is the command to use?

❍ a. **time**

❍ b. **date**

❍ c. **env**

❍ d. **set**

Question 41

To find what directory you are currently in, what is the command to use?

❍ a. **PWD**

❍ b. **cd**

❍ c. **where**

❍ d. None of the above

Question 42

All of the following can be sources of information about the DSTECH editor except which one?

❍ a. /usr/doc/DSTECH

❍ b. **DSTECH --help**

❍ c. Accompanying .pdf files on the media

❍ d. The **dstech.com** Web site

Question 43

When creating a login name for a new user, which rule(s) should you adhere to?

❍ a. Use something unlikely to be easily guessed.

❍ b. Keep it simple.

❍ c. Change it often.

❍ d. All of the above.

Question 44

Text files created in Linux and accessible at the command line can be viewed with which utility?

❍ a. **ln**

❍ b. **type**

❍ c. **cat**

❍ d. All of the above

Question 45

The **mv** command can be used to perform which function(s)?

❍ a. Move a file from one directory to another

❍ b. Rename a file in the same directory

❍ c. Move and rename a directory

❍ d. All of the above

Question 46

Fields within a file can be delimited by what?

❍ a. Colons

❍ b. Spaces

❍ c. Pipes

❍ d. Any printable character

Question 47

Using five fields, specify the **crontab** entry for a process to run at 10:20 in the morning on every Wednesday in the month of May. [Fill in the blank]

____

Question 48

System background processes running in Linux are known as what?

❍ a. Inodes

❍ b. Superblocks

❍ c. Daemons

❍ d. Services

Question 49

Which of the following is not an example of a daemon?

- ❍ a. **ps**
- ❍ b. **init**
- ❍ c. **cron**
- ❍ d. **syslogd**
- ❍ e. **atd**

Question 50

What are runlevels?

- ❍ a. The amount of time it takes for jobs to run
- ❍ b. States that control what a machine can do
- ❍ c. Process command numbers
- ❍ d. Networking limitations

Question 51

Home directories can be determined by which of the following? [Choose all correct answers]

- ❑ a. /etc/passwd
- ❑ b. /etc/profile
- ❑ c. **$HOME**
- ❑ d. System administrators

Question 52

Which of the following characters signifies the beginning of comments within a HOSTS file?

- ❍ a. @
- ❍ b. $
- ❍ c. !
- ❍ d. #

Question 53

The command **grep a[o-t]** would find which of the following matches? [Choose all correct answers]

❑ a. task

❑ b. act

❑ c. tort

❑ d. at

❑ e. a

Question 54

Which of the following commands contain an error that will prevent them from executing?

❑ a. **ls-l *.txt**

❑ b. **ls -l -t *.txt**

❑ c. **TERM = vwpt**

❑ d. **chown 777 fileone**

Question 55

The command **fgrep karen kristin** will do what?

❍ a. Find all files containing "karen" and "kristin" in their file names

❍ b. Not run—**grep** is needed

❍ c. Find every occurrence of "karen" in the file "kristin"

❍ d. Find every occurrence of "kristin" in the file "karen"

Question 56

The command **grep banner[^s] fileone** will do what?

❍ a. Find every occurrence of words starting with "banner"

❍ b. Find every word starting with "banner" at the beginning of a line

❍ c. Find every word starting with "banner" at the end of a line

❍ d. Find "banner", "bannering", and so on, but not "banners"

Question 57

What is the numeric value of the permissions **-rwsrw-rw-?**

- ❍ a. 766
- ❍ b. 755
- ❍ c. 744
- ❍ d. 722
- ❍ e. 711
- ❍ f. 1766
- ❍ g. 1744
- ❍ h. 2766
- ❍ i. 2744
- ❍ j. 4766
- ❍ k. 4777
- ❍ l. 4744
- ❍ m. 4666

Question 58

Which /usr/man subdirectory would contain the manual pages for root operator utilities?

- ❍ a. man1
- ❍ b. man4
- ❍ c. man5
- ❍ d. man8

Question 59

Which of the following utilities can be used to compress multiple files into a single archive?

- ❍ a. **gzip**
- ❍ b. **cpio**
- ❍ c. **tar**
- ❍ d. **zcat**

Question 60

Gerald has an archived file named 10_23.tar, and he wants to extract bubble.txt from it after he accidentally deleted that file from his system. Knowing the name of the file he wants to extract, and the archive file, give the minimal syntax needed to extract this file. [Fill in the blank]

____

Question 61

Jerry wants to use the **find** command to get a list of all the files on his system with the extension .txt. Once found, he wants to search through each of them (using **grep**) to see which ones contain the phrase "CDRW purchase proposal". What should he use to combine the **find** and **grep** operations?

❍ a. A semicolon (;)

❍ b. **xargs**

❍ c. The output redirect character (>)

❍ d. **join**

Question 62

The file "oursystem.commands" was created on an ancient terminal that had only uppercase characters. The file was supposed to be a shell script and now will not run because all commands appear in uppercase. The entire file needs to be converted to lowercase. What utility can be used for this purpose?

❍ a. **tac**

❍ b. **od**

❍ c. **tr**

❍ d. **expand**

Question 63

Harold has a file with a large number of figures in it. He sorted the file, trying to put it in order from lowest to highest dollar amount spent, but it came out in an odd order (1, 10, 11, 100, 111, 2, 3, and so on). What option should Harold use to sort the file in the order desired?

❍ a. **-n**

❍ b. **-r**

❍ c. **-b**

❍ d. **-f**

Question 64

What is the command to make a symbolic link to the file "options.bmp" by the name "figure_one.bmp"? [Fill in the blank]

____

Question 65

What command is used to show running processes and dynamically update them in the display? [Fill in the blank]

____

Question 66

By default, beneath which directory would nonchanging system information and documentation most likely be found?

❍ a. /etc

❍ b. /var

❍ c. /usr

❍ d. /home

Question 67

Which entry in the inittab file identifies the runlevel the system should attempt to go to on the next boot?

❍ a. id

❍ b. s0

❍ c. bw

❍ d. pf

Question 68

Which runlevel would be equal to completely powering the system off?

❍ a. 0

❍ b. 1

❍ c. 2

❍ d. 5

❍ e. 6

Question 69

Which of the following commands will return the current time?

❍ a. **echo ‘date‘**

❍ b. **echo ‘date‘**

❍ c. **echo “date”**

❍ d. **echo $DATE**

Question 70

Which command can be used to count the number of words in a text file?

❍ a. **tr**

❍ b. **tc**

❍ c. **cw**

❍ d. **wc**

Answer Key

1. f
2. a
3. c
4. **HISTFILE**
5. a
6. d
7. c
8. b
9. a
10. e
11. c
12. d
13. a
14. **mkfs -t msdos /dev/sda3**
15. b
16. c
17. c
18. d
19. b
20. b
21. a
22. c
23. c, d
24. b, c
25. b
26. **man 2 nice**
27. b
28. d
29. b
30. f
31. a, c
32. a
33. a
34. c
35. /etc/syslog.conf
36. b
37. d
38. d
39. c
40. b
41. d
42. b
43. b
44. c
45. d
46. d
47. 20 10 5 * 3
48. c
49. a
50. b
51. a, c, d
52. d
53. a, d
54. a, c
55. c
56. d
57. j
58. d
59. c
60. tar xf 10_23.tar bubble.txt
61. b
62. c
63. a
64. **ln -s options.bmp figure_one.bmp**
65. **top**
66. c
67. a
68. a
69. a
70. d

Question 1

The correct answer is f. To see only 10,000 lines out of 56,000, Martin must start with number 46,001 and view the remaining lines. Answer a would show 10,001 lines at the end of the file, whereas answer b would start with 10,000 and end up displaying 46,001 lines. Answer c would display the last 46,000 lines, and answer d is invalid because **head** does not have a + option. Answer e would display the first 10,000 lines and not the last.

Question 2

The correct answer is a. Until the variable is exported, it will not show up in the environment (answer b) but will display with the **set** command. Answers c and d are invalid options for this question (they don't exist).

Question 3

The correct answer is c. This will send the errors to the file, but not the standard output. Answer a will send standard output to the file, but not the errors. Answer b will send both errors and standard output to the file. Answer d will append standard output to the file, but not redirect errors.

Question 4

The correct answer is **HISTFILE**. This variable points to the location of the .bash_history file. By default, it is within each user's home directory.

Question 5

The correct answer is a. When the files share something in common (the first field in this case), the **join** utility can combine them together. If they share absolutely nothing in common, then **paste** (answer b) can be used. The other commands will not combine files together in the way specified.

Question 6

The correct answer is d. The **split** command will chop the file into smaller entities. The **nl** command (answer a) simply numbers the lines of output. The **cut** command (answer b) will remove fields of output, but it won't change the size of the file. The **fmt** command (answer c) can format display-per-line size and other variables but does nothing for reducing a file's size.

Question 7

The correct answer is c. Answer a will find all entries ending in "c", regardless of the number of characters in the file names. Answer b will find all names containing a "c", regardless of whether they have more or less than five characters and regardless of where "c" appears in the name. Answer d will find all files that have "c" as the fifth character, but these files could have any number of characters following.

Question 8

The correct answer is b. This will sort the file and display the output to the screen as well as save the output in the file. Answer a will display nothing on the screen, sending both output and error to the same place. Answer c will fail because the semicolon is used to connect dissimilar commands, and **tee** cannot stand on its own. Answer d will fail because "defg" is a file and not an application (among other reasons).

Question 9

The correct answer is a. There is a special "nowhere" defined as /dev/null. Answer b would send the output to the home directory of the root user, whereas answer d would send the output to the /dev directory. The directories in answers c and e do not exist.

Question 10

The correct answer is e. Once a job is running, only **renice** can change the priority. When the job is started, **nice** (answer a) should be used. The other commands listed here will show jobs but not allow the priority of them to be changed.

Question 11

The correct answer is c. The name of the application must be given, then the ampersand (&) is used to send it to the background. All other choices would fail due to improper syntax.

Question 12

The correct answer is d. Spencer will not be able to type anything on his keyboard until he first suspends the job, and this is accomplished on a job running in the foreground by pressing Ctrl+Z (^Z). All other keyboard sequences would be ignored or would stop the running job.

Question 13

The correct answer is a. **grep** is used to find lines within a file. The **find** command (answer b) is best suited for finding files on a system, not entries within the files. The **sed** utility (answer c) is best suited for changing values, and it will not find matching lines with the syntax given here. There is no Linux standard utility called **search** (answer d).

Question 14

The correct answer is **mkfs -t msdos /dev/sda3**.

The full syntax must be given for the partition to be formatted as desired.

Question 15

The correct answer is b. A relative path is always given relative to the current position. As such, it will always contain "./" or "../". The other answers are invalid for specifying paths.

Question 16

The correct answer is c. The comma can be used between the settings, and the colon (answer a) and semicolon (answer d) will not work. The command in answer b does not set the group to include the write permission.

Question 17

The correct answer is c. To finish creating a file, Tony must press Ctrl+D once if he is on a blank line and twice if he is anywhere else within the line. Pressing Ctrl+Z (all other choices) does not end/save the file but rather merely suspends it from the foreground.

Question 18

The correct answer is d. This will show disk usage. Answer a is used to establish a quota, and answer b is used to turn that quota on. The quotas will prevent Maude from saving above a certain amount, but they're not the right tool for telling you how much she is using. Answer c, **df**, will report how much disk space is free on the drive but not how much is in use in a particular directory.

Question 19

The correct answer is b. This is the file system table. Answer a is the initialization table that determines what occurs at different runlevels. Answer c is the group definitions for system groups (not filesystems). Answer d is a device, not a file, and irrelevant for this question.

Question 20

The correct answer is b. You must be able to write to a directory to be able to save files there. The read permission is necessary to be able to see the file, once it is there, or to list the entries. The execute permission is needed to be able to run a program from the directory.

Question 21

The correct answer is a. By default, newly created files are assigned the value of 666 (**-rw-rw-rw-**). The **umask** is subtracted from the default (666 - 44 = 622), thus making the permissions (**-rw--w--w-**). All other answers are invalid. The permissions for answer b are 222. For answer c, they're 644; for answer d, they're 444.

Question 22

The correct answer is c. By default, newly created directories are assigned the value of 777 (**drwxrwxrwx**). The **umask** is subtracted from the default (777 - 44 = 733), thus making the permissions (**drwx-wx-wx**). All other choices are invalid. The permissions for answer a are 333. For answer b, they're 300. For answer d, they're 744. For answer e, they're 644; for answer f, they're 444.

Question 23

The correct answers are c and d. The file must be run by what is perceived to be root. Setting the SGID (answer c) will temporarily make the user a member of the root group, whereas setting the SUID (answer d) will temporarily make the user root. Answer a makes the file executable but does not give it the needed permissions to run. Answer b loads the application into memory (making it "sticky") but does not grant the needed permissions to execute.

Question 24

The correct answers are b and c. By default, the home directory is not a part of your path. Therefore, the command cannot be called by itself (answer a). You must reference it by its absolute path (answer b) or a relative path (answer c). Answer d is invalid because it looks for the file in the parent directory (/home), but the file does not exist there.

Question 25

The correct answer is b. The /var/log/messages file is the system log where the majority of messages are written to. The file in answer a does not exist, and the files in answers c and d are configuration files for booting rather than system logs.

Question 26

The correct answer is **man 2 nice.**

This tells the **man** utility to look only in the man2 subdirectory.

Question 27

The correct answer is b. The **whatis** command will show the manual entries and nothing more. The **whereis** command (answer a) will show entries but also the executable and related entries. The **which** command (answer c) shows which directory in your path statement first holds the executable. It's not relevant for this question. Answer d displays the first manual page it finds for **nice**, and that's all.

Question 28

The correct answer is d. The **PAGER** variable can be set to **more**, **less** (the most common), or any other similar utility. The **more** utility (answer a) is a possibility that **PAGER** can be set to; if it existed as a variable, however, it would have no effect on the operation of man. The other two variables (answers b and c) are invalid entries.

Question 29

The correct answer is b. When third-party software is added to the system, it should write its documentation in the /usr/doc directory. Furthermore, it should create a subdirectory with the name of the program, a hyphen, and the version number. All other answers are invalid.

Question 30

The correct answer is f. Passwords and usernames are stored in the /etc/passwd file, not /usr/passwd (which does not exist). Within the /etc/passwd file, the fifth field is free text. All other answers are incorrect.

Question 31

The correct answers are a and c. The passwords can be in /etc/passwd, if security is not a concern, or in /etc/shadow, if security is a concern. The group and gshadow files are used to store passwords for groups (versus users).

Question 32

The correct answer is a. All template files—such as .profile and related configuration files—should be placed beneath /etc/skel. All other answers contain invalid options that do not exist.

Question 33

The correct answer is a. Entries in the /etc/profile file apply to all users, and adding it here will make the directory appear in each user's path. Answer c is also valid, but it's not the best answer because you must edit 16 existing .profiles and remember to add the value for every new user as well. Answer b is invalid for existing users. The sixth field of /etc/passwd (answer d) is the home directory of each user, and the last thing you want to do is give them all the same home directory, let alone send them to a directory used to hold executables.

Question 34

The correct answer is c. Adding a pound sign (#) to the beginning of the line makes the entire line a comment. This prevents anyone from using the account, and you can remove the pound sign when Karen returns. Deleting her .profile (answer a) will not disable the account but merely remove her own environmental variables (the variables will still be there, though, from /etc/profile). Changing her password (answer b) is an option, but it's not the best option because you will need to change it again when she comes back, and this still leaves the account accessible to anyone who can figure out the password. The **userdel** utility (answer d) will delete an account and cannot be used to disable one temporarily.

Question 35

The correct answer is /etc/syslog.conf.

This file is used by the **logrotate** utility to determine what automatic actions should take place and to which files.

Question 36

The correct answer is b. A differential backup will always get all the files that have been modified/added since the last full backup. An incremental backup (answer a) will get all files since the last full or incremental backup. The other two answers are not valid choices as backup types.

Question 37

The correct answer is d. The first field holds the minute, and the second field holds the hour. The third field is used to specify the day of the month, and the fourth field is used to specify the month. The fifth field identifies the days of the week. All other answers are incorrect.

Question 38

The correct answer is d. The at.deny file (beneath /etc) holds the names of the users who cannot use the **at** service. Anyone who does not show up in this file (and in the absence of an at.allow file) will be able to use the **at** service. All other answers are incorrect.

Question 39

The correct answer is c. When you attempt to write to a file with a single greater-than sign (>), the file is first created before anything else is done. Because the file already exists in this case, its contents are lost. After the file is zeroed, it is opened for reading but now has no contents. All other answers are incorrect.

Question 40

The correct answer is b. The **date** command will display both the date and time. There actually is a **time** command (answer a), but it's used to measure how long a process takes to run and does not have anything to do with displaying the current time. The **env** and **set** commands (answers c and d) show the defined variables—none of which is the current time.

Question 41

The correct answer is d. As a general rule, all commands are in lowercase, and variables are in uppercase. Because Linux is a case-sensitive operating system, if you enter "PWD" at the command prompt, an error will be returned because there is no such command. You must enter "pwd" in order to see the present working directory.

Question 42

The correct answer is b. Because the editor is not a standard component of Linux, the **--help** syntax should not be used. When installed, documentation should be written to the /usr/doc directory (answer a), and you should always look for files on the media as well as the vendor's Web site (answers c and d).

Question 43

The correct answer is b. Login name is how most users will refer to this user (via email, write, and other resources), and for that reason it should be a simple entry that can be used to determine who the user is. Using a difficult entry (answer a), or changing it often (answer c) are good answers for passwords but are not recommended for usernames.

Question 44

The correct answer is c. The **cat** command can be used to view text files at the Linux command prompt. The **ln** command (answer a) is used to create links to files but not to view them. The **type** command (answer b) exists in other operating systems to do the same function as **cat** does here, but it does not display text files in Linux. Also, because answers a and b are incorrect, answer d is incorrect.

Question 45

The correct answer is d. The **mv** command is a powerful one. It can be used to move and rename both files and directories.

Question 46

The correct answer is d. Any printable character can be used as a delimiter between fields in a file. This would include colons (answer a), which are often used in system files, as well as white space (answer b) and pipes (answer c).

Question 47

The correct answer is 20 10 5 * 3.

Because the day of the month does not matter, that field (the fourth field) must be left blank, but all other fields must be filled with the values specified.

Question 48

The correct answer is c. In other operating systems, background processes are often known as *services* (answer d), but they're known as *daemons* in Unix and Linux. Inodes and superblocks (answers a and b) are components of the filesystem, not of background processes.

Question 49

The correct answer is a. All other answers are processes that run in the background and pertain to system functions, but **ps** is a command that is given at the command line to show process status. A good rule of thumb is if the entry ends with a *d* (as in **syslogd** and **atd**), it is often a daemon. Although this does not hold true for all daemons (as with **init** and **cron**), it does with many.

Question 50

The correct answer is b. A runlevel determines what can transpire on the system at this time. As you switch runlevels, you add or remove functionality that the system is offering (for example, multiple users versus a single user). All other answers are incorrect.

Question 51

The correct answers are a, c, and d. The home directory can be specified in the /etc/passwd file, and that value is set to the **$HOME** variable (for use when you type "cd" on the command line). It is the system administrators who determine what the home directories will be and set up the accounts. The /etc/profile (answer b) sets variables for use by all users and does not specify individual entries.

Question 52

The correct answer is d. The pound sign (#) is used to signify the beginning of comments within a HOSTS or LMHOSTS file, or any other text file. The other answers are incorrect.

Question 53

The correct answers are a and d. These two entries match the search specification of the letter "a" followed by any other letter between "o" and "t". None of the other entries match the search criteria.

Question 54

The correct answers are a and c. The command given in answer a is incorrect because there is no command named "ls-l", and a space must be used before the hyphen. And the command given in answer c is incorrect because there is no command named "TERM", and the spaces on both sides of the equal sign must be removed for the entry to be seen as a variable. The command in answer b will run even though it could be better written as **ls -lt *.txt**. The command in answer d will run. It assumes that you have a user named 777 to whom you are giving ownership of the file.

Question 55

The correct answer is c. The syntax for **fgrep** is the same as for **grep**: You must specify what you are looking for and where you are looking for it. All other answers are incorrect.

Question 56

The correct answer is d. The command is asking to find all matches to the word "banner" followed by anything else, as long as the next character is not an "s".

Question 57

The correct answer is j. In the absence of the "s", the permissions would be 766. Because the SUID character is present (s), a value of 4000 must be added to this (4000+766 = 4766). The only other answer remotely possible from the list of possibilities is answer m; if this were the permissions, the case of the "s" would change to this: **-rwSrw-rw-**. All other answers are incorrect.

Question 58

The correct answer is d. The man8 subdirectory holds root utilities pages. The man1 subdirectory (answer a) is used for shell commands, man4 (answer b) is used for device definitions, and man5 (answer c) is used for file format pages.

Question 59

The correct answer is c. The **tar** utility can be used to compress multiple files into a single archive. The **gzip** utility (answer a) will compress individual files, and **cpio** (answer b) copies files from one location to another. The **zcat** utility (answer d) displays the contents of compressed files, just as **cat** does for uncompressed files.

Question 60

The correct answer is tar xf 10_23.tar bubble.txt.

The **x** option is needed to extract, and the **f** option is needed to specify an individual file to come from the archive.

Question 61

The correct answer is b. The **xargs** utility can make the output of one operation serve as the input of the next. Joining the operations with a semicolon (answer a) makes them two separate operations and will not work—nor will the redirection symbol (answer c). The **join** command (answer d) is used to paste fields together from two files and is not a valid option for this question.

Question 62

The correct answer is c. The **tr** utility can translate from one character set to another (in this case, uppercase to lowercase). The **tac** utility (answer a) merely displays a file in reverse order of **cat**. The **od** utility (answer b) performs an octal dump, which is not of any use for converting characters. The **expand** utility (answer d) changes tabs to spaces.

Question 63

The correct answer is a. The **-n** option will sort in numeric order. The **-r** option (answer b) sorts in reverse order but still does not make the entries numerically correct. The **-b** option (answer c) ignores leading blanks, and the **-f** option (answer d) sorts uppercase and lowercase characters as if they were all uppercase.

Question 64

The correct answer is **ln -s options.bmp figure_one.bmp**.

You must use the **-s** parameter to make a symbolic link (otherwise, it's a "hard" link), and you must give the existing file's name first, followed by the name of the link.

Question 65

The correct answer is **top**.

Unlike **ps**, which displays the entries and then exits, **top** stays active and dynamically updates the display.

Question 66

The correct answer is c. The /usr directory holds such subdirectories as /doc, where documentation is written by third-party applications, HOWTO files, and other entities. The /etc directory (answer a) is always changing and not a good location for documentation; nor is /var (answer b), which holds the log files and such. The /home directory (answer d) is used to hold user home directories.

Question 67

The correct answer is a. The entry typically resembles "id:5:initdefault:". The s0 entry (answer b) is for system initialization. The bw entry (answer c) defines bootwait, and the pf entry (answer d) is for powerfail.

Question 68

The correct answer is a. A runlevel of 0 is equal to a shutdown. A runlevel of 6 (answer e) is equal to a warm boot (power is never removed during a reboot). The other answers represent runlevels where the system continues to be accessible.

Question 69

The correct answer is a. The back quotes will cause the command to be executed and then echoed to the terminal. Both the single and double quotes (answers b and c) will display the word "date". If there is a **DATE** variable within your environment, its value will be returned by the command in answer d. Otherwise, a blank line will be displayed.

Question 70

The correct answer is d. The command **wc** will count the number of words in a file. The **tr** command (answer a) converts from one character set to another. There are no such commands as **tc** and **cw** (answers b and c).

Glossary

! (exclamation mark)
This is known as a *bang* in Linux, and it can be used to enter commands and rerun commands from the command prompt.

Absolute path
This is the opposite of a relative path. When using an absolute path, you must give the full path to the file, regardless of where you currently are. An example would be /home/edulaney/file.

American Standard Code for Information Interchange (ASCII)
ASCII is the eight-bit coding scheme created to standardize the transferring of data between systems.

Authentication
This is the process of validating a user's access to a system. Authentication is typically employed by comparing a username and password against an authorized list.

Background
This is a location where jobs can run without requiring interaction from the user. There can only be one job running in the foreground, but there can be an unlimited number (bound by resources) of jobs running in the background.

Backup
This is the process of saving files to another location in case something unforeseen happens to the existing copy. Backups should be performed on a regular basis and done to removable media.

bash
This is the Bourne Again shell, which is an interpreter between the user and the operating system.

Bitmap
This was originally an array of bits but is now expanded to include arrays of bytes or even 32-bit quantities that specify the dot pattern and colors that describe an image on the screen or printed paper.

Boot
This is the process of powering on a system and starting services.

Bourne shell
This is the original shell used in Unix (sh). It is limited in what it can do, and although still around, in most systems it is a link to bash.

C
This is a high-level programming language developed at Bell Labs. C is both powerful and flexible and is used to program a variety of applications.

C++
This is an object-oriented version of the C programming language.

Child
A child is an entity that is subservient to another. For example, a child directory is a subdirectory beneath another, and a child process is a process called by another to perform a subset of the commands that need to run.

Cold boot
This involves restarting the system after taking away the power. This is accomplished by changing to runlevel 0.

Console
The console is the primary terminal for the system. This is usually the terminal associated with the root user.

Cookie
This is a text file sent from a Web server to a client. A cookie holds values about a user's preferences locally on his or her machine, and it's most commonly used to provide personalized Web content.

csh
This is the C shell, which is an interpreter between the user and the operating system.

Daemon
A daemon is a process that runs in the background on Linux to provide services to users. Examples of services provided include email, printing, and so on.

Delimiter
A delimiter is a character used to separate fields within a file. The two most common delimiters are white spaces and colons.

Device
A device is a physical item that can be accessed with Linux. Examples include hard drives, floppy drives, and so on.

Directory
A directory is a folder that can contain files or other directories (subdirectories). A home directory should exist for every user, and there are a number of system directories created during the installation of Linux (such as /bin and /etc).

Disk caching
This is a method to improve performance of the filesystem. A section of memory is used as a temporary holding place for frequently accessed file data.

Domain Name System (DNS)
This is a static, hierarchical name service for TCP/IP hosts.

Domain Name System (DNS) Server
This is a computer system that converts domain names to IP addresses using a database of hostnames and IP addresses.

Dynamic Host Configuration Protocol (DHCP)
This is a protocol for automatic TCP/IP configuration that provides static and dynamic address allocation and management.

Echo
An echo returns back the exact same value, string, or entity sent. By default, most echoing is done to the terminal, but it can be redirected.

Electronic mail (email)
Email is electronic text messages exchanged over public and private networks.

Execute permission
This is the permission necessary to be able to run an application or shell script.

FAQs (Frequently Asked Questions)
This is a collection of responses (usually in electronic text format) to the most common questions asked on a topic.

File permissions
These are the rights assigned to a file or directory that determine who can use it and what they can do with it.

File Transfer Protocol (FTP)
This is the standard method of transferring files using TCP/IP. FTP allows you to transfer files between dissimilar computers, with preservation of binary data and optional translation of text file formats.

Filesystem
This is the cumulative partition with which Linux can interact. A filesystem must first be mounted before it can be accessed by users.

Foreground
This is a location where jobs run and can accept interaction from the user. There can only be one job running in the foreground, but there can be an unlimited number (bound by resources) of jobs running in the background.

GNU
This is an acronym for *GNU's Not Unix*. GNU is a project run by the Free Software Foundation to create utilities.

Graphical User Interface (GUI)
This is a computer system design in which the user interacts with the system using graphical symbols, tools, and events rather than text-based displays and commands. An example is the normal Windows user interface.

Group
This is a collection of users who share the ability to own resources and access items within Linux.

Host
A host is any device that is attached to the internetwork and uses TCP/IP.

Host ID
This is the portion of the IP address that identifies a computer within a particular network ID.

HOWTO
This is an electronic document similar to a FAQ, but more tutorial in nature, that addresses an individual topic.

Hyperlink
This is an element found on a hypertext document that, when clicked, connects the user to a linked file.

Hypertext Markup Language (HTML)
HTML is a set of codes or markup used to define how text and other elements will be displayed in a Web browser.

Hypertext Transfer Protocol (HTTP)
This is the protocol that defines how requests are communicated between Web clients and Web servers.

Internet
The Internet is the worldwide interconnected wide area network, based on the TCP/IP protocol suite.

Internet Protocol (IP)
This is the Network layer protocol of TCP/IP, responsible for addressing and sending TCP packets over the network.

IP address
This is used to identify a node on a network and to specify routing information on an internetwork. Each node on the internetwork must be assigned a unique IP address, which is made up of the network ID, plus a unique host ID assigned by the network administrator. The subnet mask is used to separate an IP address into the host ID and network ID. In Windows 2000, you can assign an IP address either manually or automatically using DHCP.

Job
A job is a running process that can be moved between the foreground and background, as well as suspended or stopped.

Kernel
This is the compiled file that is needed to act as the heart of the operating system. In the absence of almost any file but the kernel, the operating system can usually limp along. In the absence of the kernel, however, there is no operating system.

Kill
This means to terminate an entity. In relation to Linux, the killing is often done to processes that are no longer needed.

LILO
This is the Linux Loader. It is used to bring up the operating system or a menu that allows you to choose which operating system you wish to load if there are more than one on the system.

Line Printer Remote (LPR)
This is a TCP/IP protocol for sending commands to network dot-matrix printers.

Logging
This is the act of writing messages to log files. These files can be examined (audited) by the administrator to determine what is happening on the system.

Login
This is the act of entering a valid password and username and beginning a session with the Linux operating system.

Logoff
This involves an individual user ending his or her session within the Linux operating system.

Linux
This is a version of Unix developed by Linus Torvalds.

man
This is a set of documentation (manual pages) available in all vendor versions and flavors of Linux.

Mount
This involves making an external resource available for local use. The most common use is to mount remote filesystems.

Multiboot
This is the ability to have more than one operating system on a computer and choose which one you want to boot into each session.

Netstat
This is a TCP/IP utility used to display protocol statistics and connection information.

Network
This is a group of computers and other devices that can interact by means of a shared communications link.

Network ID
This is the portion of the IP address that identifies a group of computers and devices located on the same logical network. It is separated from the host ID using the subnet mask.

Network Interface Card (NIC)
This is an adapter card that connects a computer to a network.

Packet Internet Groper (ping)
This is a utility for determining connectivity between a connection.

Parent
A parent is one level back from the current entity. In terms of a parent directory, it is the directory of which the current directory is a subdirectory. In terms of a process, it is the process that started the current one.

Partition
This is a workable unit of the hard drive.

Password
This is a security measure used to restrict access to computer systems. A password is a unique string of characters that must be provided before a logon or an access is authorized.

Point-to-Point Protocol (PPP)
This is the industry standard that is implemented in dial-up networking. PPP is a line protocol used to connect to remote networking services, including Internet Service Providers. Prior to the introduction of PPP, another line protocol, SLIP, was used.

POST (Pre-Operating System Test)

This is an internal check done by every computer during boot, prior to loading the operating system.

PostScript

This is a page-description language, developed by Adobe Systems, that offers flexible font capability and high-quality graphics. PostScript uses English-like commands to control page layout and to load and scale fonts.

Process

A process is any running instance of an application or service.

Protocol

This is a set of rules and conventions by which two computers pass messages across a network. Protocols are used between instances of a particular layer on each computer.

PS1

This is the primary prompt a user sees when working on the command line. When incomplete commands are given, the prompt changes to PS2.

PS2 through PS4

These are prompts available to the user other than his or her primary prompt. These are most often used to indicate that more data must be given before the command can be executed.

Read permission

This is the permission necessary to be able to view the contents of a file or create a copy of it.

Reboot

This is the act of shutting down the system and then restarting it. If power is ever removed during the process, it is known as a *cold boot* (shutdown). If power is never removed, it is known as a *warm boot* (restart).

Recursive

This refers to when you go through something and everything beneath it. When you recursively delete a directory, you also delete all files and subdirectories beneath it. When you recursively end a process, you end the process and all other processes for which it was the parent.

Redirection

This refers to sending output to a location other than where it would normally default to.

Relative path

This is the opposite of an absolute path. When using a relative path, you must specify where to go based on what the current directory is. Relative paths always utilize either "." or "..". An example would be ../file.

Removable media

This is any type of resource that files can be copied onto and then removed from the system. The most popular is tape used for backups.

Requests for Comments (RFCs)

These are the official documents of the Internet Engineering Task Force that specify the details for protocols included in the TCP/IP family.

Restore
This is the act of recovering data after a failure. It's most often used as the counterpart to a backup.

Root
This refers to the main entity. For example, the *root directory* is the directory beneath which all others are subdirectories, and the *root user* is the user who can stop any process and change the permissions of any file or user (in other words, the chief administrator for the system).

Runlevel
This is the current level at which the system is operating. There are seven possible runlevels, each offering different services.

Samba
This is an interpreter between the Linux operating system and Windows-based operating systems. It converts message blocks for proper interoperability between the two operating systems.

Server
This is a computer or program that responds to requests from clients.

Shell
This is the command interpreter that acts as an agent on behalf of the user when interacting with the operating system. Numerous shells are available, each with a slightly different feature set. The most common are bash, csh and tcsh.

Shutdown
This is the act of properly closing open files and ending services to bring the system to a powered-off state.

Standard error
The expected (default) location where error messages will be displayed. In most instances, this is the terminal.

Standard input
This is the expected (default) location from which input will come. In most instances, this is the keyboard/user.

Standard output
This is the expected (default) location where output will go. In most instances, this is the terminal.

Subnetwork
This is a network that is part of a larger network.

Swap
This is the act of changing one thing for another. This phrase is most often used in relation to a *swap file*, which holds needed information that the system is using, but due to system constraints cannot hold it all in RAM at one time. When such is the case, data is swapped—as needed—between the hard drive and RAM.

tcsh
This is Tom's C shell, an interpreter between the user and the operating system.

Telnet
This is the Application layer protocol that provides virtual terminal service on TCP/IP networks.

Terminal
This is a monitor from which a user can log in and work with the Linux operating system.

Text file
This is a file containing only ASCII letters, numbers, and symbols, without any formatting information except for carriage return/linefeeds.

Transmission Control Protocol (TCP)
This is a connection-based protocol, responsible for breaking data into packets that the IP protocol sends over the network. This protocol provides a reliable, sequenced communication stream for internetwork communication.

Transmission Control Protocol/Internet Protocol (TCP/IP)
This is a protocol stack developed by the U.S. Department of Defense, composed of a suite of protocols used to connect hosts on the Internet. TCP/IP is the de facto standard communications protocol for the Internet.

Unix
This is one of the original multiuser, multitasking network operating systems.

Unmount
This refers to making an external resource no longer available for local use. The most common use is to unmount remote filesystems.

User
This refers to anyone allowed access to resources on the Linux system. A valid user account requires a password and username in the /etc/passwd file.

Warm boot
This refers to restarting the system without ever taking away the power. This is accomplished by changing to runlevel 6.

Web browser
This is the client software used to browse the Web.

Web server
This is a server responsible for Web content using the HTTP protocol.

White space
This is a blank used to separate entities in a file (a delimiter). It can be either a tab character or a space.

Wide Area Network (WAN)
This is a geographically widespread network. When LANs are joined together, they typically form a WAN.

Wildcard
This is any character that can represent other characters. The two most common wildcards within Linux are the question mark (?) and the asterisk (*). The former is used to represent any one character, whereas the latter represents zero or more characters.

Write permission
This is the permission necessary to be able to create or modify a file.

X
This is short for *X Windows System*, which provides a graphical interface to Linux.

Index

Bold page numbers indicate sample exam questions.

S

X

Y

Z

EXAM CRAM INSIDER

The Coriolis Exam Cram Personal Trainer

An exciting new category in certification training products

The Exam Cram Personal Trainer is the first certification-specific testing product that completely links learning with testing to:

- **Increase your comprehension**
- **Decrease the time it takes you to learn**

No system blends learning content with test questions as effectively as the Exam Cram Personal Trainer.

Only the Exam Cram Personal Trainer offers this much power at this price.

Its unique Personalized Practice Test Engine provides a real-time test environment and an authentic representation of what you will encounter during your actual certification exams.

Much More than Just Another CBT!
Most current CBT learning systems offer simple review questions at the end of a chapter with an overall test at the end of the course, with no links back to the lessons. But Exam Cram Personal Trainer takes learning to a higher level.

Its four main components are:

- The complete text of an Exam Cram study guide in HTML format
- A Personalized Practice Test Engine with multiple test methods
- A database of 150 questions linked directly to an Exam Cram chapter

Plus, additional features include:

- **Hint:** Not sure of your answer? Click Hint and the software goes to the text that covers that topic.
- **Lesson:** Still not enough detail? Click Lesson and the software goes to the beginning of the chapter.
- **Update feature:** Need even more questions? Click Update to download more questions from the Coriolis Web site.
- **Notes:** Create your own memory joggers.
- **Graphic analysis:** How did you do? View your score, the required score to pass, and other information.
- **Personalized Cram Sheet:** Print unique study information just for you.

Windows 2000 Server Exam Cram Personal Trainer
ISBN: 1-57610-735-3

Windows 2000 Professional Exam Cram Personal Trainer
ISBN: 1-57610-734-5

Windows 2000 Directory Services Exam Cram Personal Trainer
ISBN: 1-57610-732-9

Windows 2000 Security Design Exam Cram Personal Trainer
ISBN: 1-57610-772-8

Windows 2000 Network Exam Cram Personal Trainer
ISBN: 1-57610-733-7

Windows 2000 Migrating from NT4 Exam Cram Personal Trainer
ISBN: 1-57610-773-6

A+ Exam Cram Personal Trainer
ISBN: 1-57610-658-6

CCNA Routing and Switching Exam Cram Personal Trainer
ISBN: 1-57610-781-7

$99.99 U.S. • $149.99 Canada

Available: November 2000

The Smartest Way to Get Certified Just Got Smarter™

Look for All of the Exam Cram Brand Certification Study Systems

ALL NEW! Exam Cram Personal Trainer Systems

The Exam Cram Personal Trainer systems are an exciting new category in certification training products. These CD-ROM based systems offer extensive capabilities at a moderate price and are the first certification-specific testing product to completely link learning with testing.

This Exam Cram study guide turned interactive course lets you customize the way you learn.

Each system includes:

- A Personalized Practice Test engine with multiple test methods
- A database of nearly 300 questions linked directly to the subject matter within the Exam Cram

Exam Cram Audio Review Systems

Written and read by certification instructors, each set contains four cassettes jam-packed with the certification exam information you must have. Designed to be used on their own or as a complement to our Exam Cram study guides, Flash Cards, and Practice Tests.

Each system includes:

- Study preparation tips with an essential last-minute review for the exam
- Hours of lessons highlighting key terms and techniques
- A comprehensive overview of all exam objectives
- 45 minutes of review questions, complete with answers and explanations

Exam Cram Flash Cards

These pocket-sized study tools are 100% focused on exams. Key questions appear on side one of each card and in-depth answers on side two. Each card features either a cross-reference to the appropriate Exam Cram study guide chapter or to another valuable resource. Comes with a CD-ROM featuring electronic versions of the flash cards and a complete practice exam.

Exam Cram Practice Tests

Our readers told us that extra practice exams were vital to certification success, so we created the perfect companion book for certification study material.

Each book contains:

- Several practice exams
- Electronic versions of practice exams on the accompanying CD-ROM presented in an interactive format, enabling practice in an environment similar to that of the actual exam
- Each practice question is followed by the corresponding answer (why the right answers are right and the wrong answers are wrong)
- References to the Exam Cram study guide chapter or other resource for that topic

The Smartest Way to Get Certified™